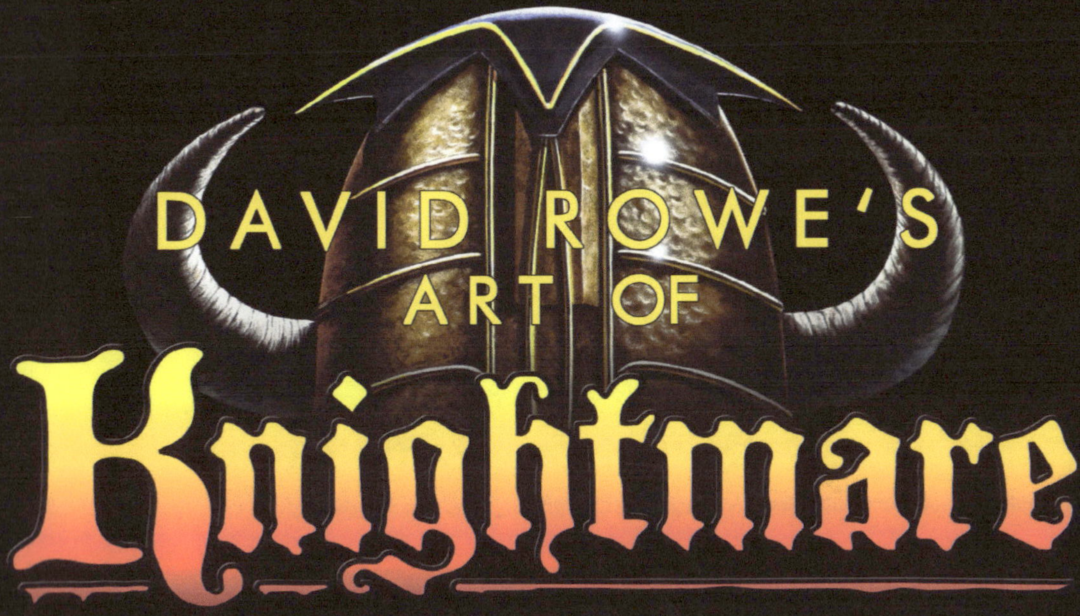

Knightmare

David Rowe

Foreword by Tim Child

Copyright

First published in 2014
This edition published in 2018 by Acorn Books
an imprint of Andrews UK Limited
www.andrewsuk.com

Dungeon Levels

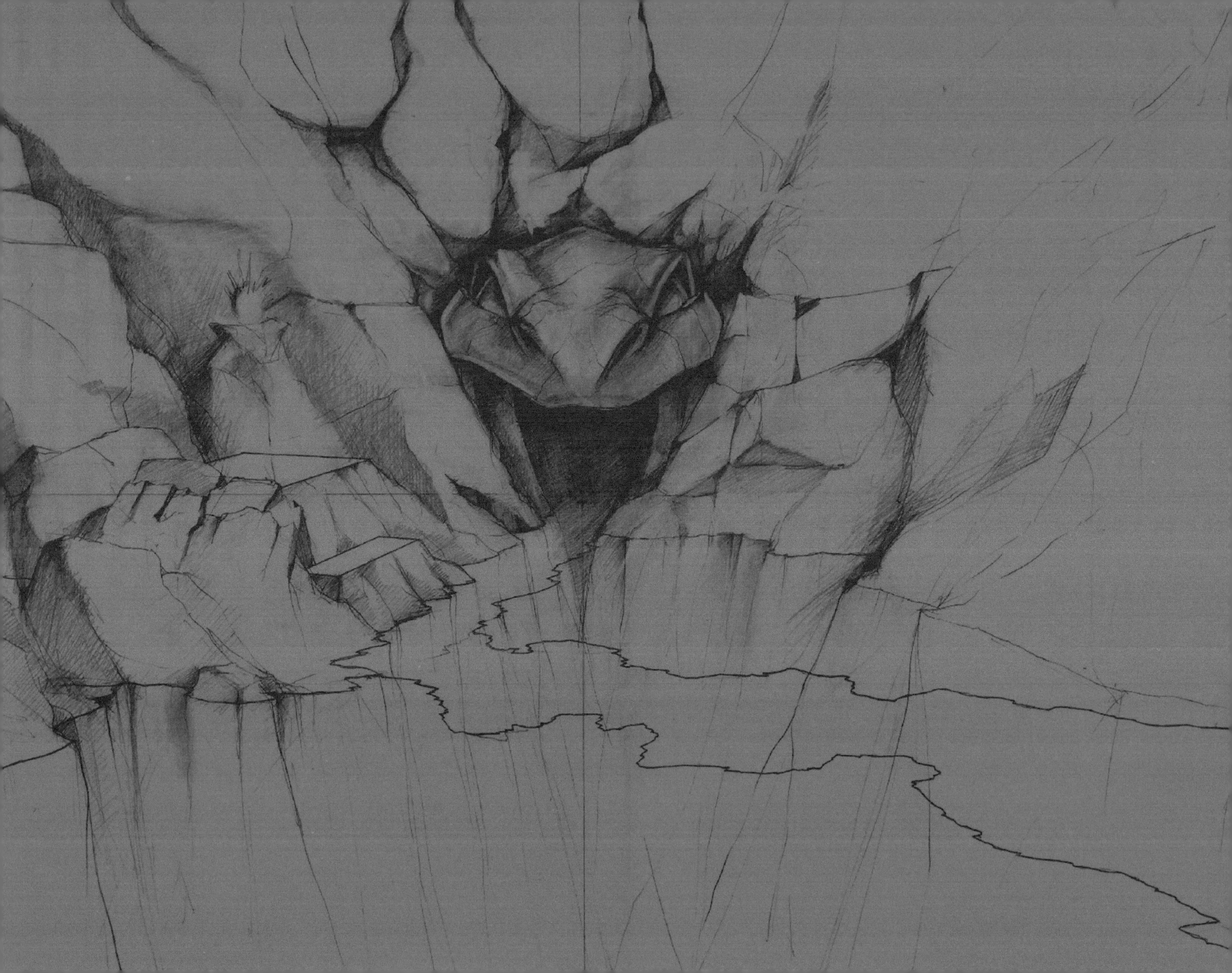

Fright Knight Trophy

The Fright Knight Trophy was awarded to successful teams who completed the dungeon. A promotional illustration was commissioned by Tim and was followed through with the customary faxed drawing before the painting was commenced.
I had the actual trophy to work from and I was hoping that Tim would forget to ask for its return. Sadly this wasn't the case...ah well!

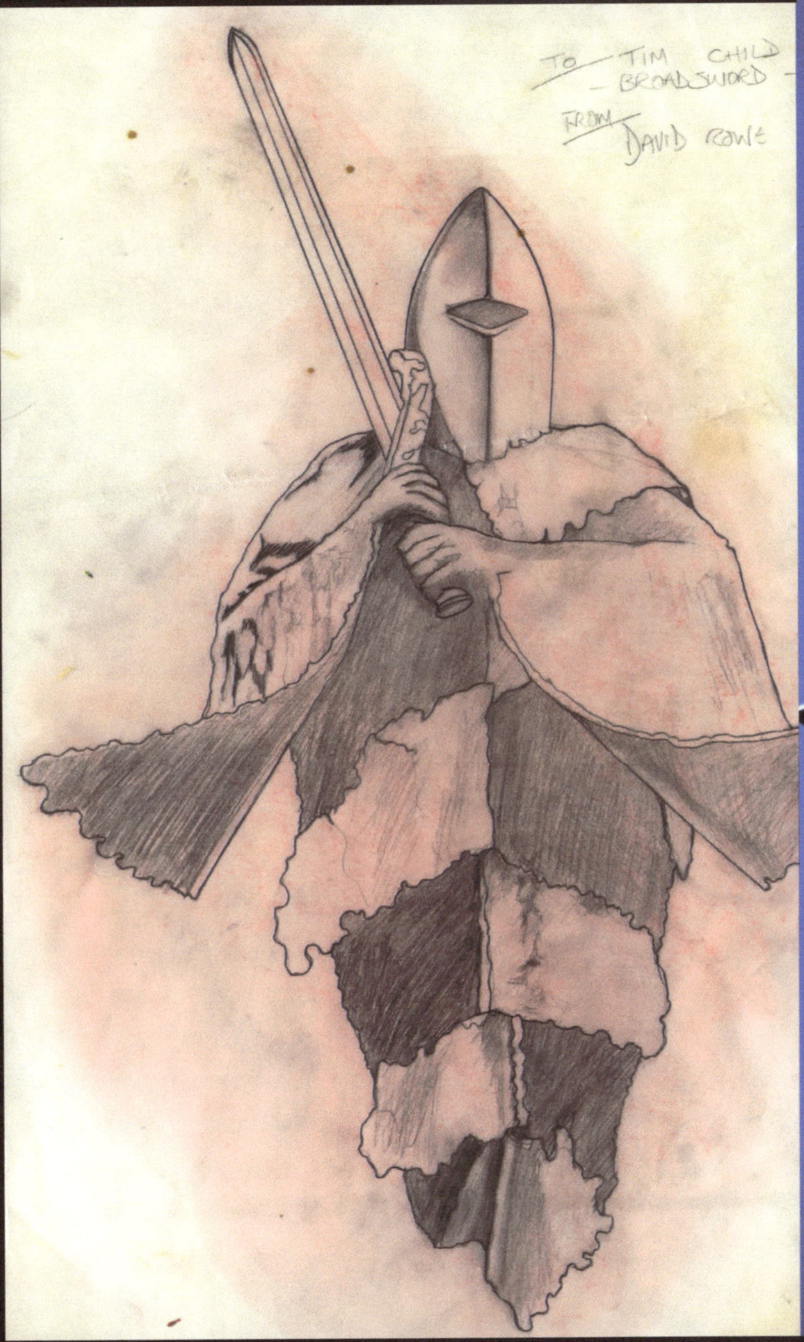

TO TIM CHILD
— BROADSWORD —
FROM DAVID ROWE

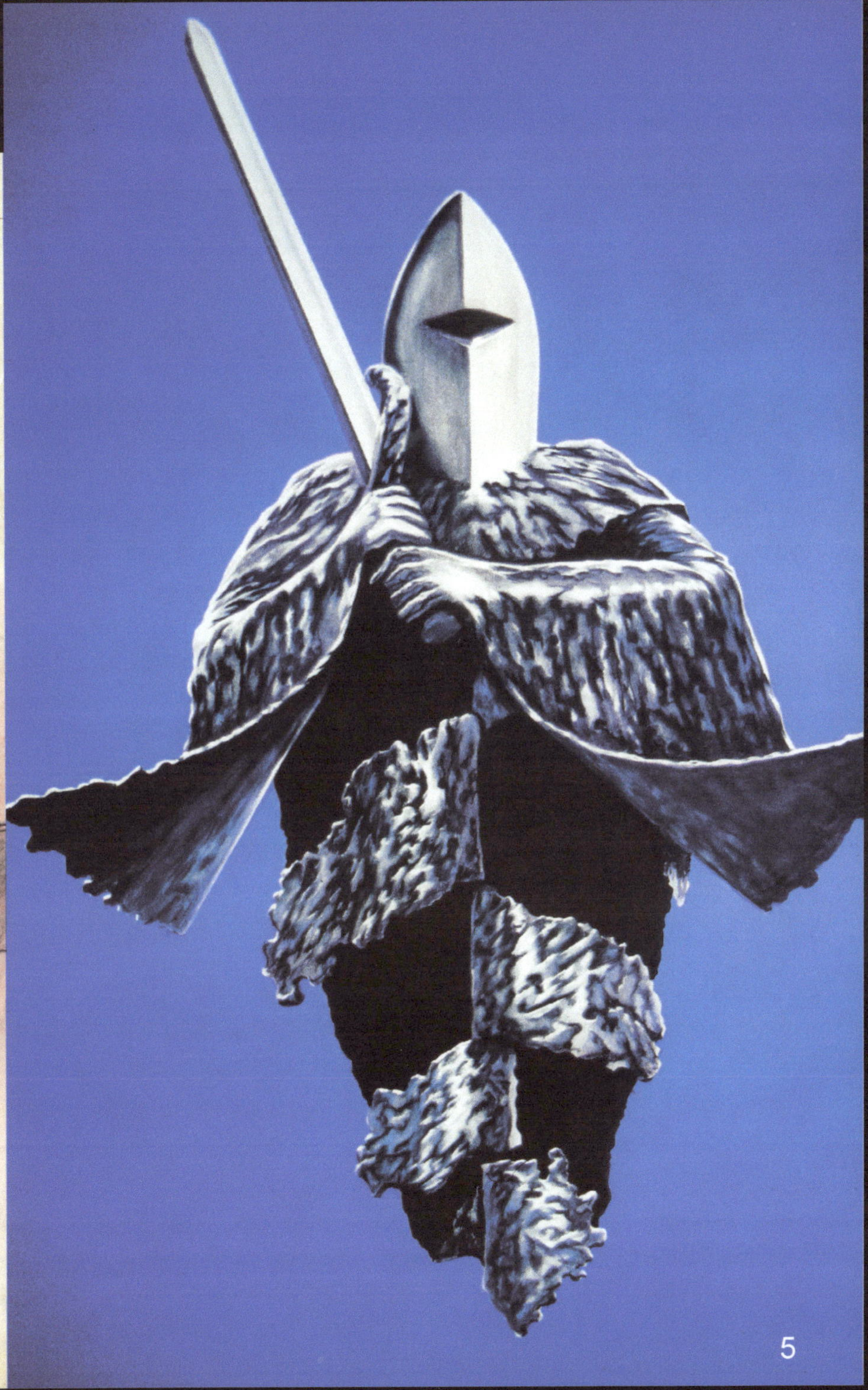

Roll of Honour

This is a list of all the wonderful people who contributed to the Indiegogo campaign fund for 'David Rowe's Art of Knightmare'. To them all I offer my most humble and sincere thanks. They also enabled the target of £3,500 not only to be reached within the campaign period, but also to be exceeded making a grand total of £4,117.

I would also like to thank the large number of Knightmare fans who helped to keep the pot boiling via social media and big thanks to the team at knightmare.com for their invaluable support and encouragement.

Andy Kitching
Glen Passman
Sarah Beamish
Francis Goodall
Andy Hawkins
Richard Hewison
Alison Hooper
Jennifer Gray
Jon Jones
Nick Gates
Alan Boyd
Gameplay Jenny
Jonathon Harris
James Howat
Michael Tucker
Jason Karl
Glenn Cooney
Amy Robinson
Andy Haigh
David Coles
Sarah Bonney
James Kontargyris
Donna Sluggett
David Cunningham
Andrew Cunningham
Amanda Baker

Alex Fruen
Neil Parry
Mevlut Dinc
Paul Morrison
Nick Galaxy
David Goldstein
David Trenholme
Mr S Mapes
Adam Walsh
Tom MacRae
Roy Jackson
Susan Jackson
Samantha Warren
Bill Hau
Rushy
Richard McClaughry
Jonjo Barrow
Simon Woor
Mik McArthur
Phillip L Ward
Michael Garry
Jonathan Bentley
David Walford
Gemma Coles
Liam Davis
Christian Langdale
Jim Whitfield

Shaktijit Dave
Harjinder Lall
Ben Groom
Liam Brierley
Michelle Jones
Amy Leete
David Hurst
Paul Blades
James Aukett
Tomas Awdry
Paul Flannery
Helen McCulloch
Matthew Richings
Chris Ballard
Bryan Howarth
Anne Stacey
Dan Reeves
Mark Peters
Paul Ward
Keith McDonald
John Hoare
Lyall McCarthy
James Alexander McMullen

Foreword

I think it was the Canadian media visionary Marshal McLuhan
who was credited with the claim that 'a picture is worth a
thousand words', and whilst some writers might counter-
claim that words allow the reader to imagine their own
settings, I think in the Adventure Game world, especially in
the era before convincing Virtual Realities, most of us need a
little help.
No one provides it with greater conviction than my friend and
collaborator for more than 25 years, David Rowe; a multi-
talented artist, and illustrator whose works have become the
stuff of magic for millions.

Tim Child

Message

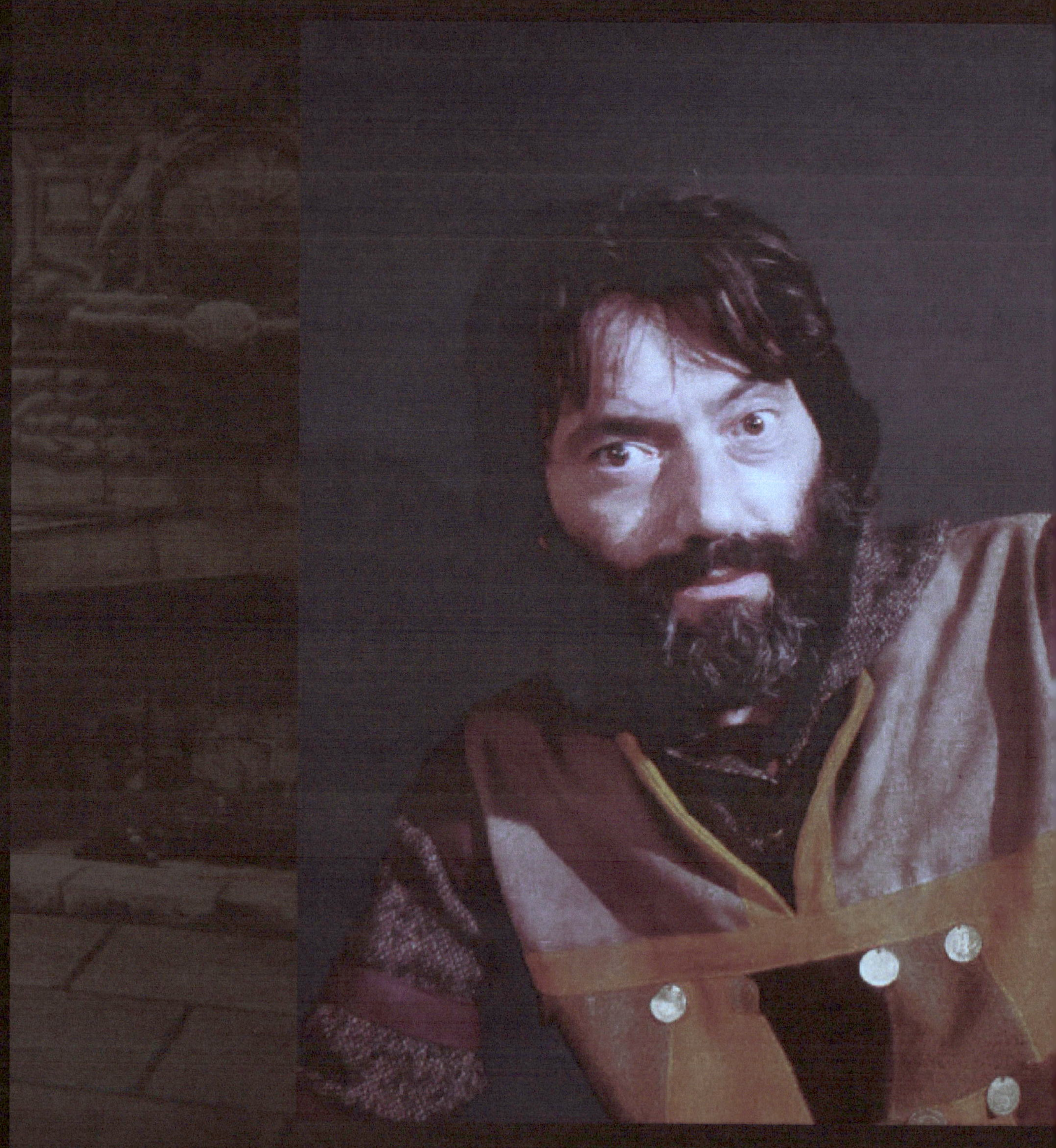

"I am with you all the way. It was your brilliant artwork that gave the show its magic. The kids truly believed they were stepping into a fantastical world. It must be preserved at all costs. To any fan, and I include myself, to have such a book would be a 'must have' item."

Hugo Myatt (Treguard)

Preface

1981 saw the dawning of the video game industry with the arrival of the Sinclair ZX81. Talented individuals quickly learned to develop additional add-ons such as sound boards and graphics cards which enabled them to create the first, albeit crude, video games similar to those, such as Pong, which had begun to appear in the pubs and arcades.

A whole world of fantastic possibilities suddenly began to take shape as the early pioneers wrestled to squeeze every ounce out of the technology to realise their vision of truly immersive, interactive game play.

I became involved with the cover artwork at this time with the enviable task of developing strong impact point of sale illustrations that gave a vision of the exciting game play that could be experienced from playing the games. My brief was usually one of playing the pre-release version of the game and then dreaming up a fantasy illustration that captured the mood.

The two main categories of game at the time were Arcade Action or Adventure, the latter usually being text only or with very simple flat coloured graphics. The momentum generated by the ever inventive game developers fuelled the development of more sophisticated and powerful home computers.

My work carried on in this vein and spread into magazine and book publishing and occasionally advertising, but I hadn't even considered television.

On an artwork delivery trip to Melbourne House Publishers, I was tipped off that someone form Anglia Television had been making enquiries about my artwork. I had my portfolio with me and asked to use their phone. I was on my way to Norwich in a trice, intrigued to find out more and to meet Tim Child who had made the enquiry.

Tim was an enthusiastic gamer who had the insight to recognise that whilst the graphics were limited in the home computer sector, they had much more scope in television and in particular with the emergent chromakey technology.

I met with Tim and the production team and was briefed on what was required. I was asked to produce a small number of test rooms which I increased by adding overlays painted on clear acetate so that they could perform tests prior to making a pilot programme that was to become Knightmare, the hugely popular hit TV series that ran from 1987 to 1994.

Up until this point chromakey was mainly used for placing weather maps or news rooms behind a presenter, often leaving a tell-take blue fringe surrounding him. Tim pushed the envelope by placing the characters in a 3D void and retaining cast shadows that anchored them to the floor.

As an illustrator, I was used to working within the constraints of a brief and it soon became apparent that in order for the illusion to work, the rooms had to match the geometry of the camera's view of the chromakey void exactly. Tim called in the help of French special effects expert Jean Peyre to create the first grid which took into account the camera lens, height and tilt angle and mimicked the camera's view precisely.

Armed with several copies of this grid I was able to create the room paintings by overlaying them with layout paper or sometimes tracing paper and developing each drawing knowing that it would be consistent with the needs of the production team members when creating the composite scene on the fly.

This production is a record of all the surviving work that went into making the early Knightmare series. You can read more here:

www.knightmare.com//home/a-history-of-knightmare

Grids and Sets

The Grids were a vital element that underpinned the production of Knightmare.
Once everybody knew that all the components that made up the composite view were going to work, the cast, crew and Dungeoneer were free to concentrate on making great television.

Top Left.
The primary grid was produced by Jean Peyre. It was essential for getting my bearings in the dungeon rooms and for producing further grids. Each room drawing was commenced on a sheet overlaying the appropriate grid for the camera view.

Bottom Left.
There was a requirement for a lower camera viewpoint on some of the rooms. I produced this grid which lowered the horizon to exactly halfway up the back wall.

Top Right.
The original set design by Mel Bibby.

Bottom Right.
A double depth grid, although the back half would be inaccessible to the Dungeoneer.

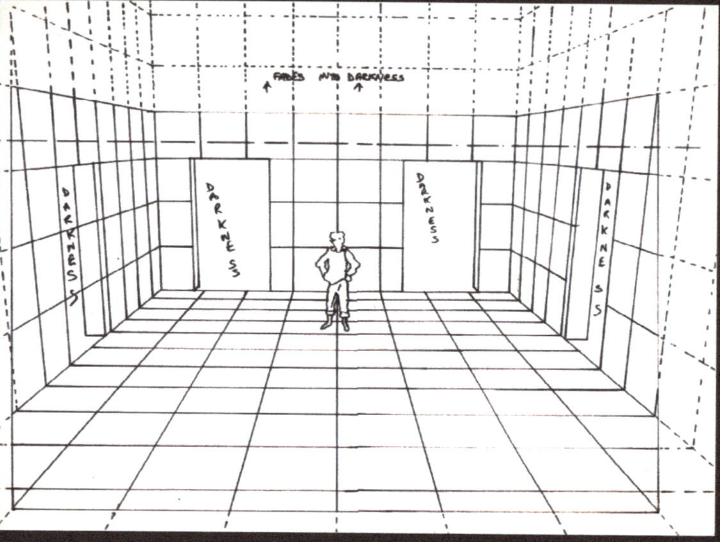

The primary grid, produced by Jean Peyre.

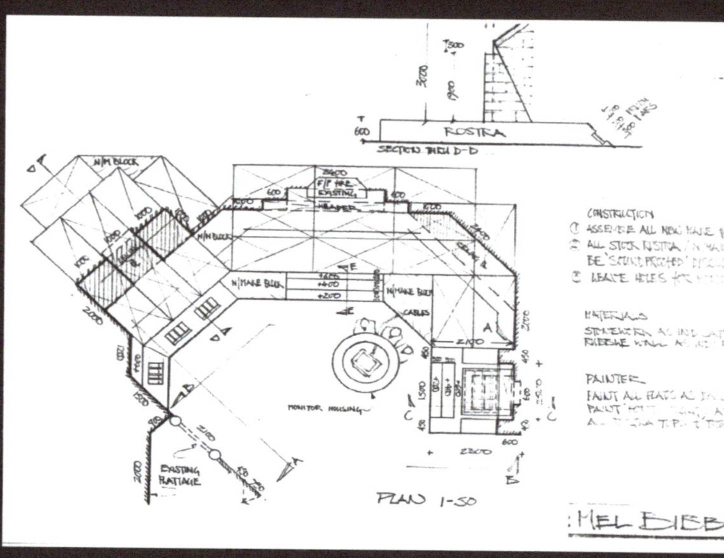

This is the plan view of Treguard's ante room showing the position for the contestants and the layout.

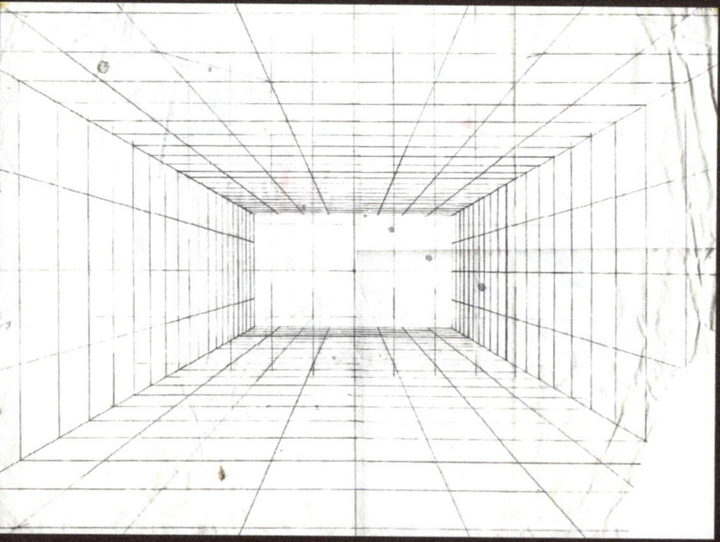

The lowered horizon perspective grid. A very mangled and stained working drawing.

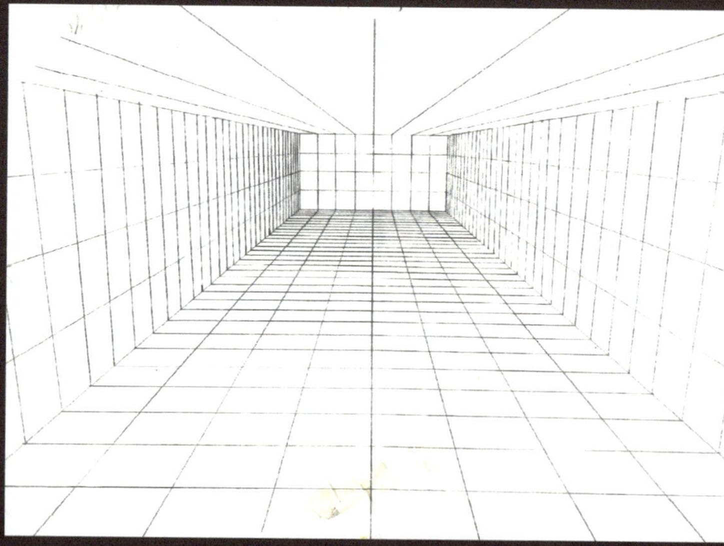

The grid that was produced as a guide for the painting of deeper rooms.

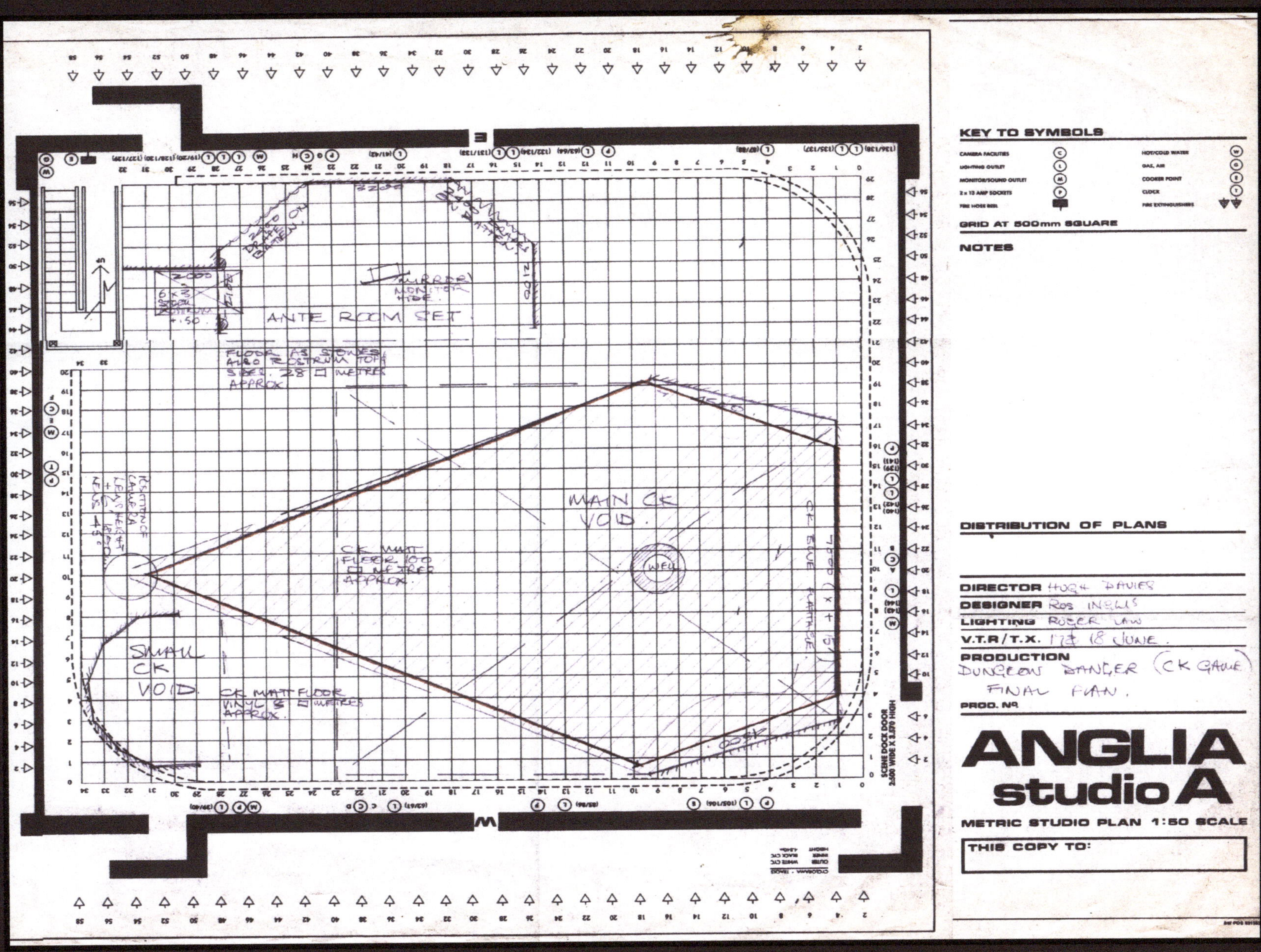

This is a plan of the construction of the Knightmare set showing the ante room where Treguard and the rest of the team were filmed. The main chromakey studio area is adjacent.

The Illustrations

Materials and equipment used:

CS10 Media 6 Illustration board.
Magic Color® Liquid acrylics
Olympos and DeVilbiss® airbrushes
Frisk Low Tack Masking Film
Gouache
Fine sable brushes sizes 2 and 3
Type writer eraser pencil.

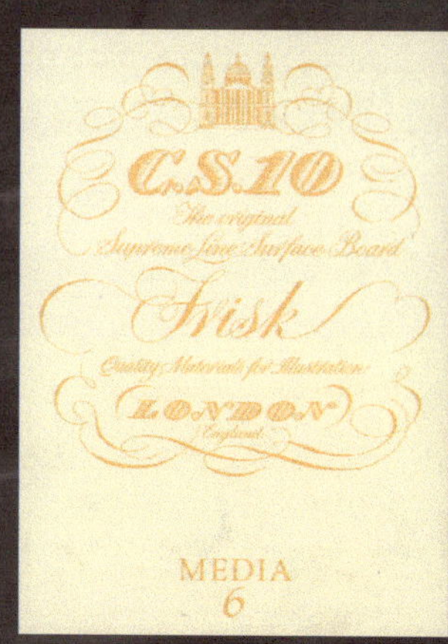

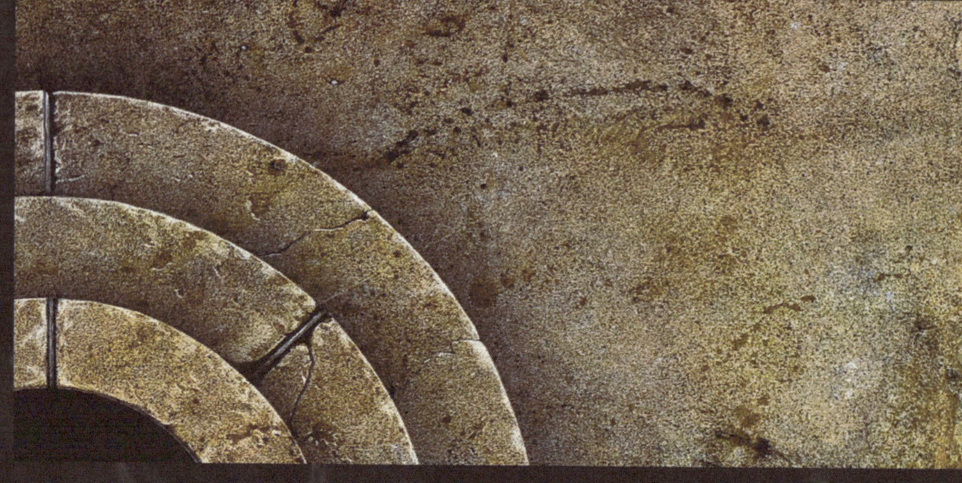

The original commission was for 31 dungeon room illustrations, but this number increased over the ensuing series. This was a large undertaking and required a disciplined approach if I was to provide the work in time. Correcting finished artwork is a real pain and so I used my tried and tested procedure of supplying rough sketches in colour if required, to indicate what would feature in the finished painting.

Communication was by fax and telephone way back in the mid Eighties, so I had invested about £2,000 in a fax machine that could send A3 sized drawings in half-tone which gave the impression of a grey scale. Any modifications were discussed over the phone or faxed back as drawn indications and then the go ahead was given.

Following the approval of the rough, the next stage was to produce the full sized drawing based upon the lines of the perspective grid. The key lines on the drawing were then drawn over using a large sheet of tracing paper. This was then rubbed on the reverse with coloured pastel or very soft lead pencil. The tracing paper was then taped to the illustration board and the lines transferred by drawing over them to copy the pastel to the final surface.

The illustration board edges were protected with low tack masking film allowing a generous 10mm bleed. Areas that required the same texture were then left exposed as the rest of the painting was protected with the film.

The stone textures in the paintings came about after a good deal of experimentation. I used air brushed spatter to achieve a fine speckled cover and noticed that by combining a number of bright primary colours a 'grey' stone effect came about. The most important discovery was that if I took the shiny, waxy backing sheet of the low tack masking film and sprayed that with a fine coating, I could then place the wet paint surface against the painting and press heavily to 'print' it onto the painting. The heavier the coating, the coarser the effect and so by applying different densities, I was able to achieve a good depth of texture.

A further bonus afforded by this technique was the way that the features that randomly appeared in the textures were able to be exploited as detail, making them look as if they were naturally occurring.

Once all the main areas had been masked in turn and given the required textures, the detail and finishing was commenced.

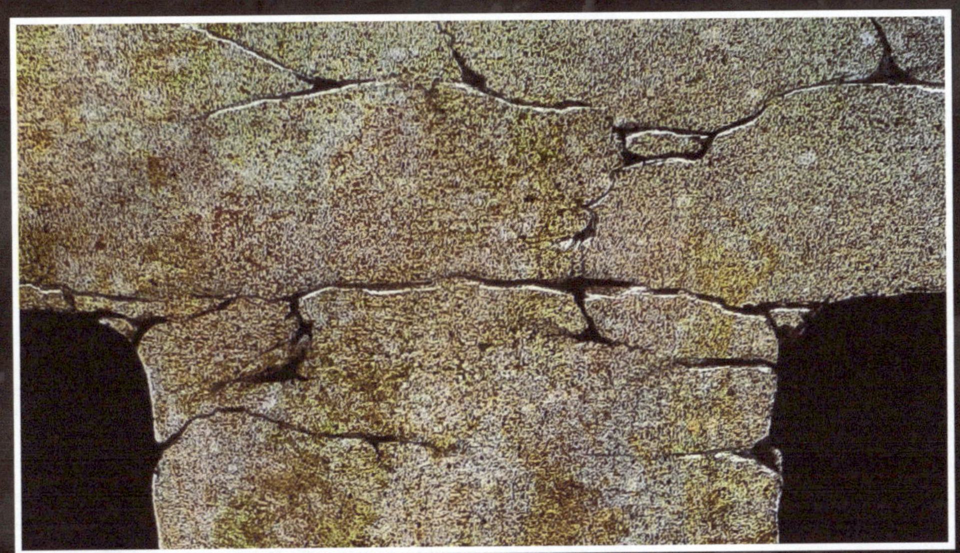

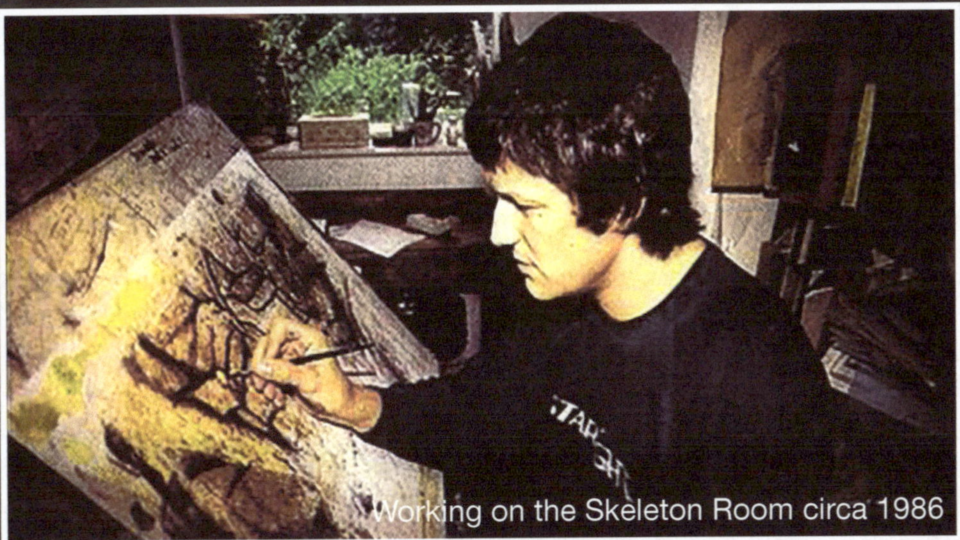
Working on the Skeleton Room circa 1986

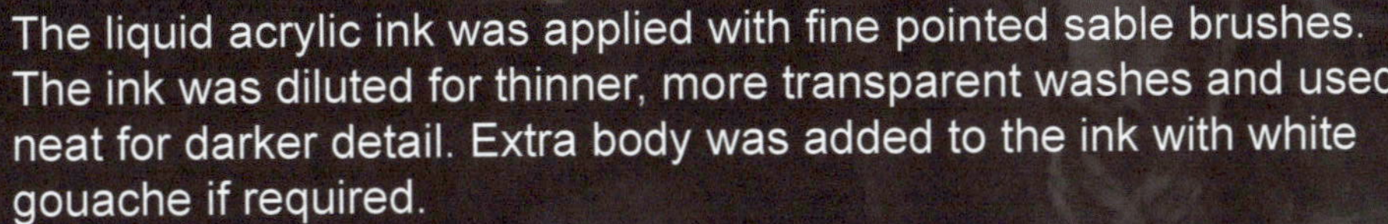

The liquid acrylic ink was applied with fine pointed sable brushes. The ink was diluted for thinner, more transparent washes and used neat for darker detail. Extra body was added to the ink with white gouache if required.

Highlights were added by using a typewriter eraser pencil to gently and partly rub through to the illustration board. Stronger highlights were added by soft scraping with a scalpel tip. The deep structure of the surface of the illustration board enabled this to happen without undue damage.

The undertaking necessitated long hours of concentration seeing the arrival of dawn on most days, but I count it as a privilege to have been 'in the creative zone' on such an inspirational project.

The paintings were worked upon under a natural daylight bulb so that consistency of colour could be maintained through both the hours of daylight and the hours of darkness.

Airbrushing acrylic inks can be hazardous and required the wearing of a heavy duty, twin filter industrial mask. The activity took place in a garage at the bottom of the garden and required a dash with the paint surface pointing down if it was raining.

There wasn't time to wait for paint to dry and so a hair dryer was kept at hand and the drying paint forced to bake onto the board allowing work to continue almost unabated.

During the process of applying the detail, the loaded paintbrush had the excess removed for the right consistency. The protective film on the painting edge was always handy so it was wiped off on that. It made for a very messy looking work in progress, but I still remember the thrill of seeing the film removed.

At the peak of activity, there were around 6 illustrations being produced per week which were then packaged and sent to Tim.

Techniques Used

The textures were applied to completely cover the surface of the illustration board before the detail was added. When creating the fade into darkness, the lit surfaces had to be carefully shielded from the spray.

The applied textures always suggested fracture lines or mossy detail which could be exaggerated with a brush and scalpel. Although the texturing was loose, the planes of the grid were always preserved.

Even rendered walls required texture and basic lighting. Detailing such as stains and cracks were added for interest and to give a sense of history to the room.

Each masked area was given different texture treatments depending on the type of surface. Random droplets of water or Magic Color® cleaning fluid added to the impression of lichen or algae.

The effect of ambient light was added to indicate form. This could be airbrushed or applied as a glaze with a sable brush and very diluted inks.

The underlying grid was key to the success of the project. The painting's ground plane could be worked upon in the certain knowledge that it was in the same perspective as the studio floor for the cast.

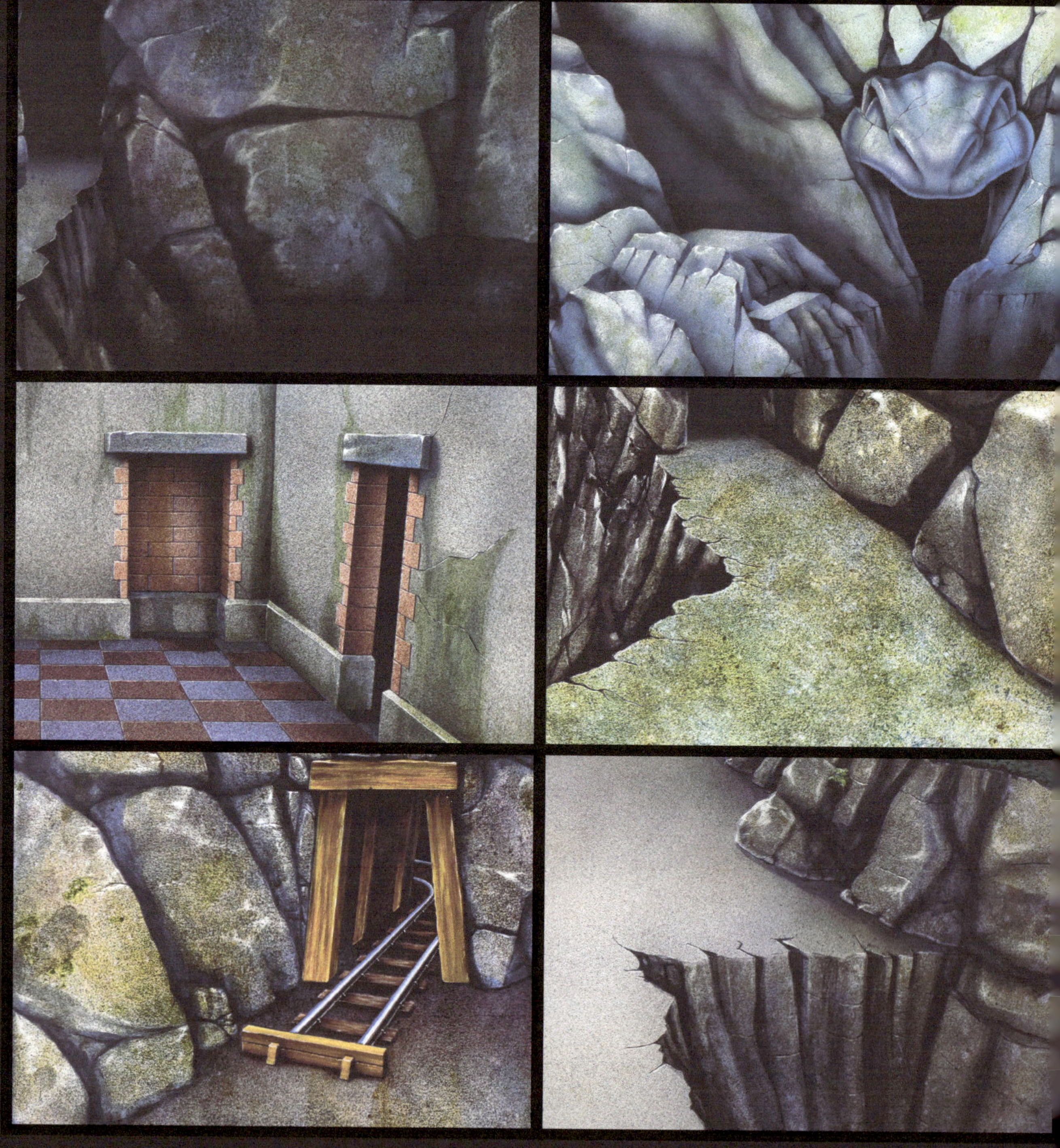

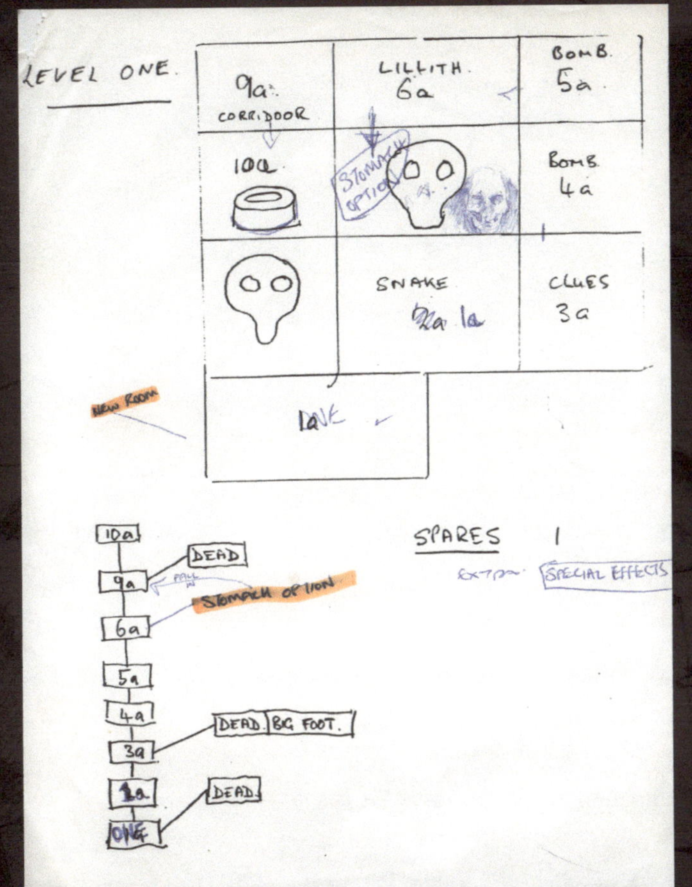

KNIGHTMARE SERIES 2 H128453-128465+H128913-128915

David R

Amended 9.5.88

Level 1

	Anteroom
1/A	Roulette Room
1/1	Door Option Room
1/1a	Snake Rm/Scorpion Rm
1/2a	Giant Room (Maggots etc)
1/3a	Granitas/Clue Rm
1/4a	1st Bomb Rm
1/5a	2nd Bomb Rm
1/6a	Lillith Rm
1/7a	Stomach Rm
1/8a	Crone Rm (also poss use in Level 2)
1/9a	Corridor Rm
1/10a	Wellway Rm
1/11a	Crossing Rm One
1/12a	Cardroom
1/13a	Roller Coaster Corridor
1/14a	2nd Wall Monster/Clue Rm
1/15a	Troll Rm
1/16a	Lion Rm
1/17a	Alt use of GIANT Rm - Scarab Rm
1/18a	Spider Rm
1/19a	Kitchen Rm

Door Option Room 1.1

This was one of the first rooms to be painted for series one.

Sufficient floor space had to be left clear for the placement of anagram letters that the Dungeoneer was directed to step on in sequence to form the word alluded to.

Most of the rooms have floor tiles of some description. They acted as a point of reference to the team when directing the Dungeoneer.

Although the lighting in the scene had to be fairly flat-lit a certain amount of modelling was necessary to indicate form which could then leave the computer graphics team to concentrate on the shafts of light and flickering flamed torches. This treatment could vary and allowed the possibility of the room being used in different ways with hues and lighting to match.

The blue chromakey sets contained props, panels and any items that could mask the Dungeoneer. Their placement had to match the corresponding painting component.

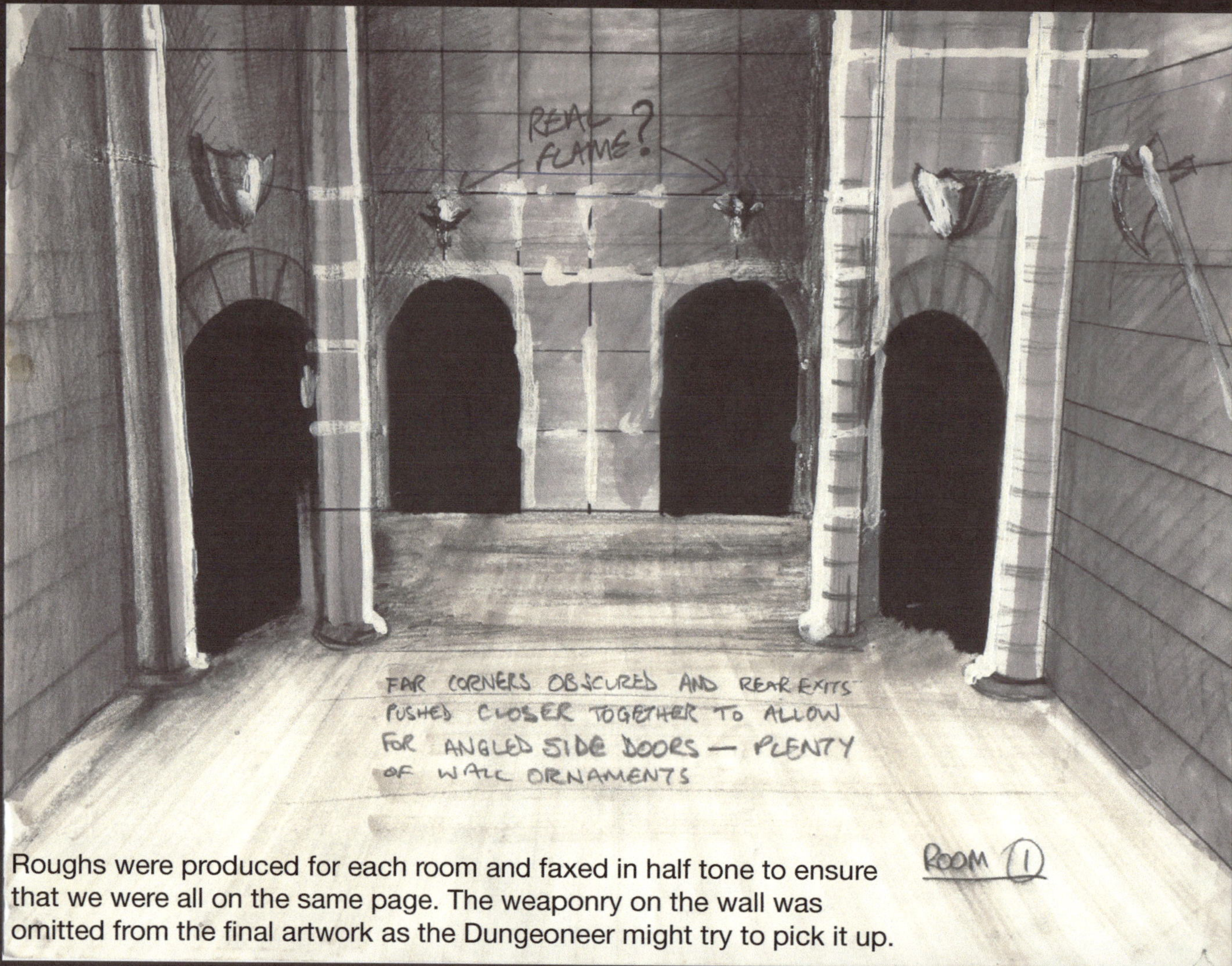

Roughs were produced for each room and faxed in half tone to ensure that we were all on the same page. The weaponry on the wall was omitted from the final artwork as the Dungeoneer might try to pick it up.

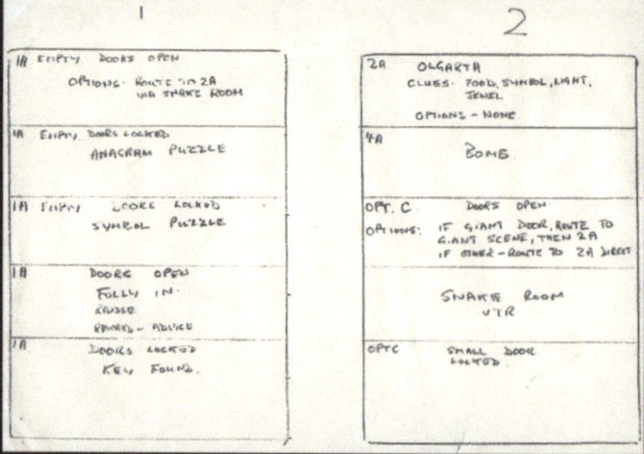

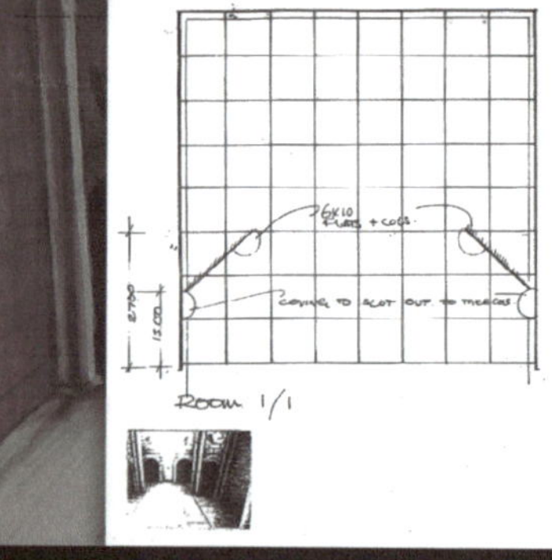

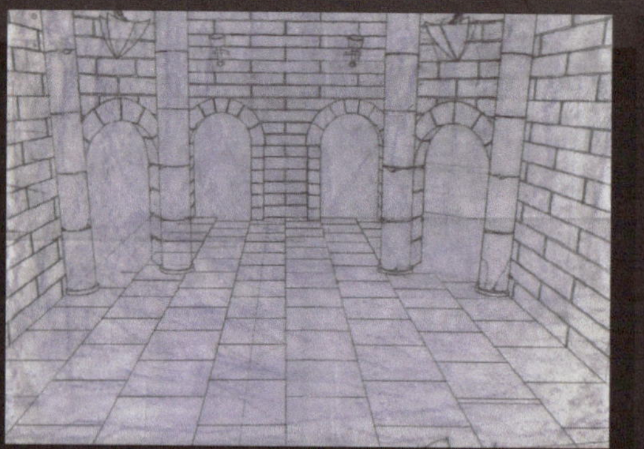

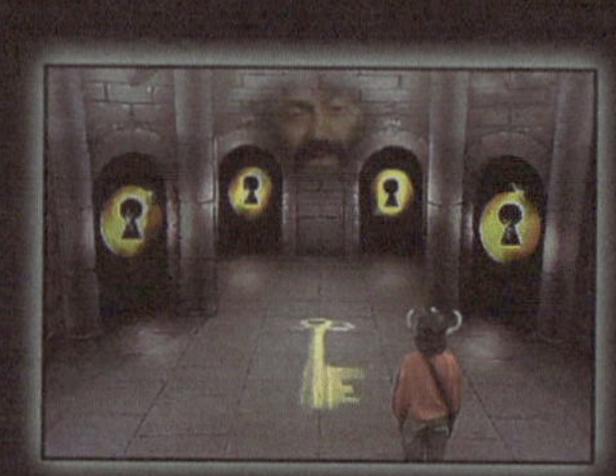

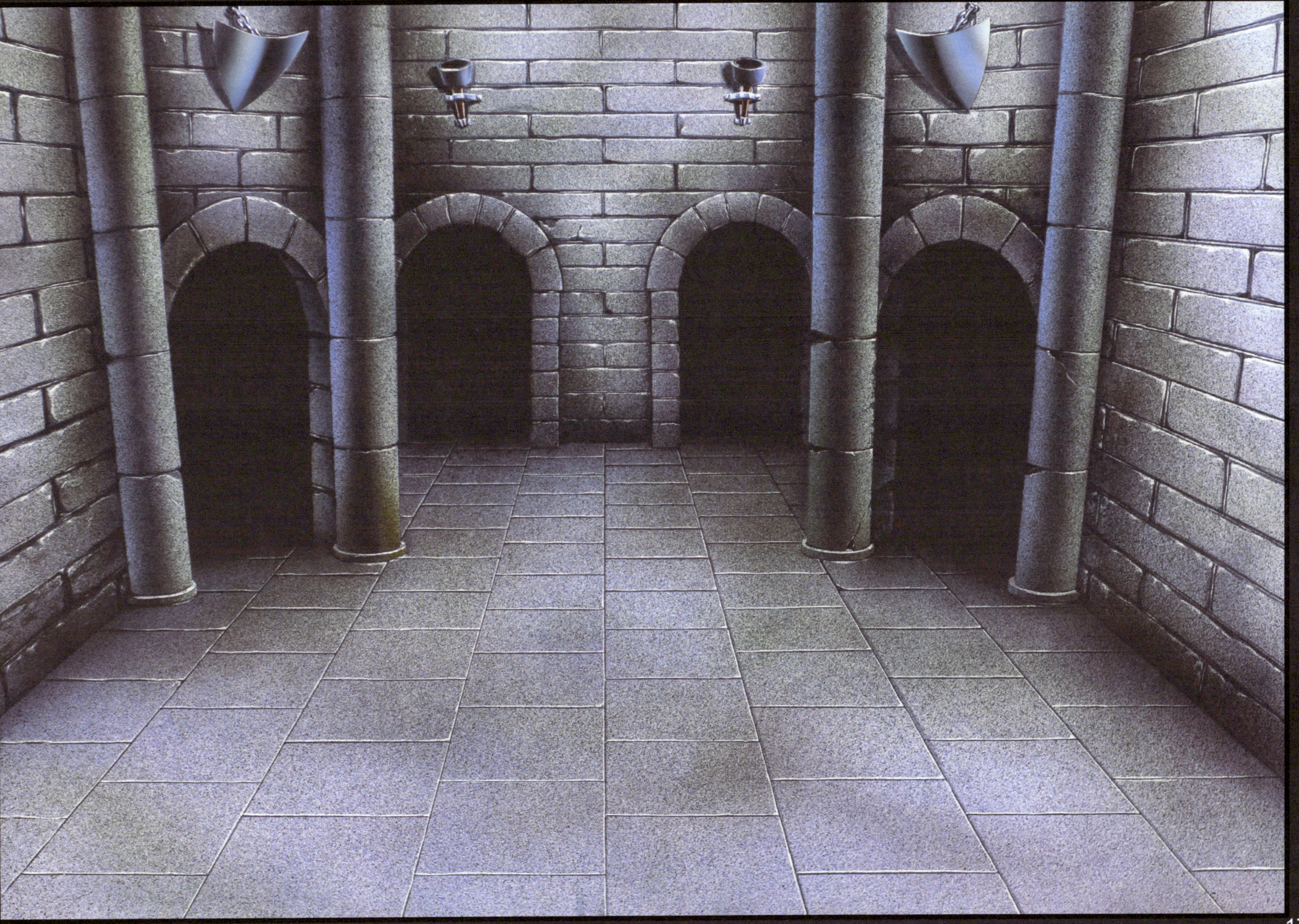

Snake/Scorpion Room 1.1a

The Snake Room was created with a view to having a final composite featuring creatures from Colchester zoo.

The lighting is relatively flat and although the room is brick red in colour the computer graphic phase could introduce any altered hue and many different dramatic lighting scenarios.

Artefacts and weapons were deliberately placed well out of reach of the adventurer in case they were asked to acquire one of them.

The original construction drawings were developed by overlaying a copy of the perspective grid with paper. If time was pressing, this would be straight onto tracing paper and then quickly transferred to illustration board by rubbing the back with coloured chalk and tracing the lines through.

Right: *Dungeon guide notes from Broadsword with hinted scenario options.*

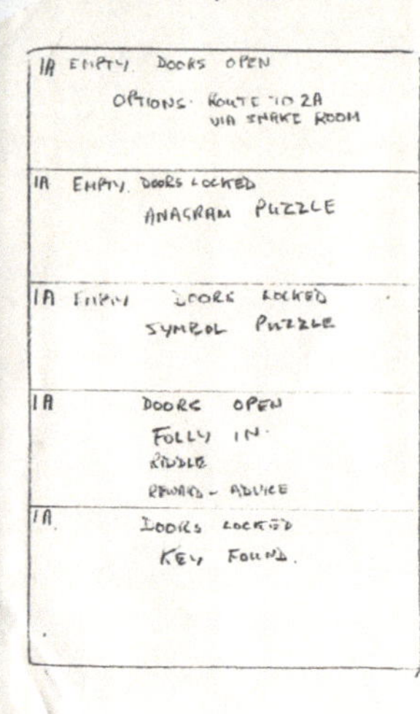

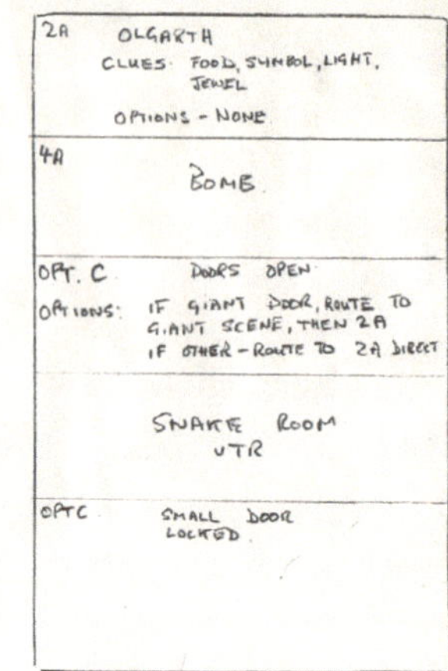

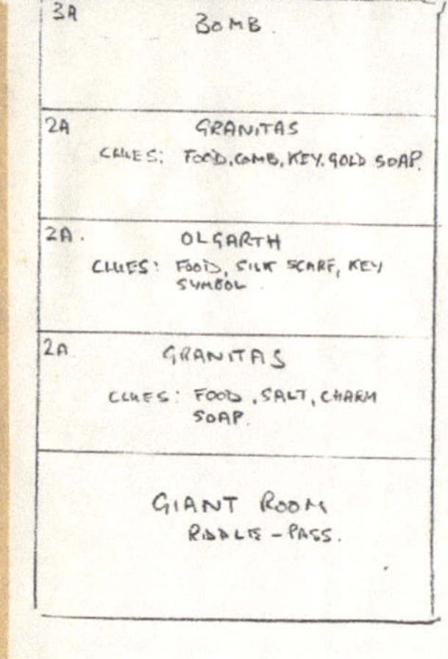

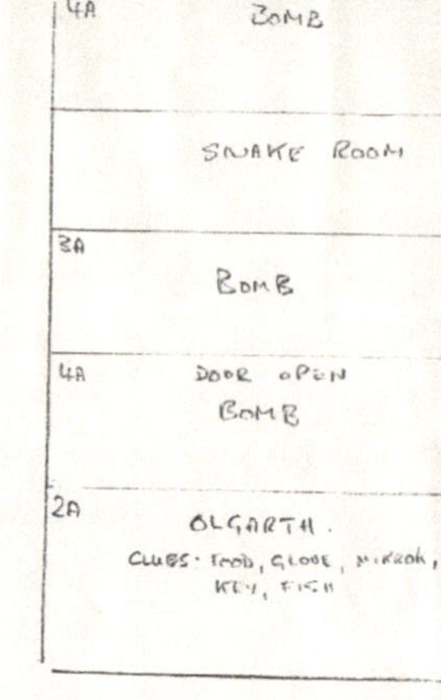

LEVEL 1. G. PLAN.

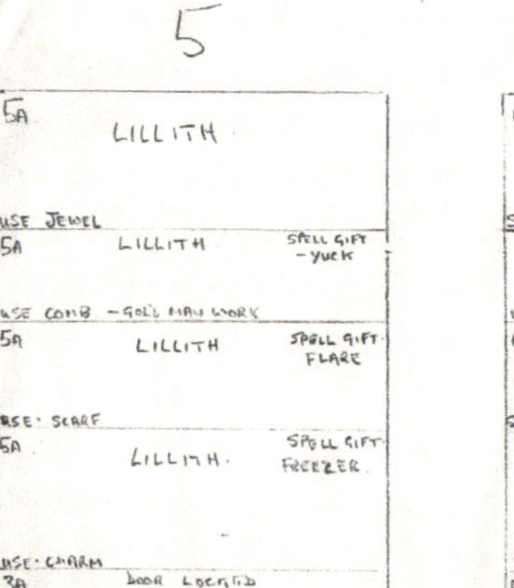

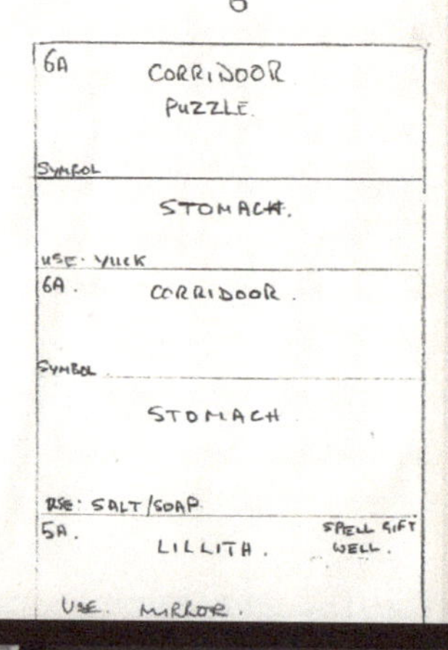

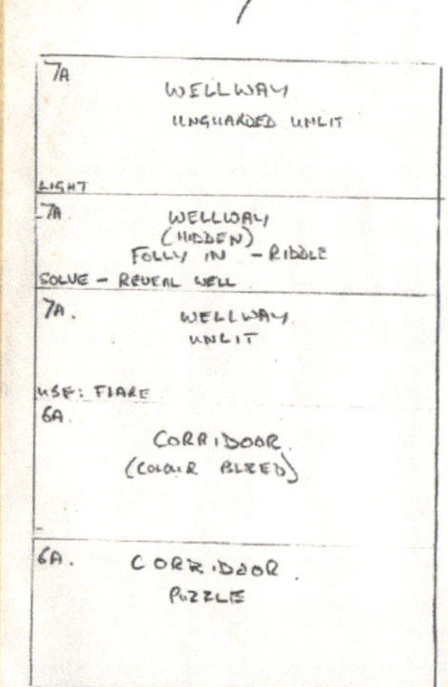

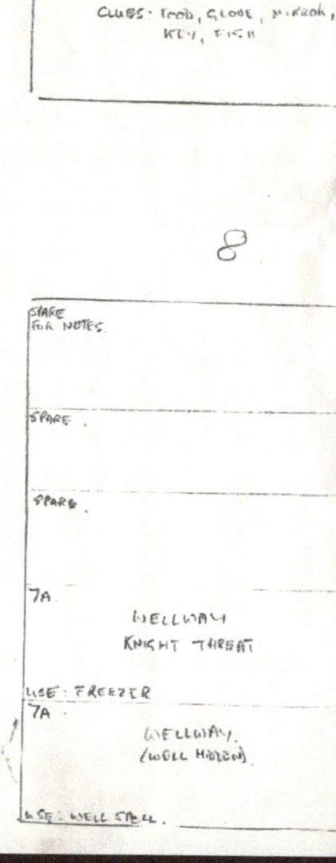

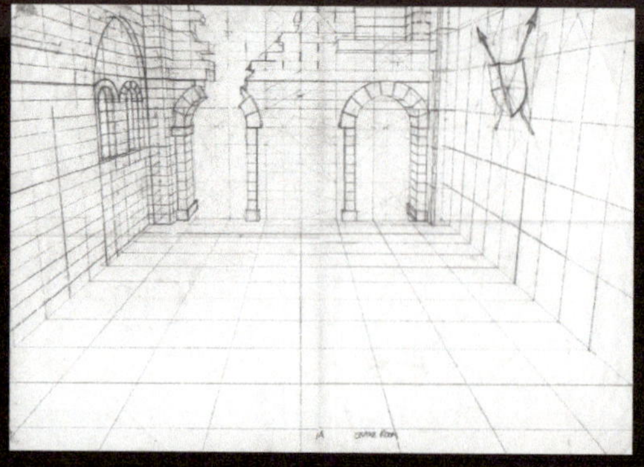

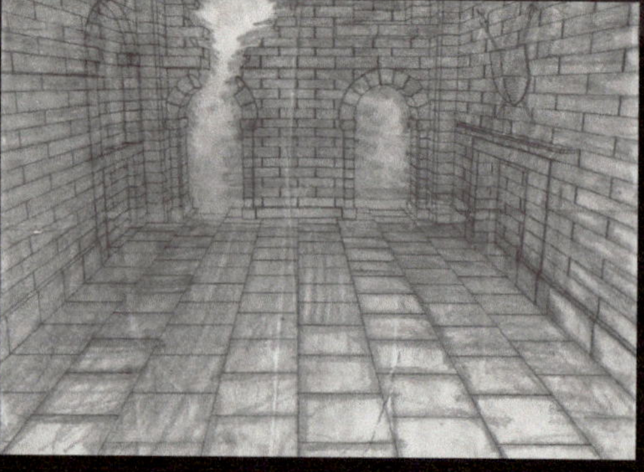

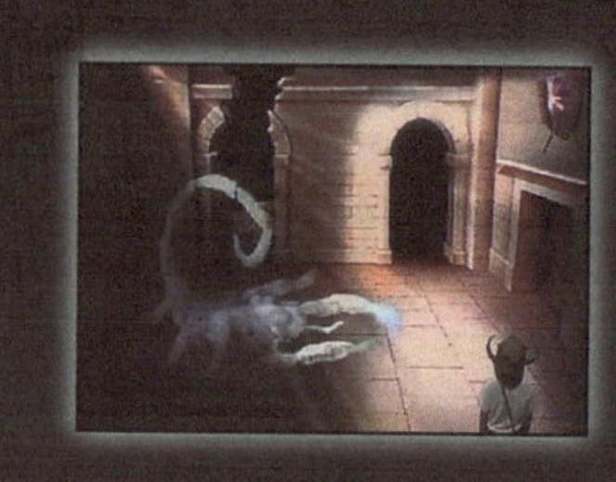

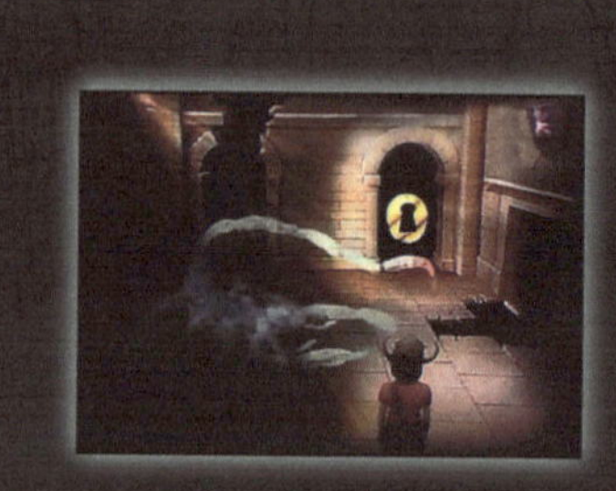

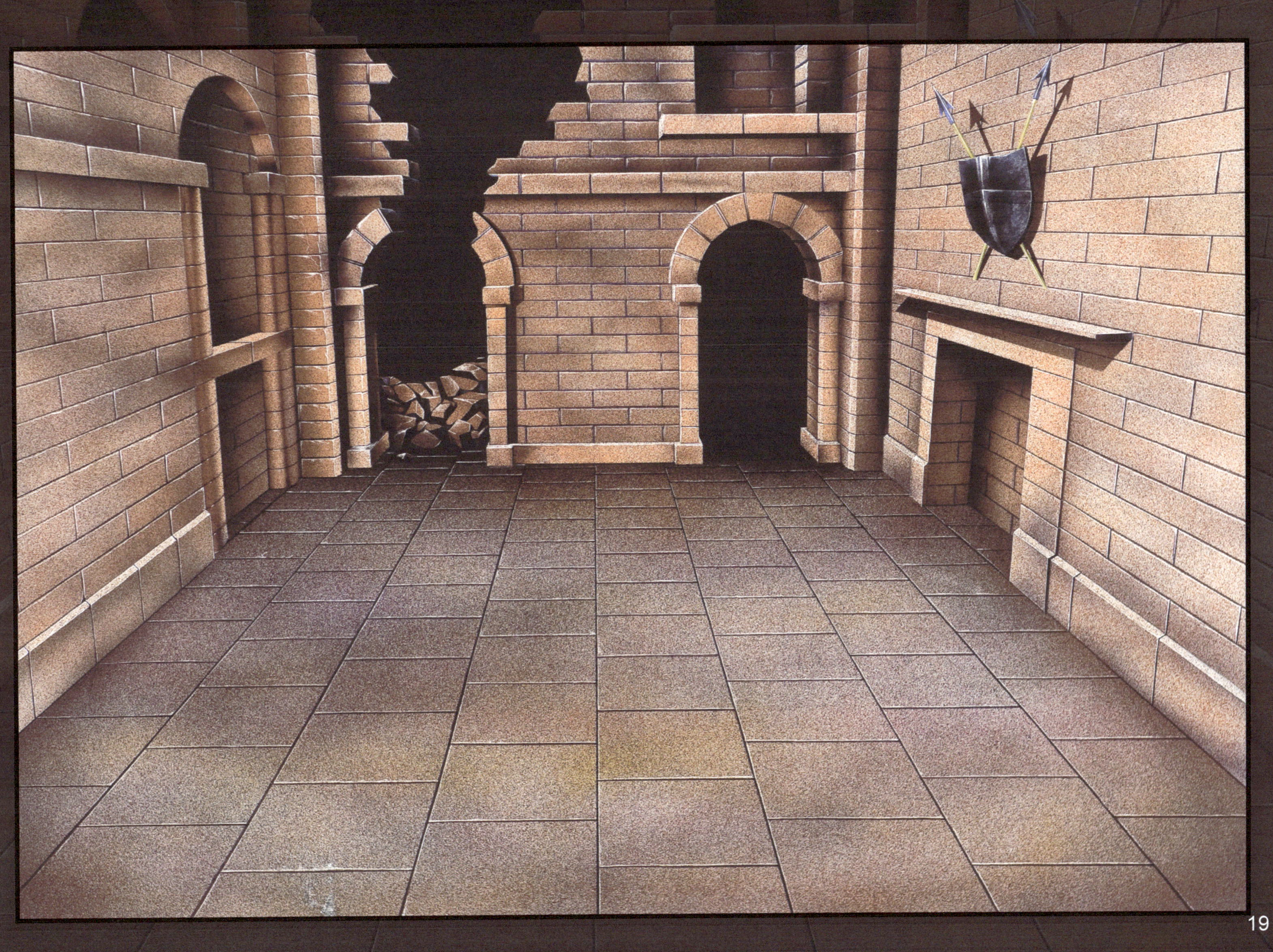

Giant Room 1.2a

The requirements for this room included the placement of a ledge to the left for the Dungeoneer to walk upon and a large pit for him to interact with the head of an enormous giant.

This room was very versatile and was also composited with a seething pit of huge maggots in place of the giant.

Another manifestation of the room was the Scarab Room (room 1.17a). This room was reconstructed with computer graphics, taking the left half of the image, duplicating it and flipping it to form a new right side. The effect was to produce a scarab-like symmetrical room. The room was then relit with glowing flames and fire.

This additional use of the original art proved less time consuming and more cost effective than producing another original painting.

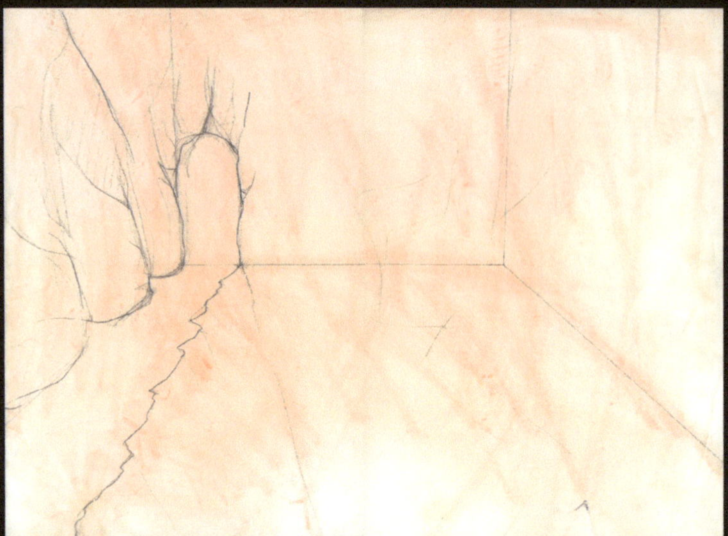

This tracing was fairly simple and straightforward. The room geometry still had to be marked in for alignment.

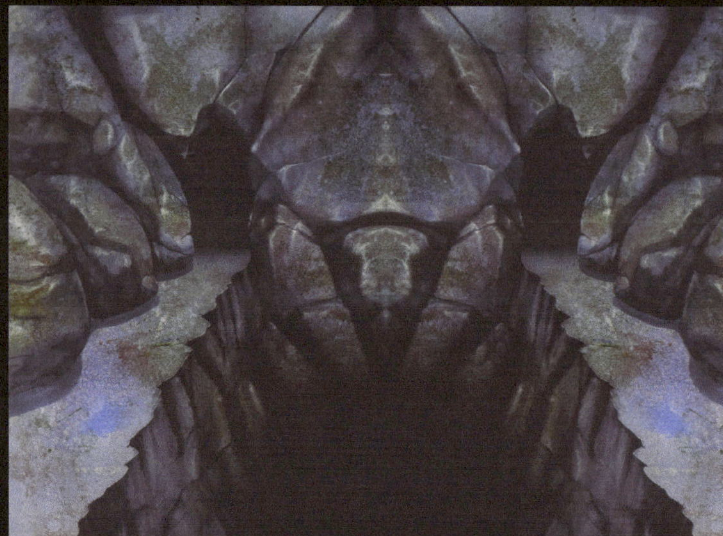

The Scarab Room was created by adding a flipped copy of the left side of the image and filling the fore-ground.

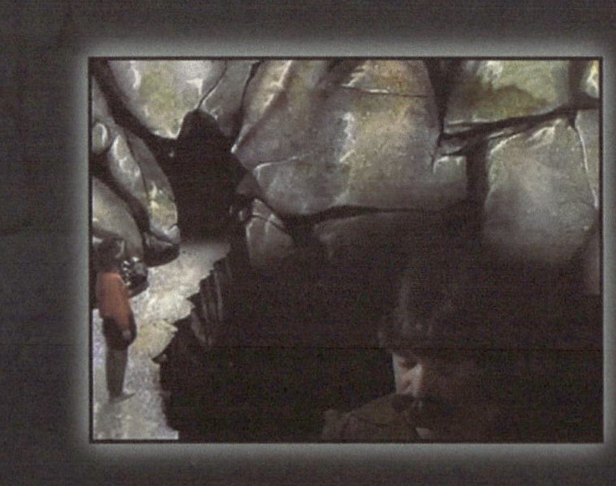

The Giant's room as broadcast.

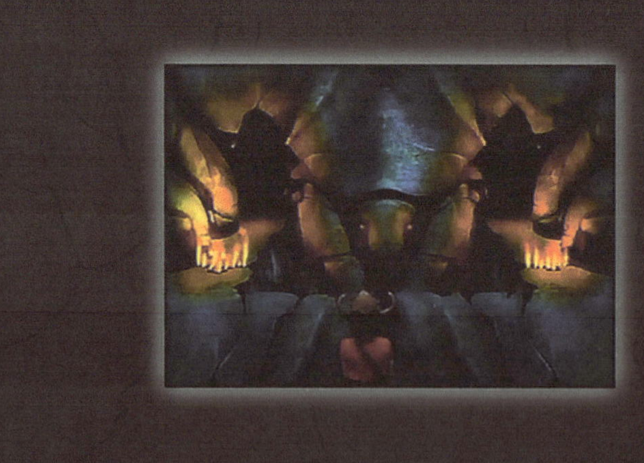

The Scarab Room as broadcast.

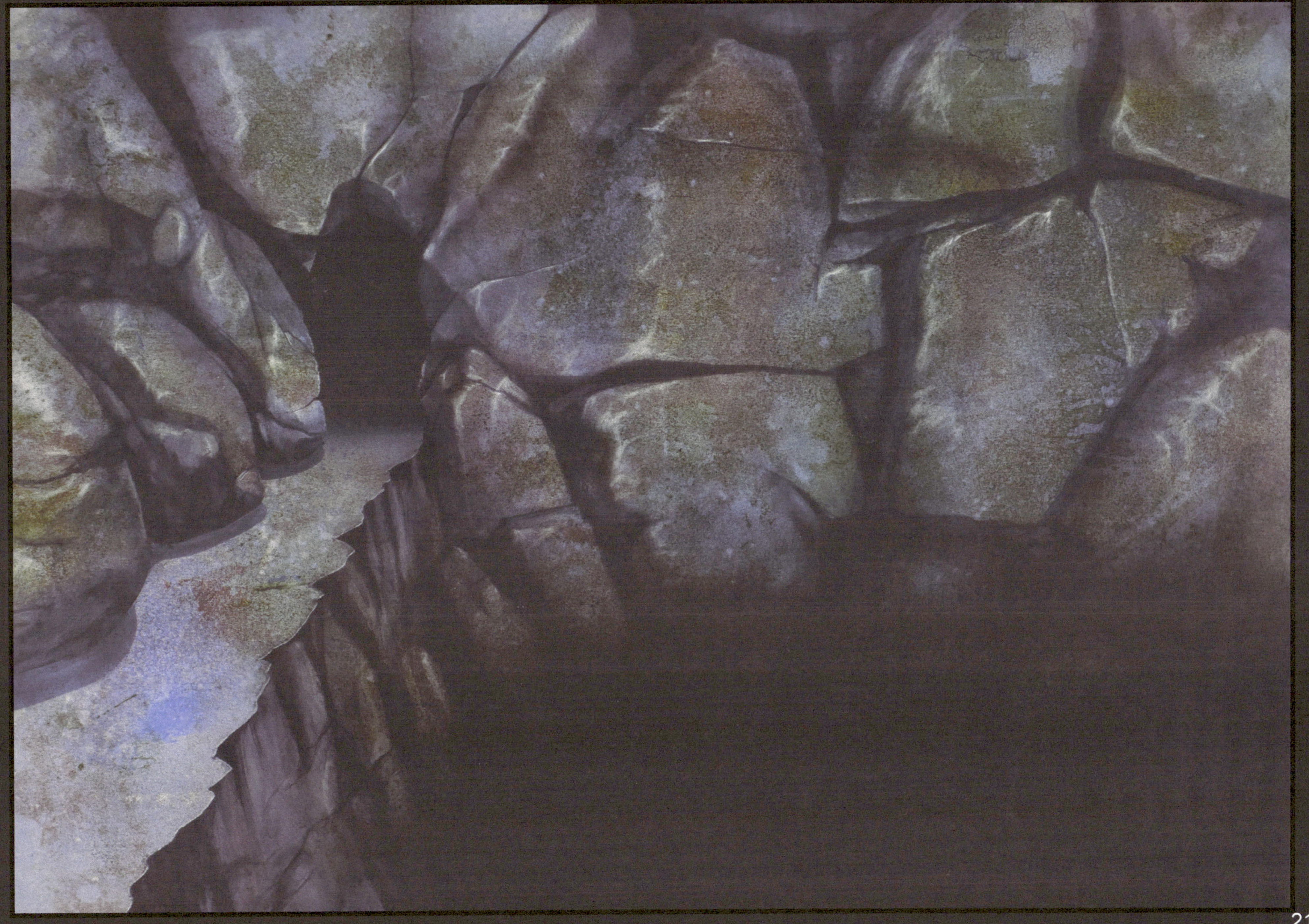

Granitas Clue Room 1.3a

This room required a blank wall at the back so that a wall monster could manifest itself. The foreground had to be clear for a table with props which the Dungeoneer could actually pick up.

Wall monster sketches had to be craggy as if formed from rocks. These were to be made into foam masks and composited with the painting.

As the room was to be fairly plain, I added damp patches, stains and cracks to provide added interest and a sense of the room having had a history.

Left to Right:
Progress Plan.

Drawing.
There is a rough indication for positioning the wall monster.

Tracing.

Wall Monster rough.

Broadcast composite. *This shows strong lighting that could capture object shadows, thus anchoring them to the floor. This was a notable breakthrough for Chromakey techniques.*

Further variation *based upon the original.*

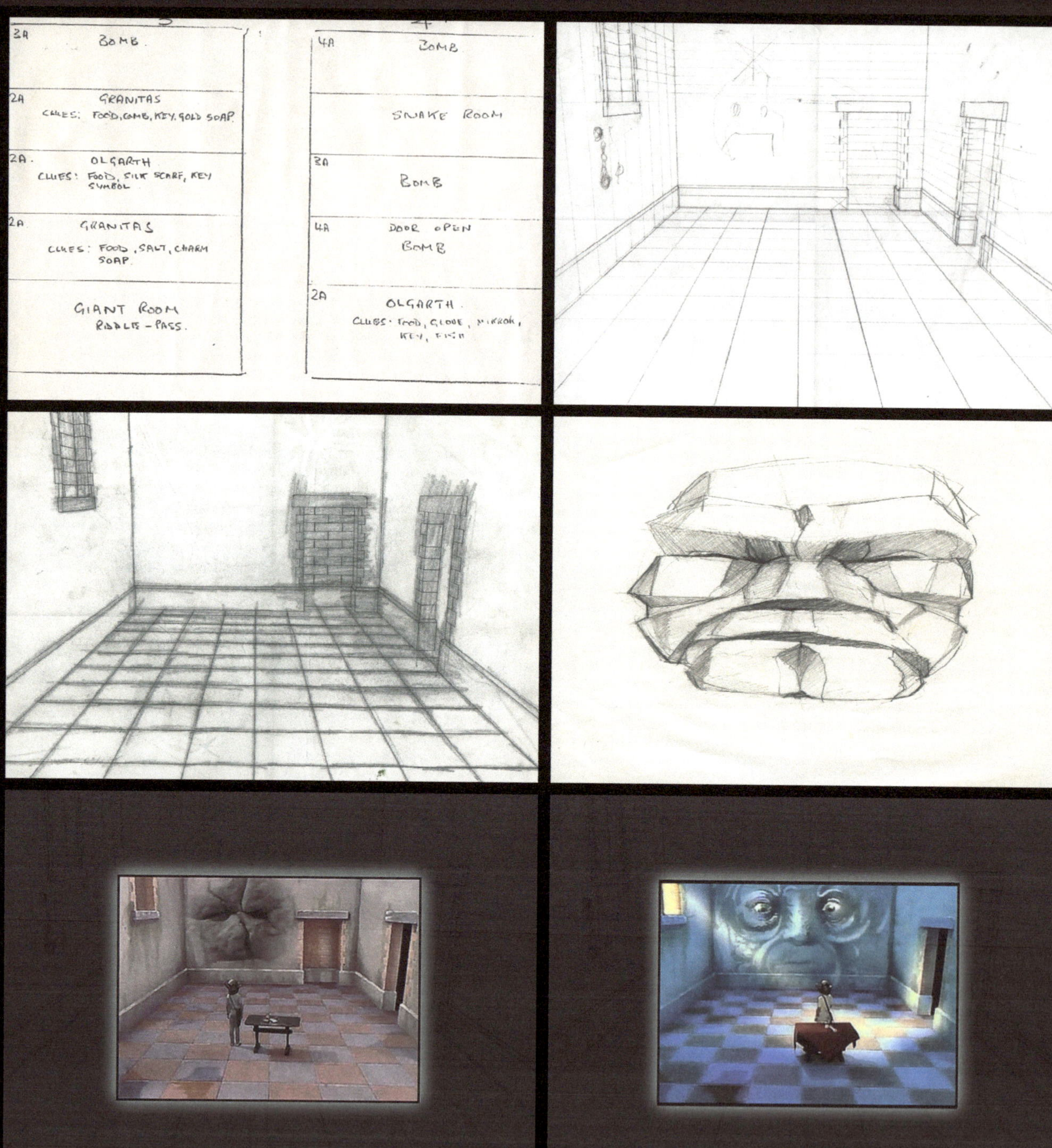

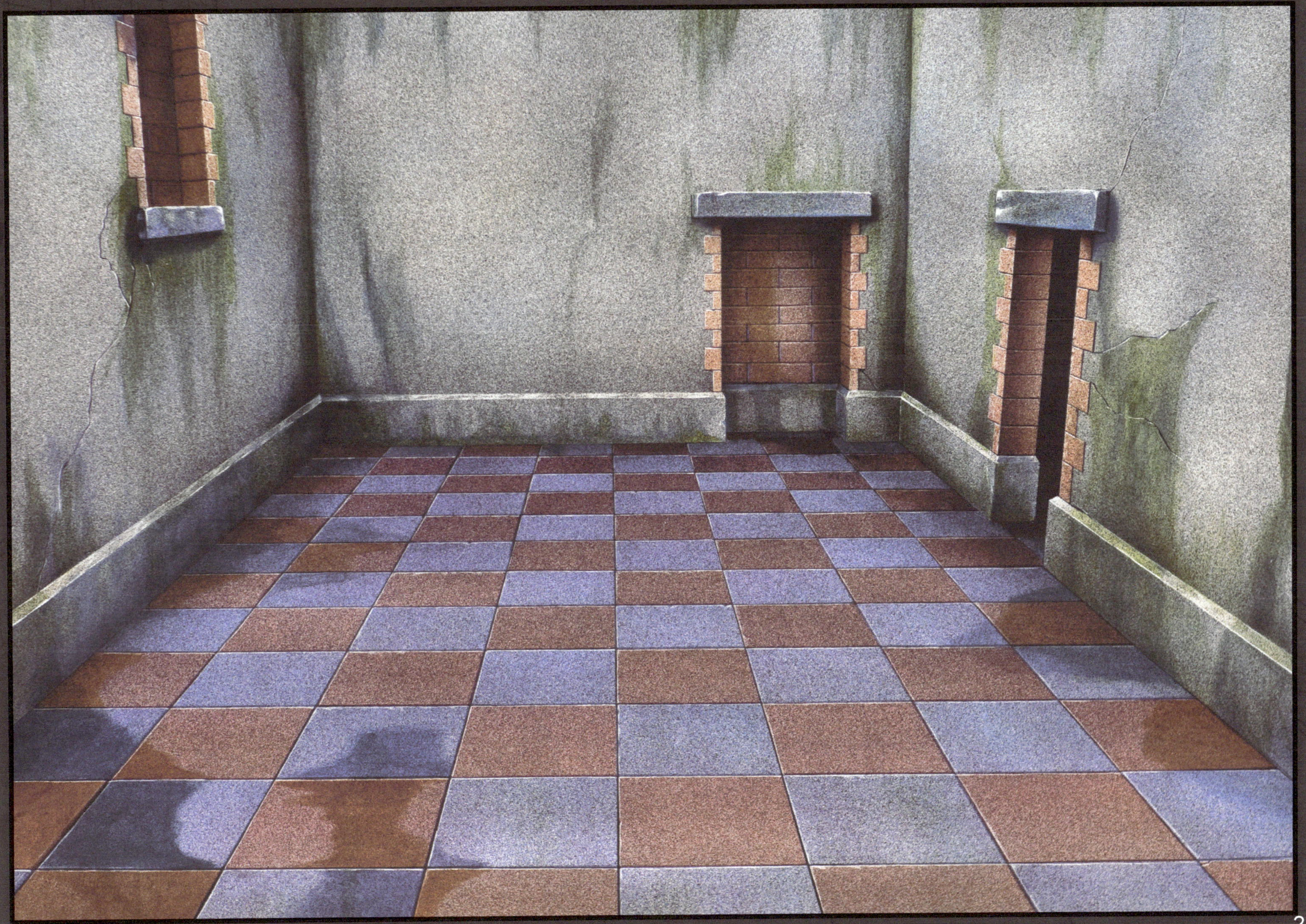

Bomb Room One
1.4a

The Bomb Room was an extremely effective 'hurry up' device. It ensured that the rapport between the Dungeoneer and the rest of team was of the highest order necessary for the impending challenges.

It was a form of natural selection that ensured that only the most able teams made progress in the dungeon.

Each grid square represented one metre of studio floor. Bisecting the squares with diagonal lines at the beginning and end of a row enabled further subdivision. This allowed more detail to be accurately placed in the painting and proved a useful guide for building physical props.

Right: *The grid was transferred to the drawing to aid the drawing of features. As can be seen here, the grid was further subdivided to aid the placement of more detailed features.*

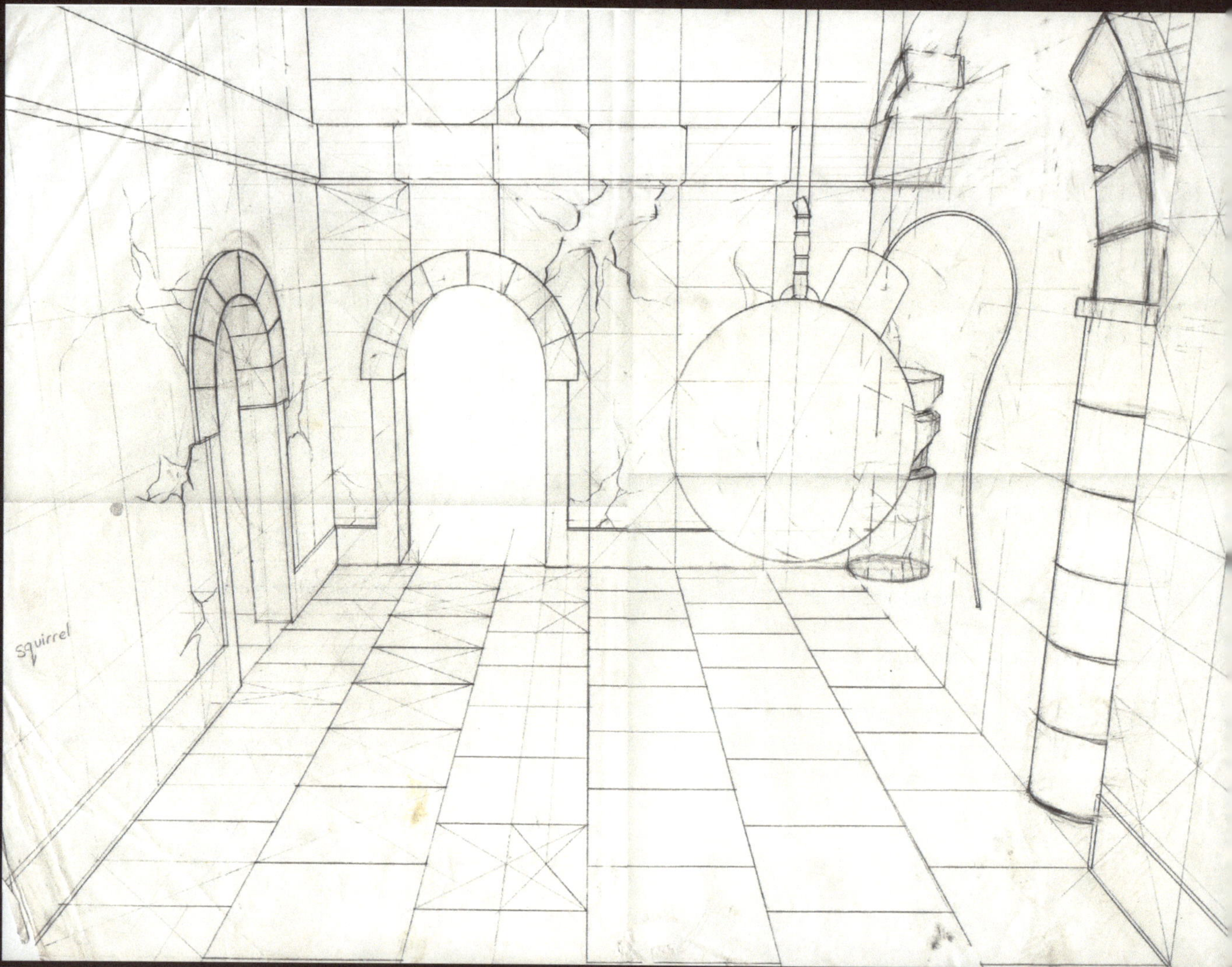

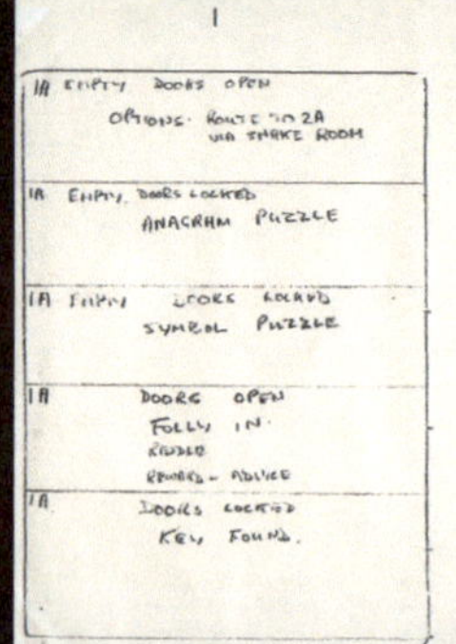

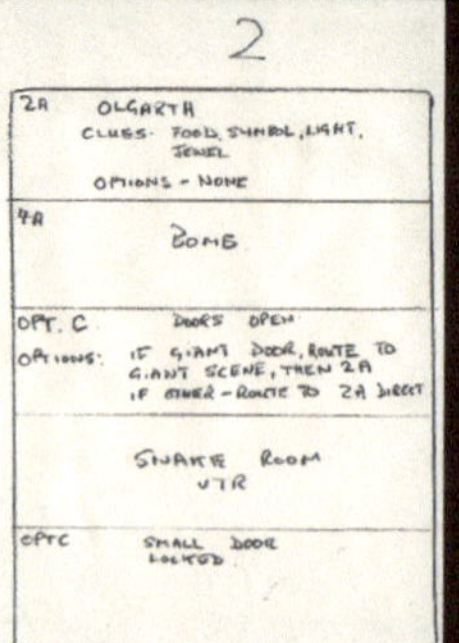

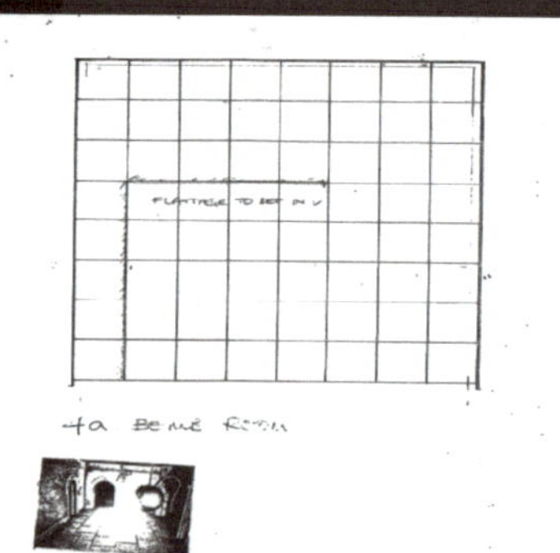

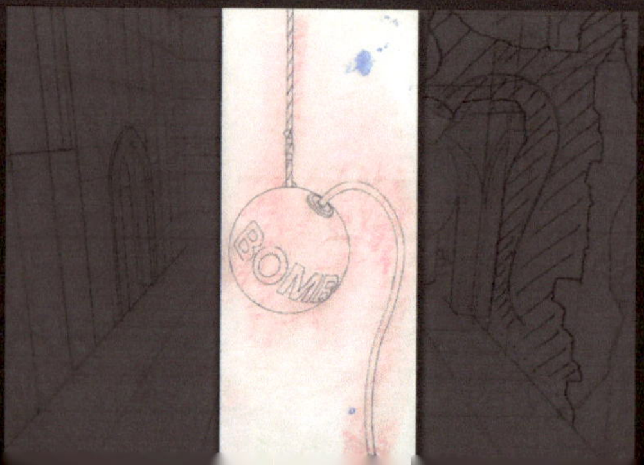

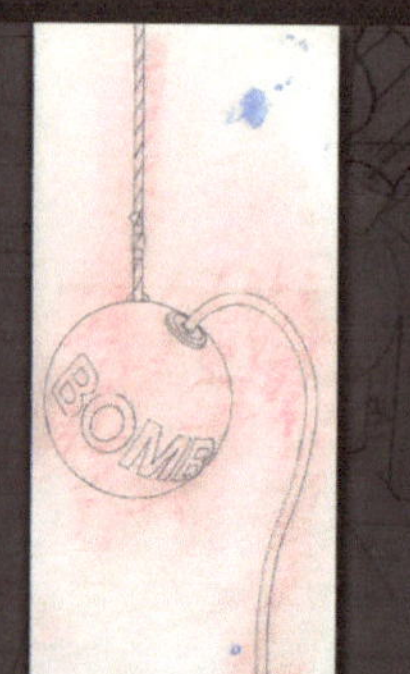

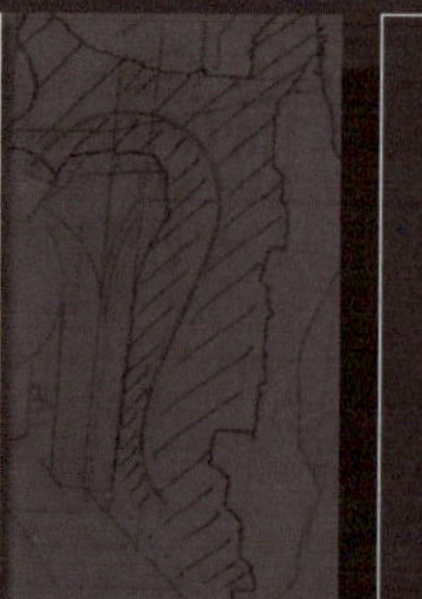

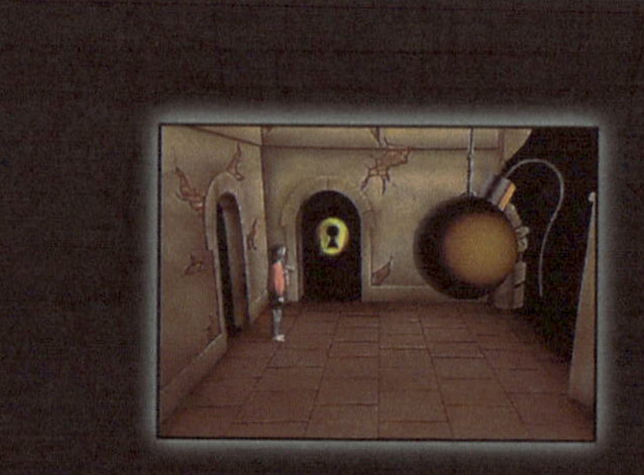

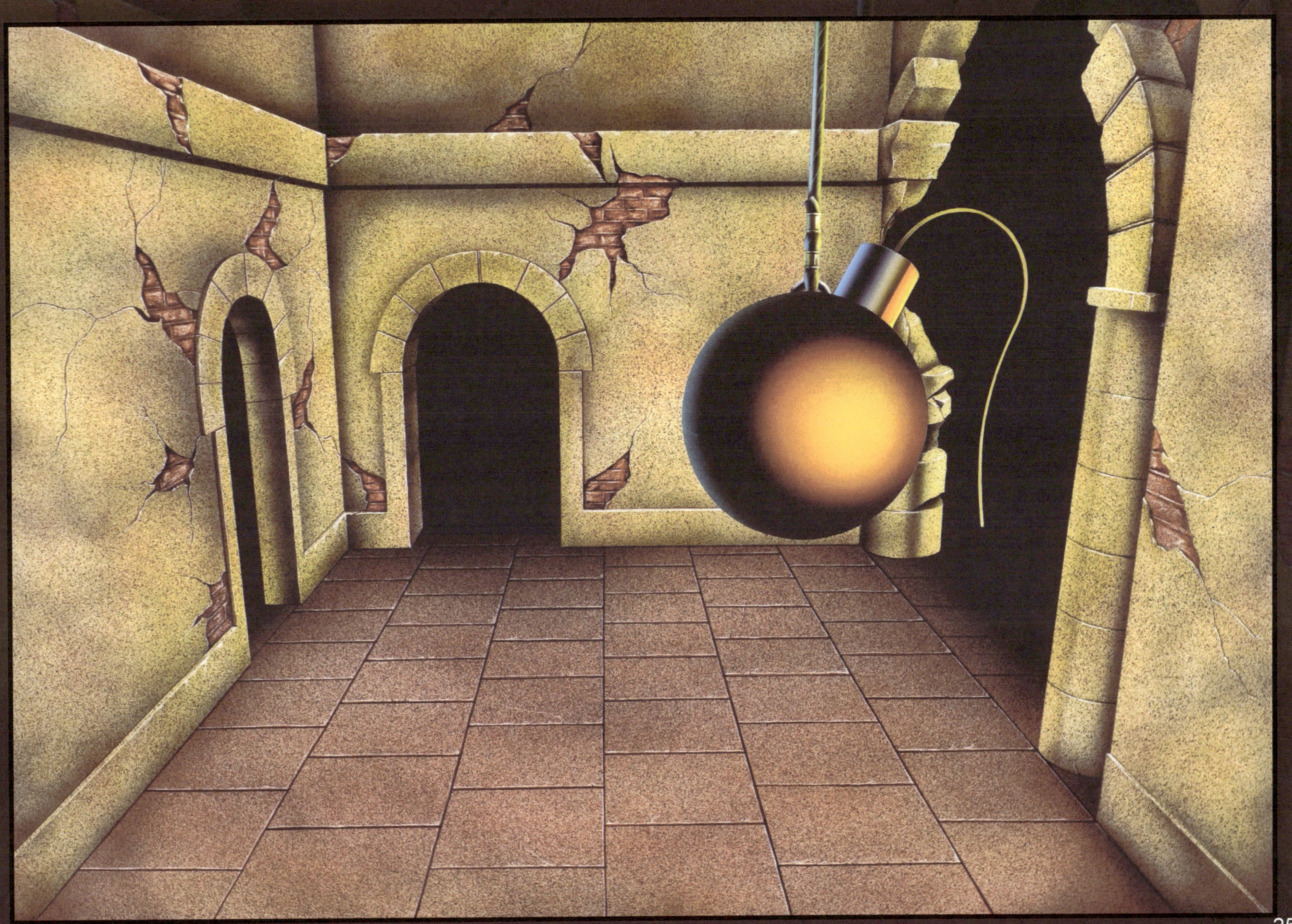

Bomb Room Two 1.5a

A second Bomb room was commissioned. It was used to provide an extra hurry up and had a much faster burning fuse.
The hatched area in the drawing was contrived as a contrasting background to make the burning fuse appear as bright as possible.
The Bomb rooms could appear as they were painted or reversed.

Right: *The drawing for the second Bomb Room. The hatched area indicated the section of broken wall that had to disappear into darkness. This conveniently gave a high contrast background for the burning fuse animation.*

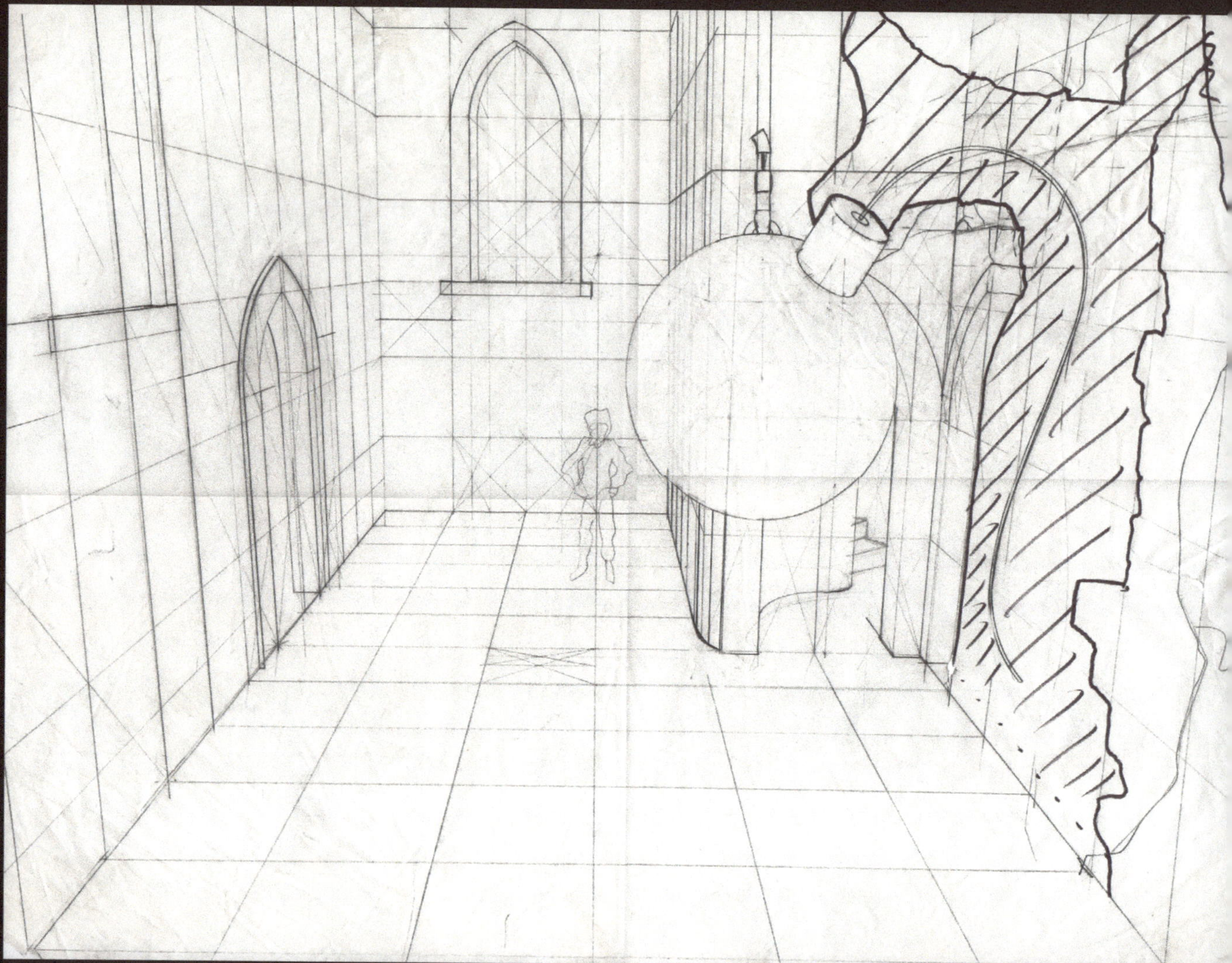

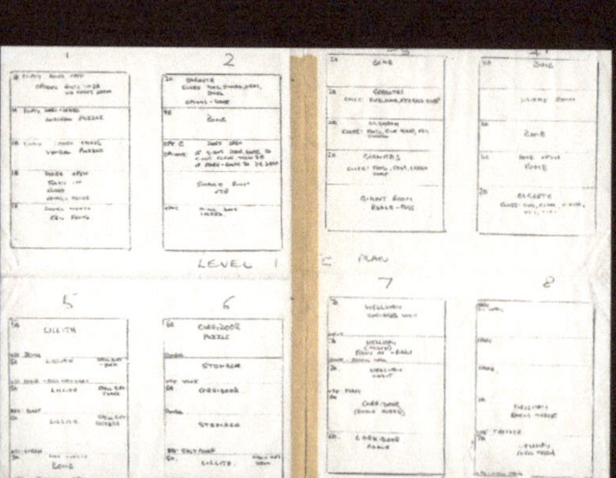

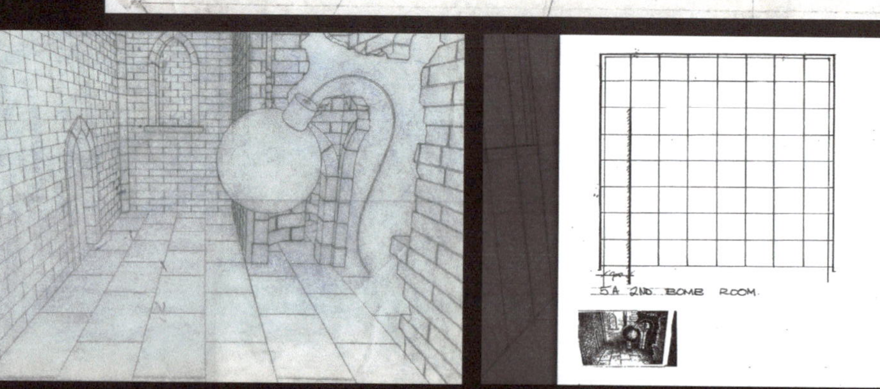

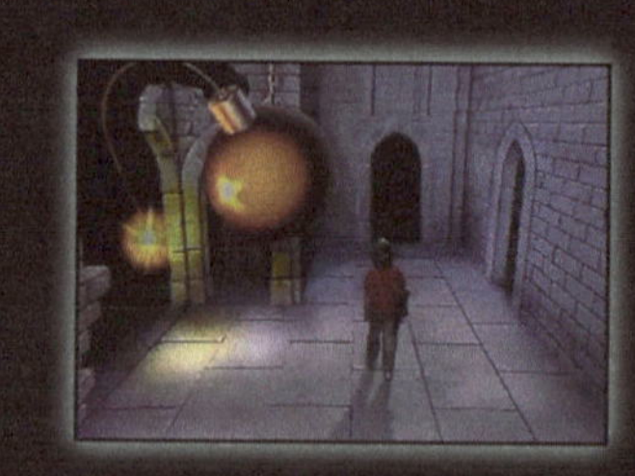

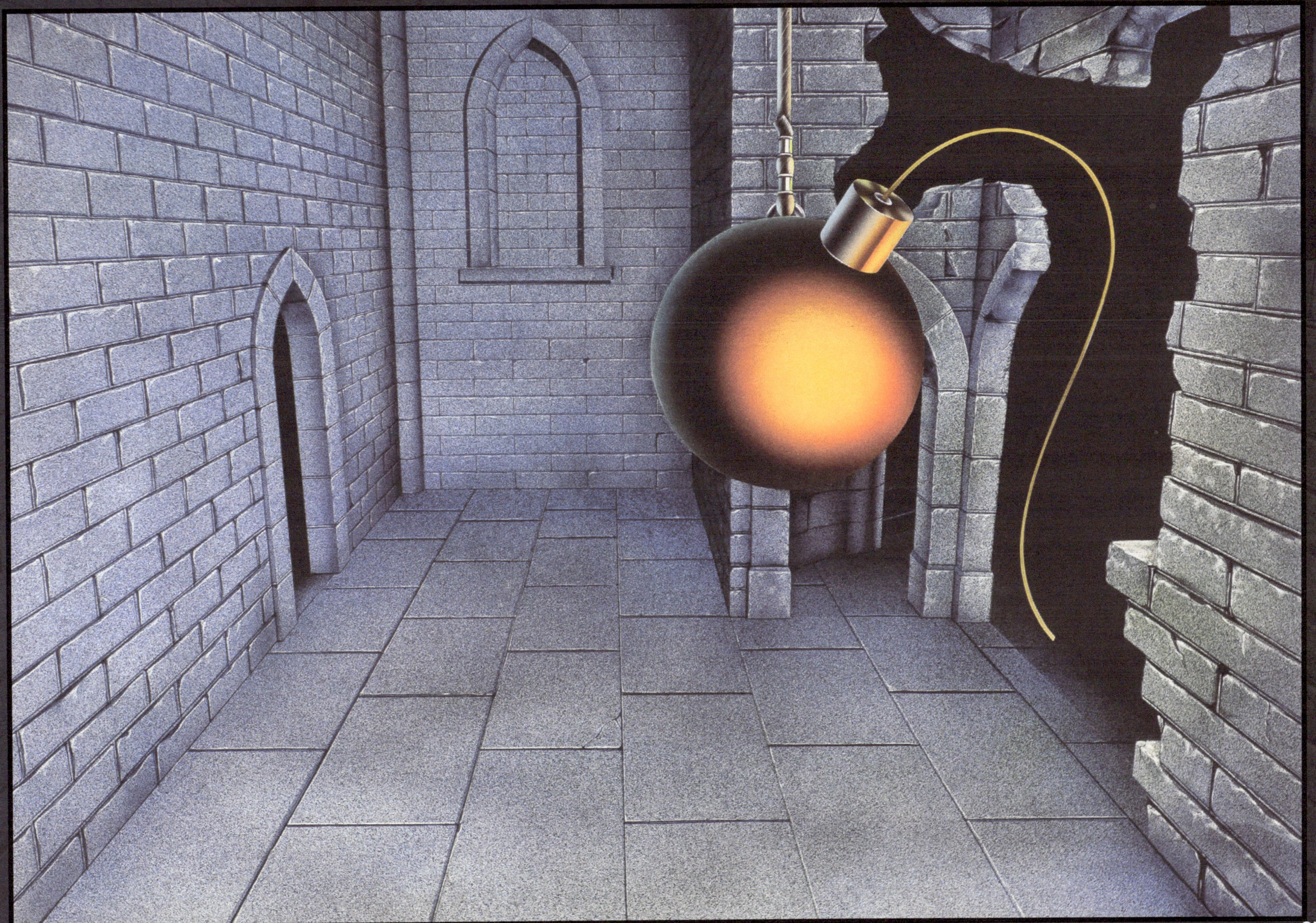

Lilith Room 1.6a

This is one of my favourite rooms. There were exact features to match so that props could be positioned accurately.
The ledges on the left acted as a seat and foot rest for Lilith. As her gown flowed over the props, I was relieved to see that it appeared to flow over the rocks in the final composite.
The continuous crack line in the rocks on either side of the chasm indicate where the floor plane would have gone through.

Right: *The Lilith room drawing showing more detail. The ledges for Lilith's seat were precisely located on the grid. A sketch of Lilith was roughed in to indicate scale and position. The causeway was omitted and added with CG.*

Far Right: *This is how the scene was observed by the actors and crew. The rest of the Dungeoneer's team saw the composite of actors and painting on the monitor in the chest within the ante room.*

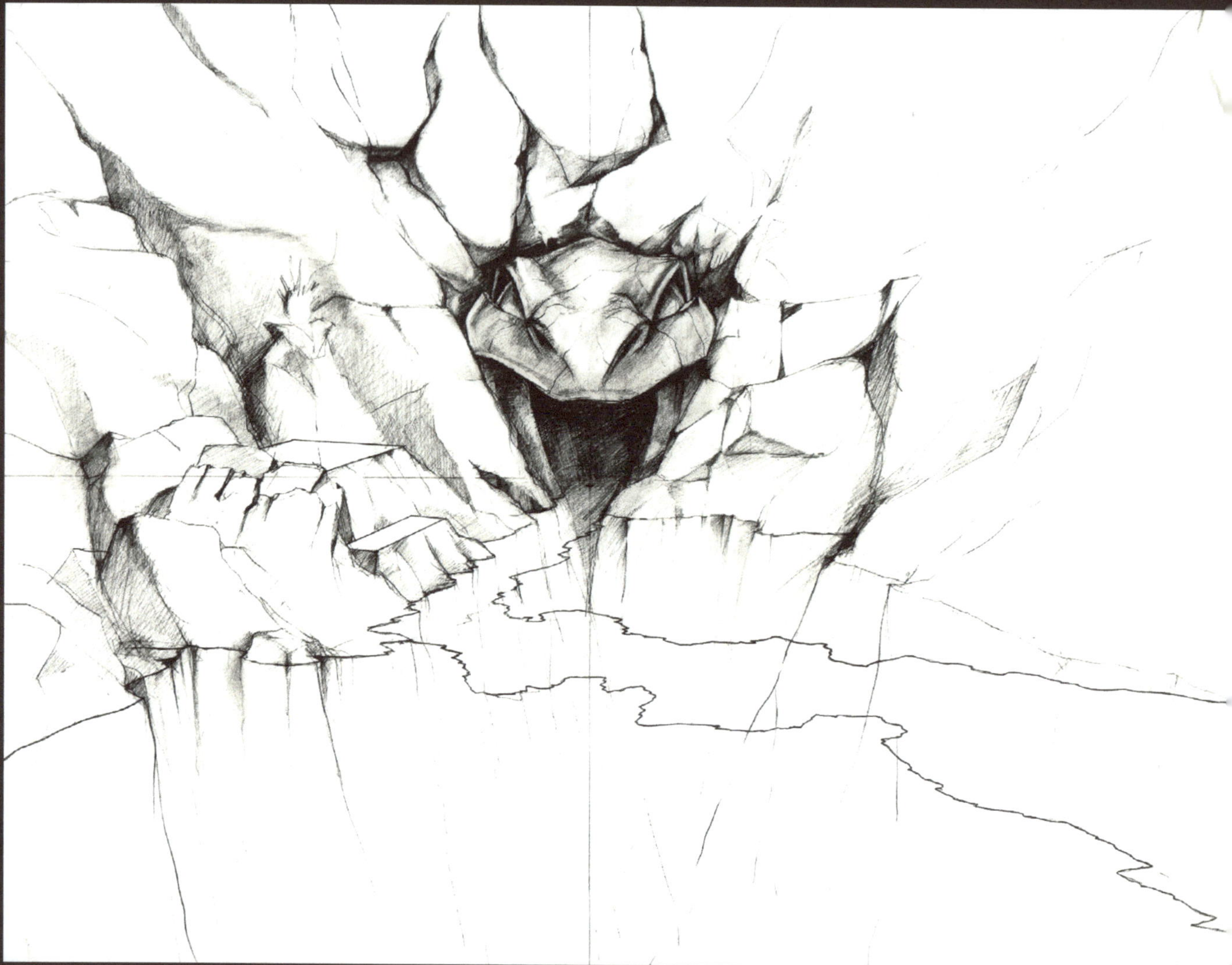

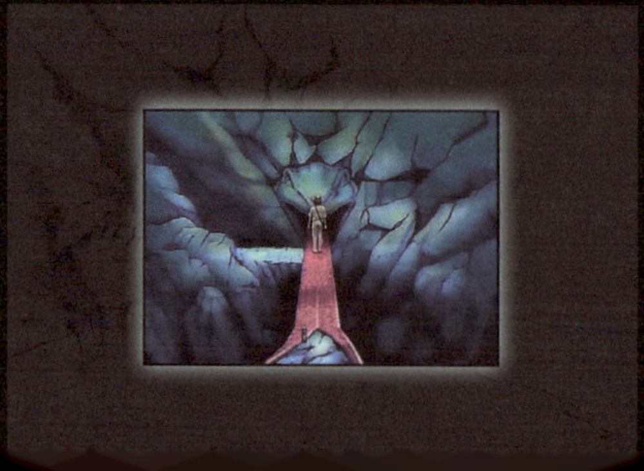

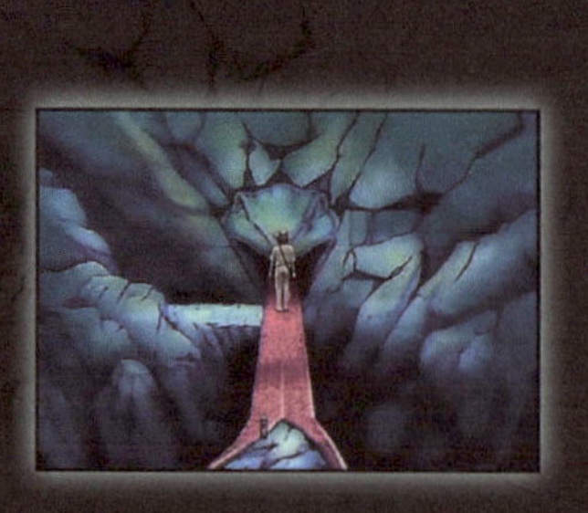

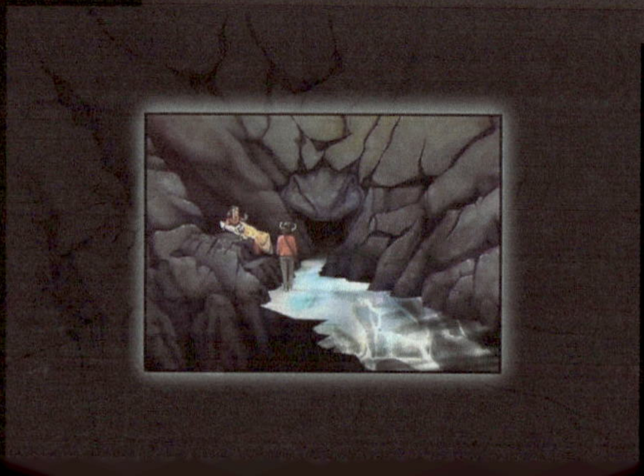

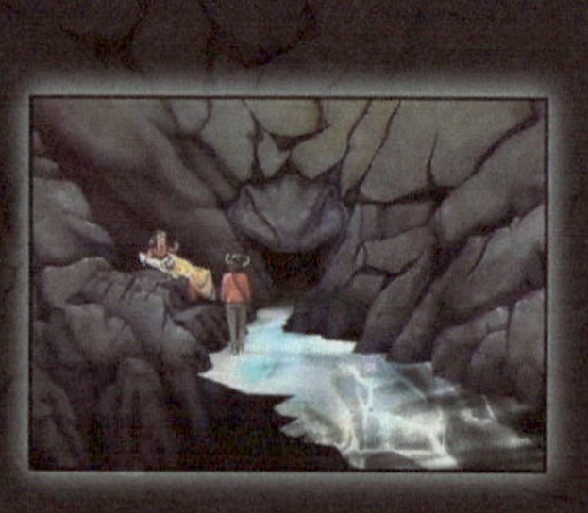

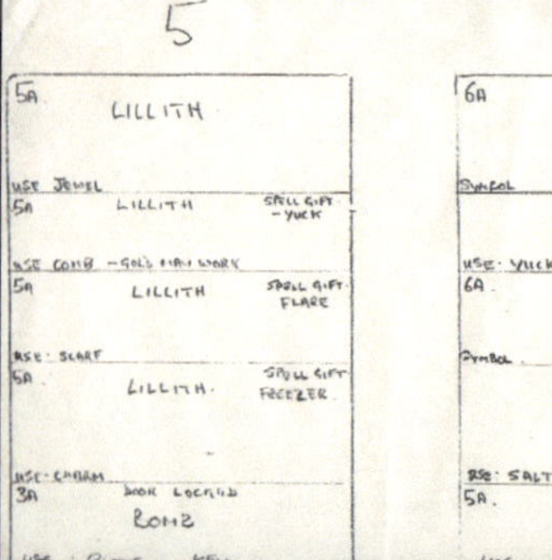

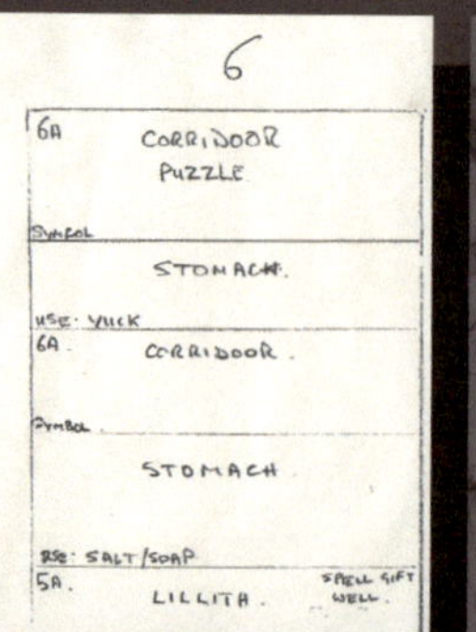

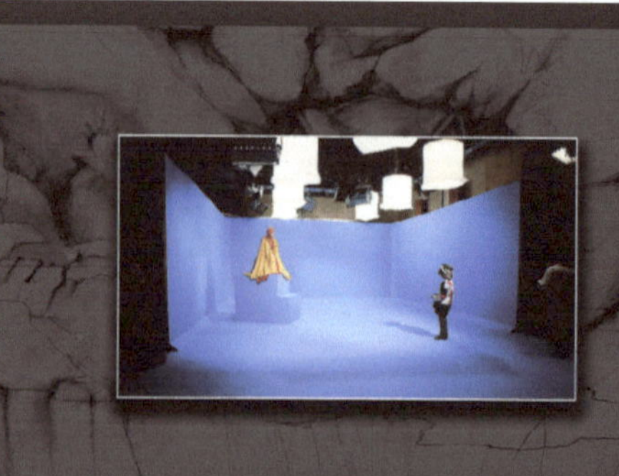

"""

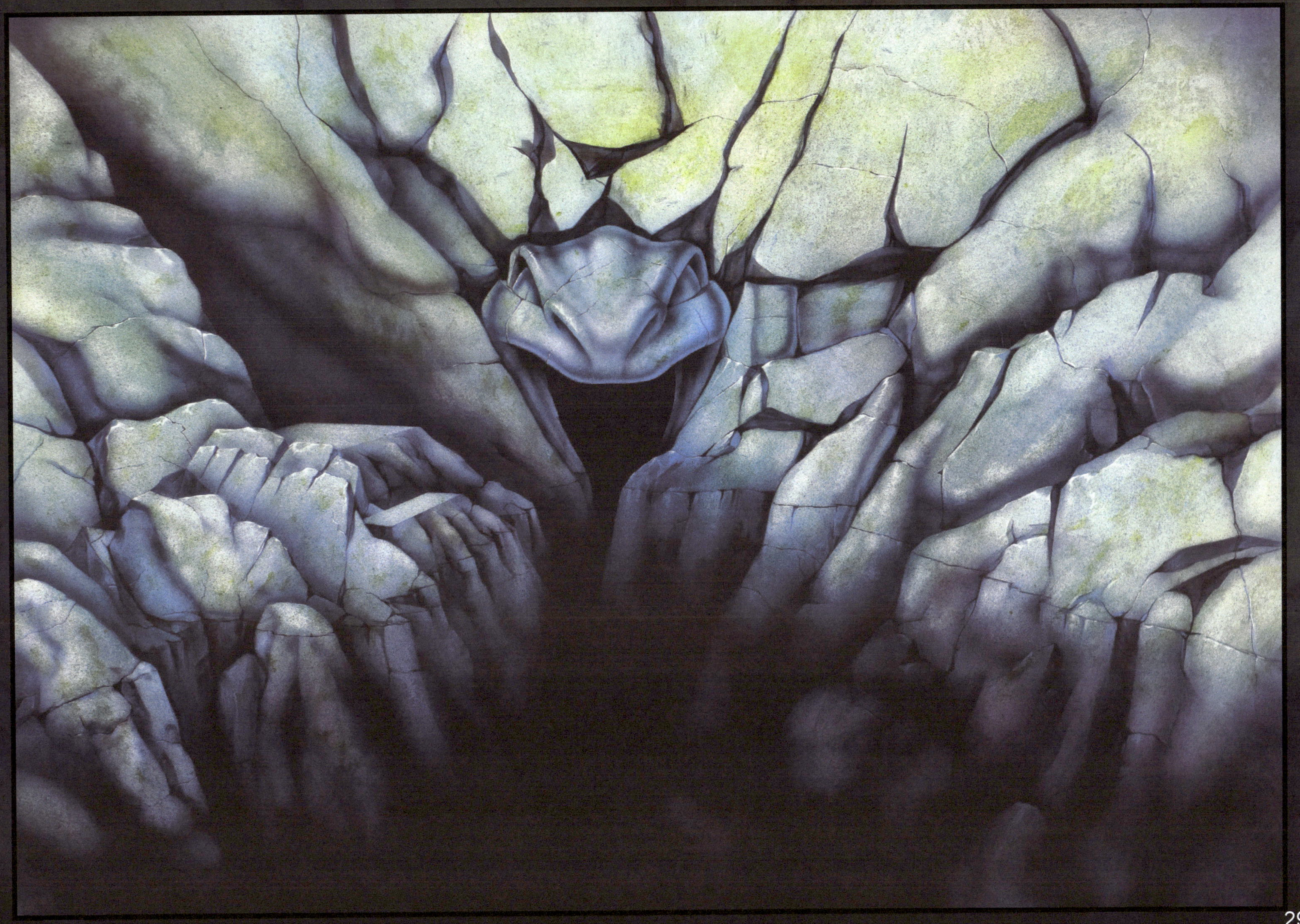

Stomach Room 1.7a

Not one for the squeamish! I had an urgent call from the designer, Ros Inglis who said that they were in the studio ready to shoot and were having trouble lining up the painting with the geometry of the room. I had been working late into the night hence the zzzzeds on the fax which I sent to show where the walls should line up.
The Dungeoneer slid into view partly obscured by a matte which followed the edge of the feature halfway in on the right. It can be seen in the floor plan image.

Top Left: *Scribbled notes over a phone call.*

Top Right: *Stomach Room colour rough.*

Middle Left: *Further layers were added and haggis wrapping inspired 'veins' of fat to give more form to the image.*

Middle Right: *This was an important fax to Ros Inglis, designer on the early Knightmare series. The position of the edges of the void were not obvious from the painting so I faxed a quick annotated overlay as a guide.*

Bottom Left: *Floor plan for the Stomach Room showing the slide entry point.*

Bottom Right: *The Dungeoneer slid down the ramp into the stomach room. The flat prop for that part of the stomach matched the painting perfectly, sustaining the illusion.*

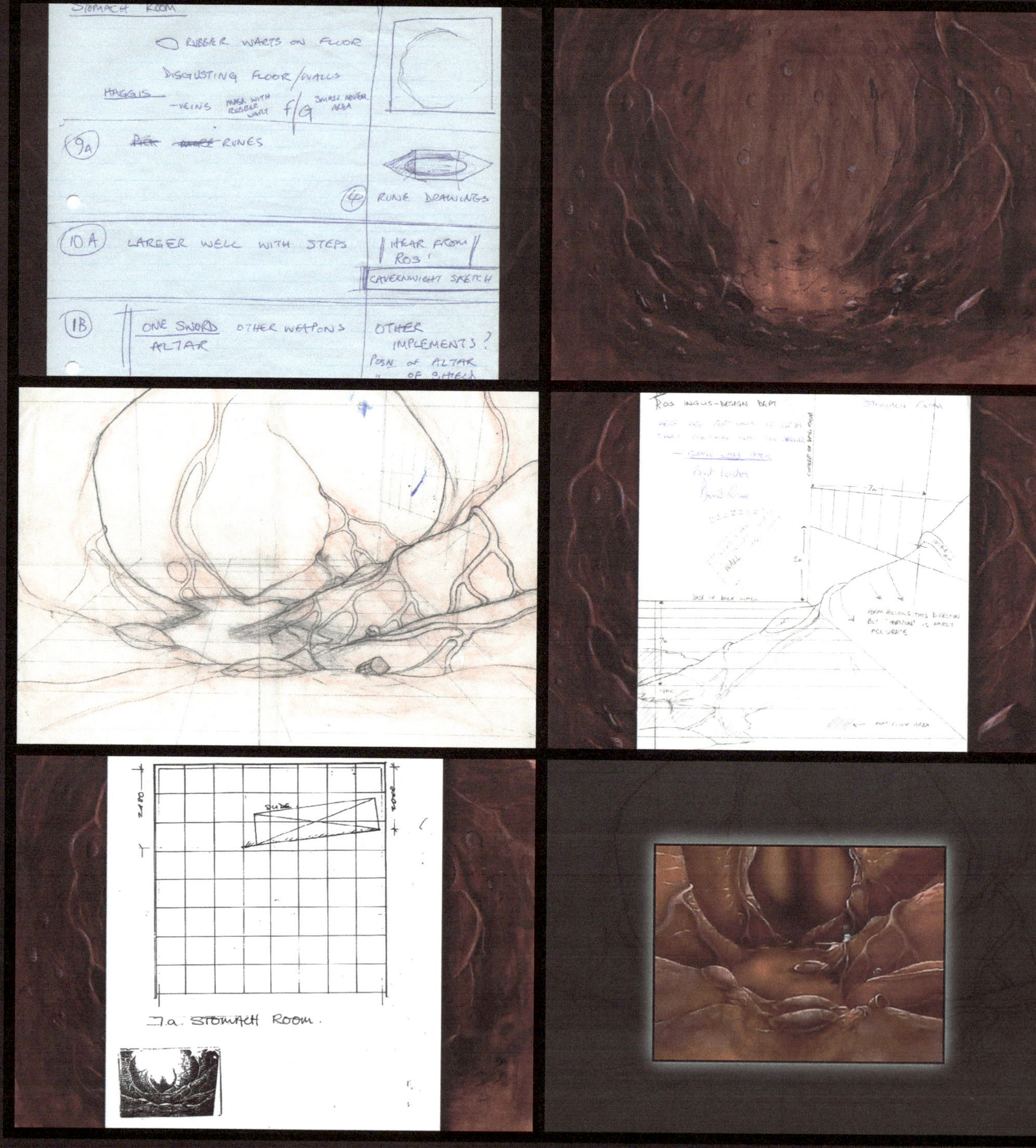

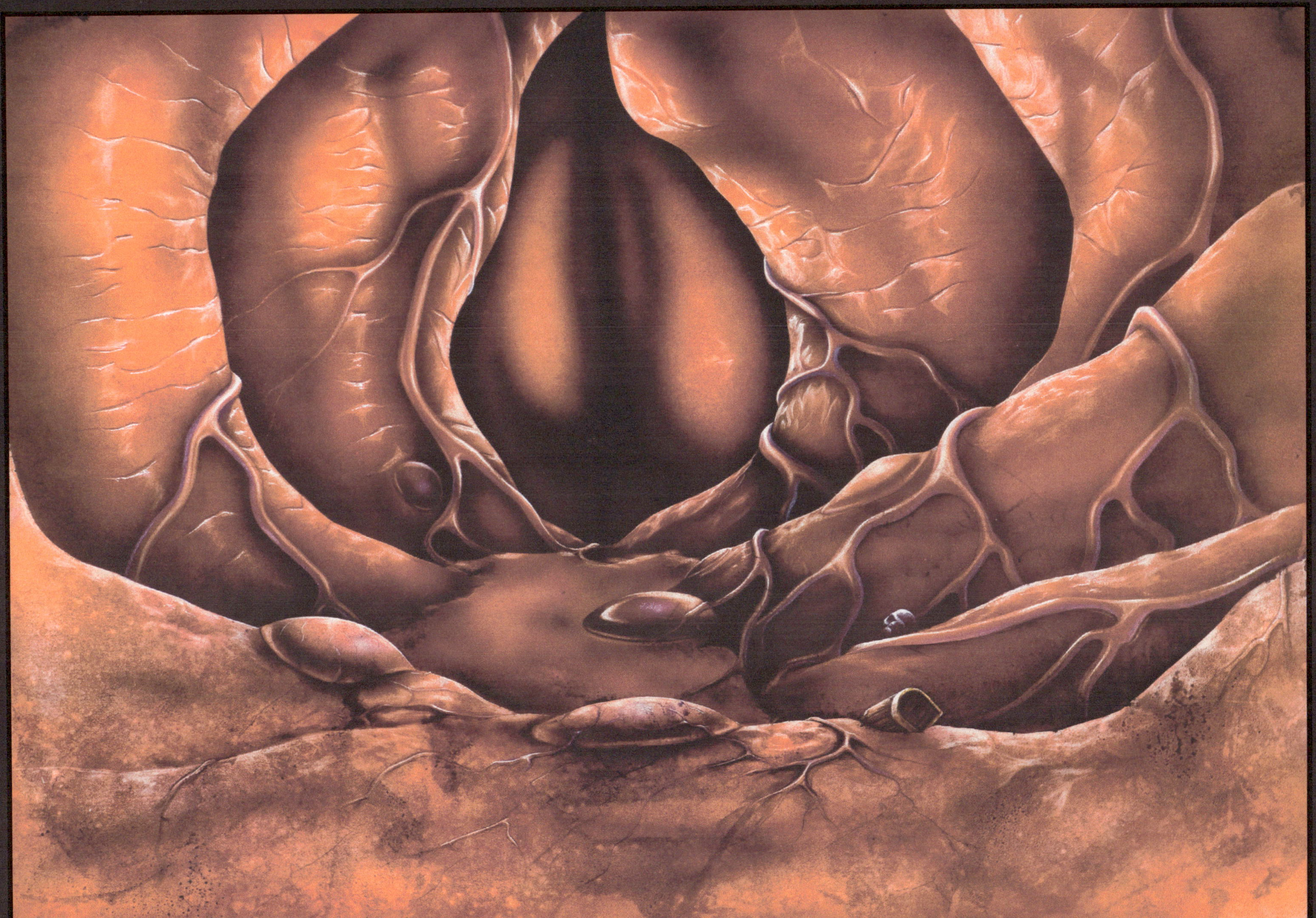

Crone Room 1.8a

This room was a witch's hovel. The alternative features of well and cauldron offered a variety of scenarios that could be played out.

The faxed rough was printed on a thermal fax roll and was badly faded, but was rescued to be at least legible using Photoshop.

The faxed room notes, Far Right had the same problem.

The notes describe the addition of the rear exit as an alternative escape route.

The well could be switched with a cauldron...ooh! Nasty!

Bottom 2nd. Left: *An annotated fax describing the steps required so that everyone understood what was needed in the final artwork. Note the objects which, as they were painted had to be placed out of reach to prevent the Dungeoneer being directed to pick them up.*

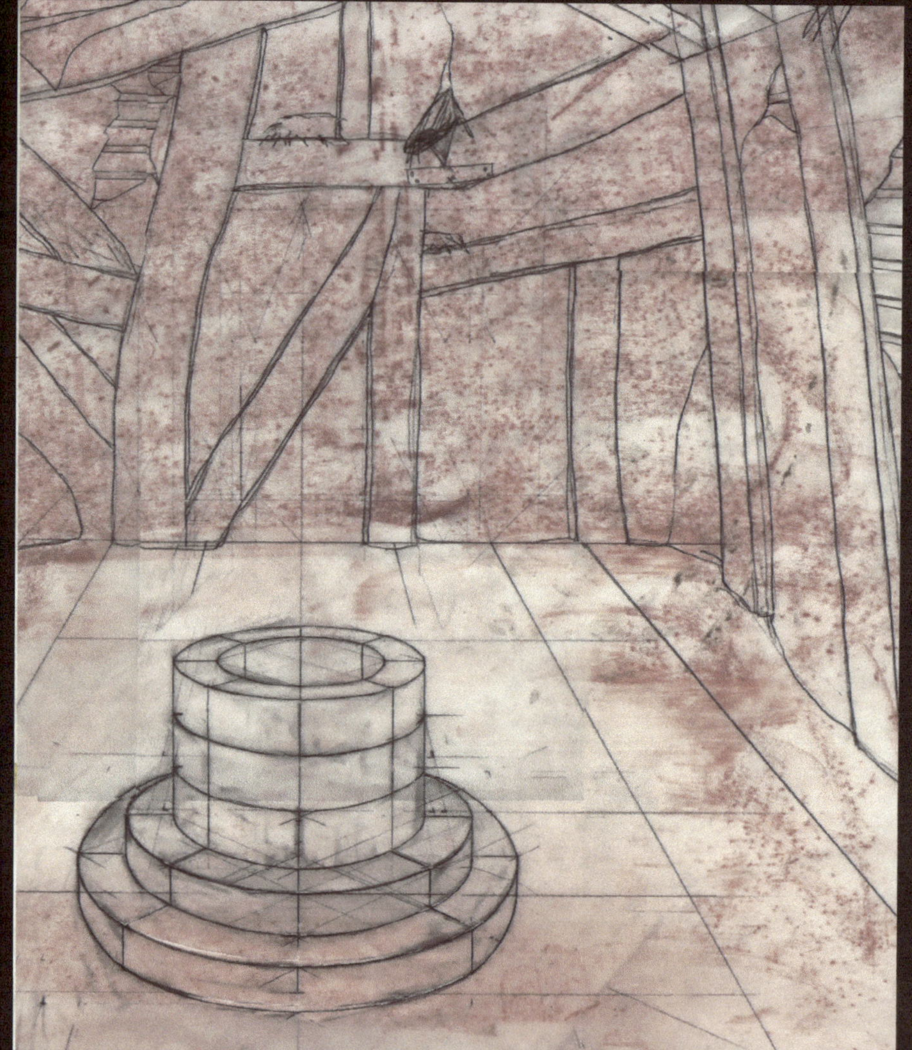

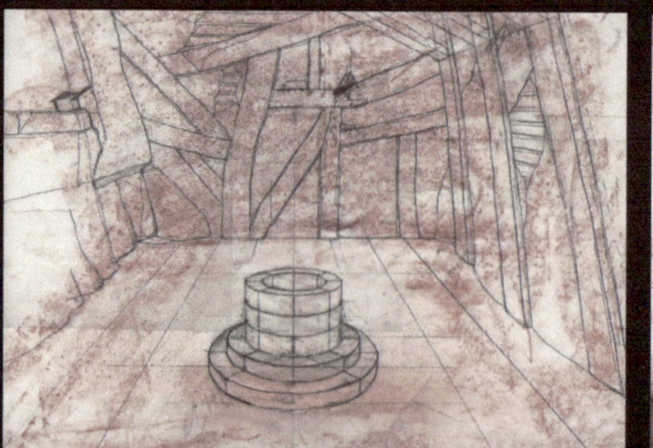

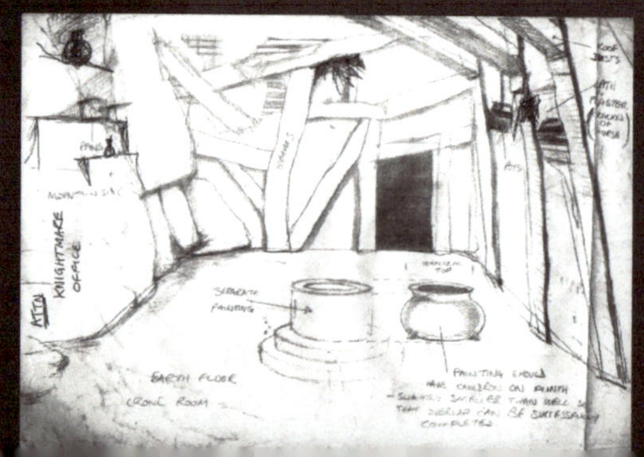

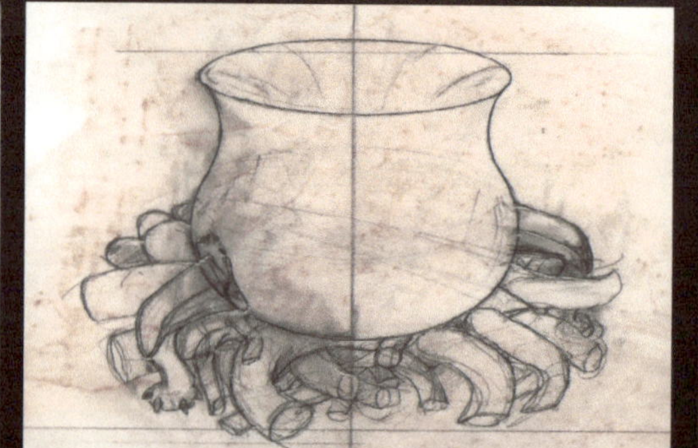

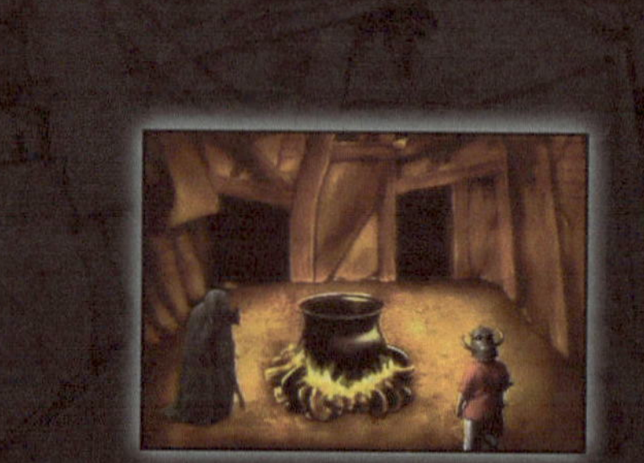

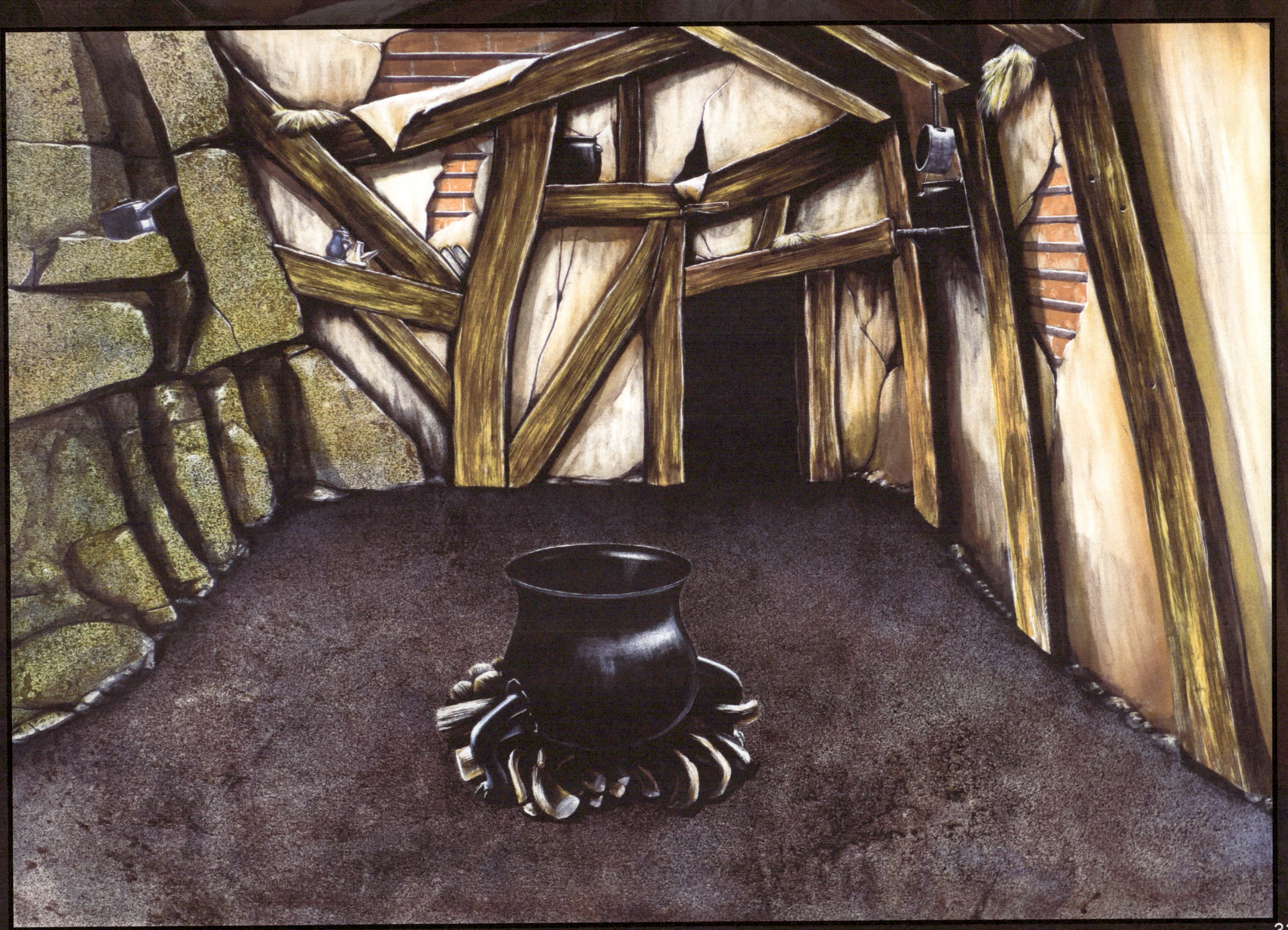

Corridor Room 1.9a

This room was known by Treguard as the great corridor of the catacombs, patrolled by the army of the dead.
The runes were placed as an extra game play option, but could be edited out by overlaying them with sampled texture from the plain hexagonal tiles. The heraldic emblems are placed suitably out of reach.

Right: *The Corridor Room drawing. This was narrower than a regular room. Construction lines aided drawing the detail in perspective.*

Bottom Left: *This faxed plan showed where the blue flattage props had to be placed so that the Dungeoneer couldn't walk through walls.*

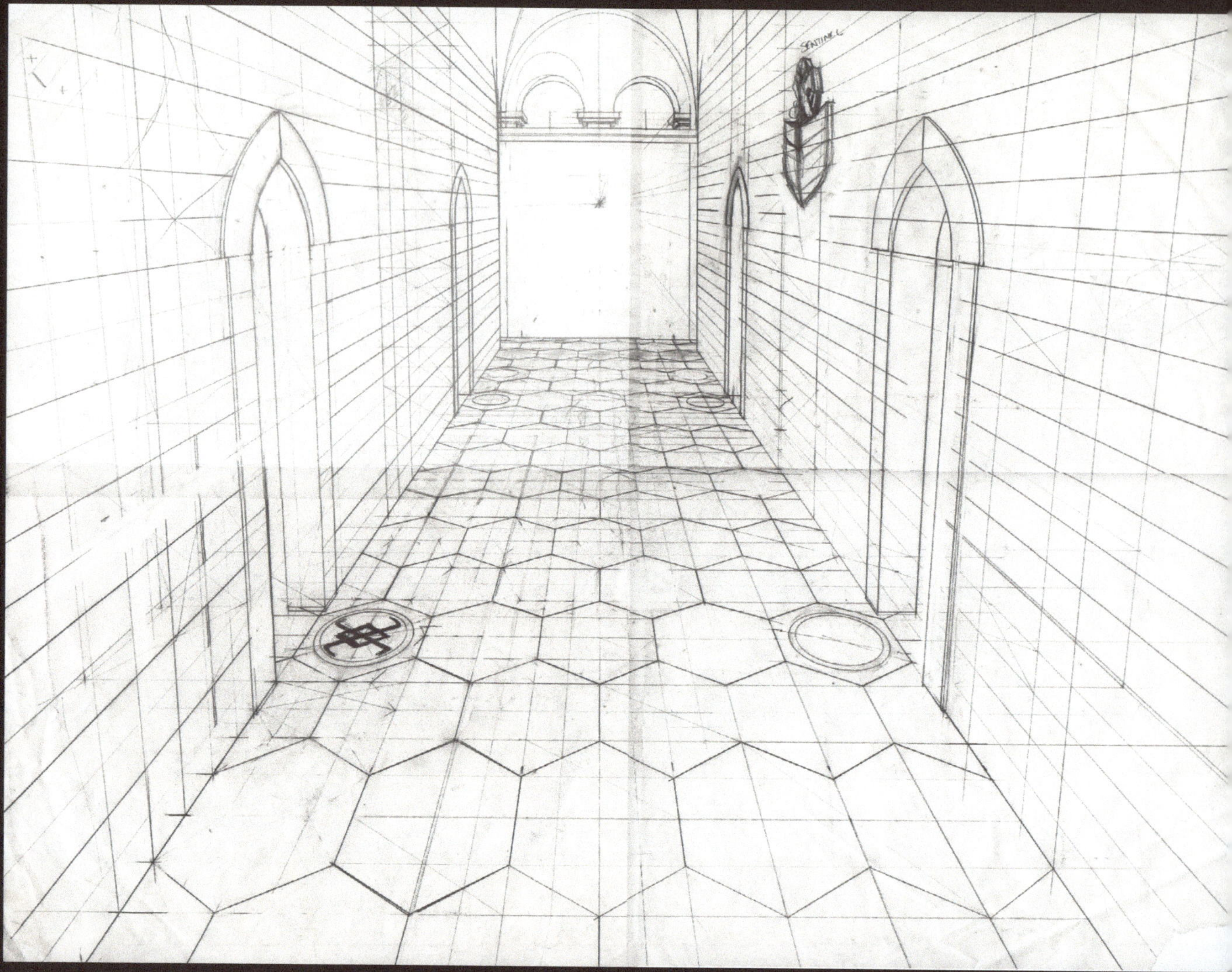

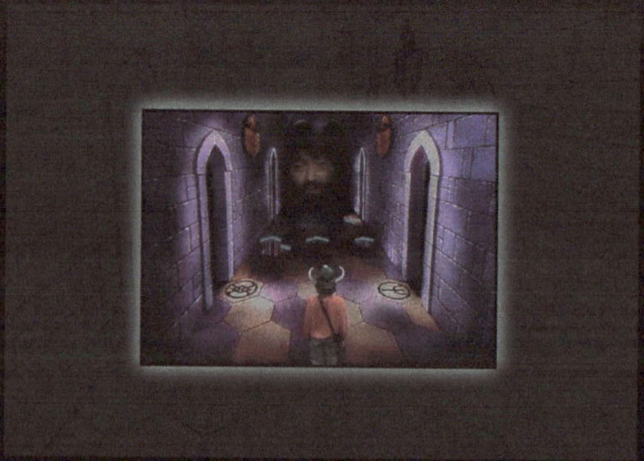

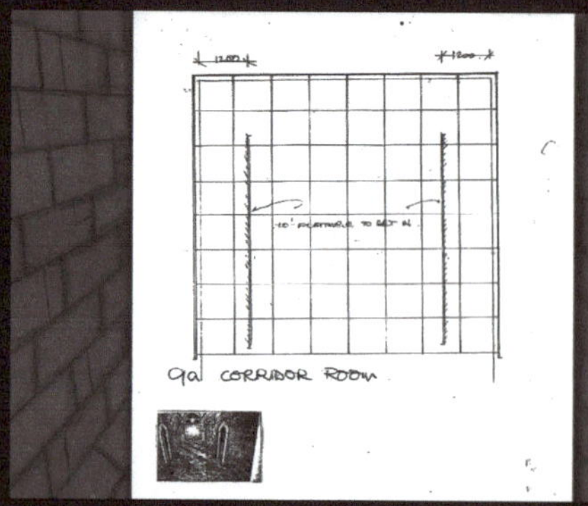
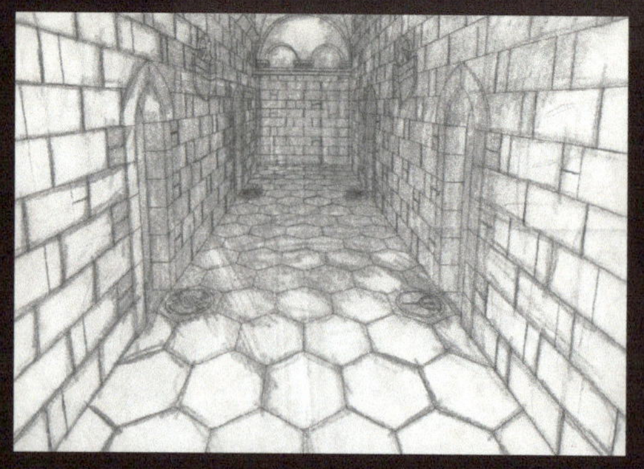
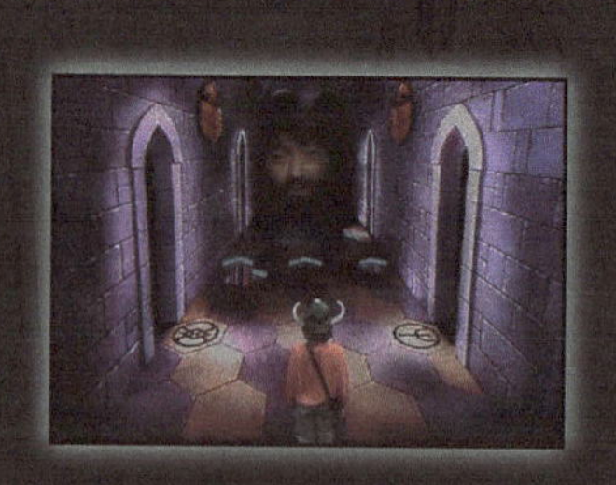
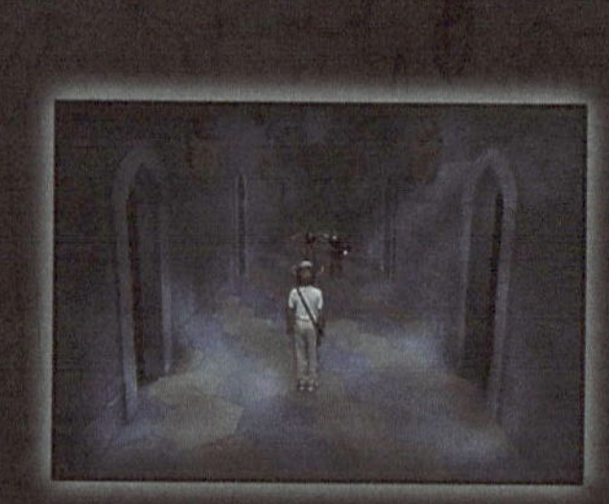

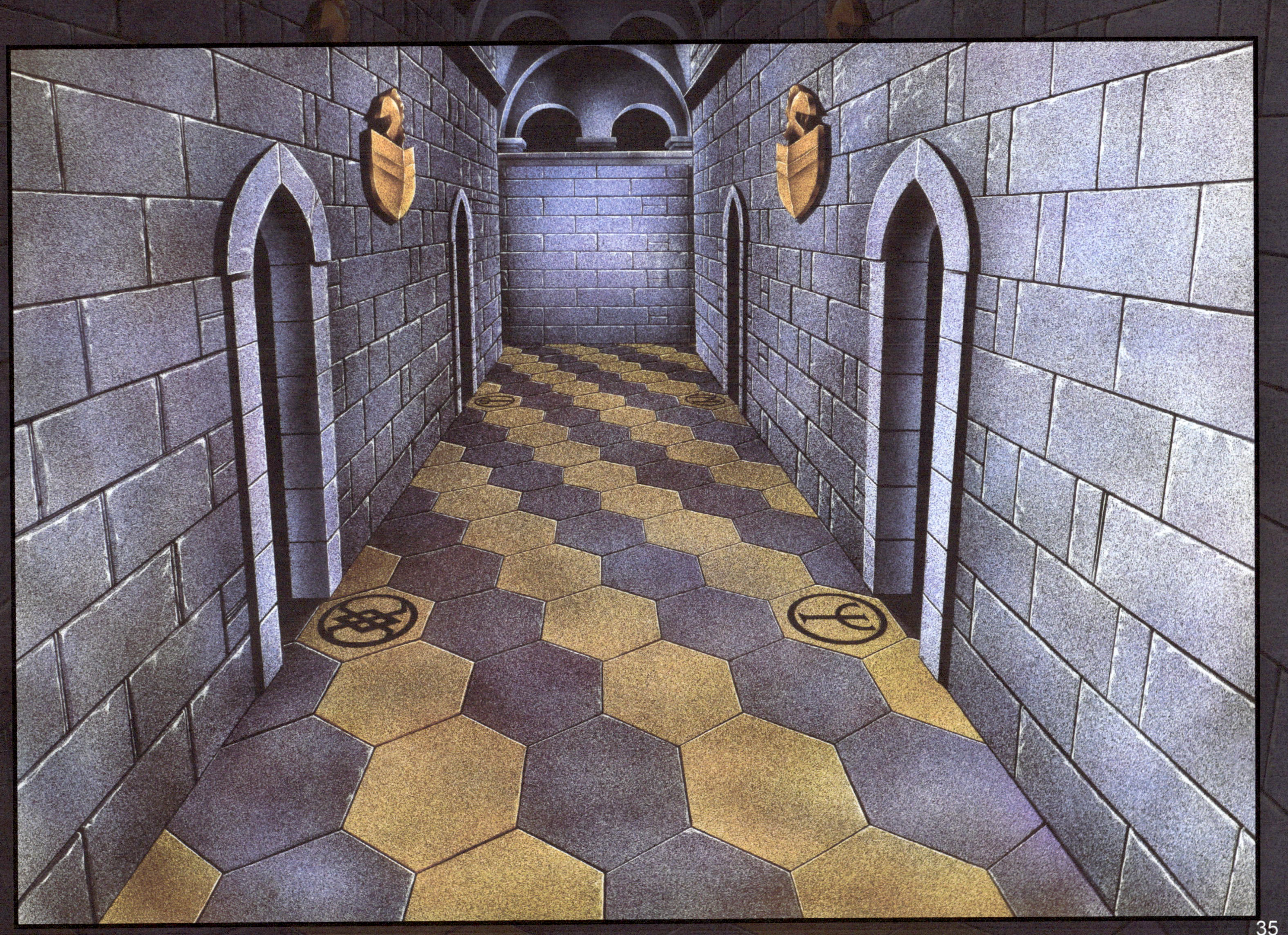

Well way Room 1.10a

The well was drawn in the correct perspective for the grid and used the exact dimensions provided in Ros Inglis's well design.
This was made as a chromakey prop and so the dimensions and positioning were critical so that the Dungeoneer could make a convincing descent through the well drawing.

Right: *The drawing. The well was missing the base steps. These would certainly have to be included in the final artwork. The construction lines were made to extrapolate to the right and create the perspective stone blocks.*

Bottom Left: *This fax from the designer Ros Inglis gave the exact dimensions of the well. It was printed out on my fax machine which used thermal paper and so had to be rescued. Great on cost at the time, but not for longevity.*

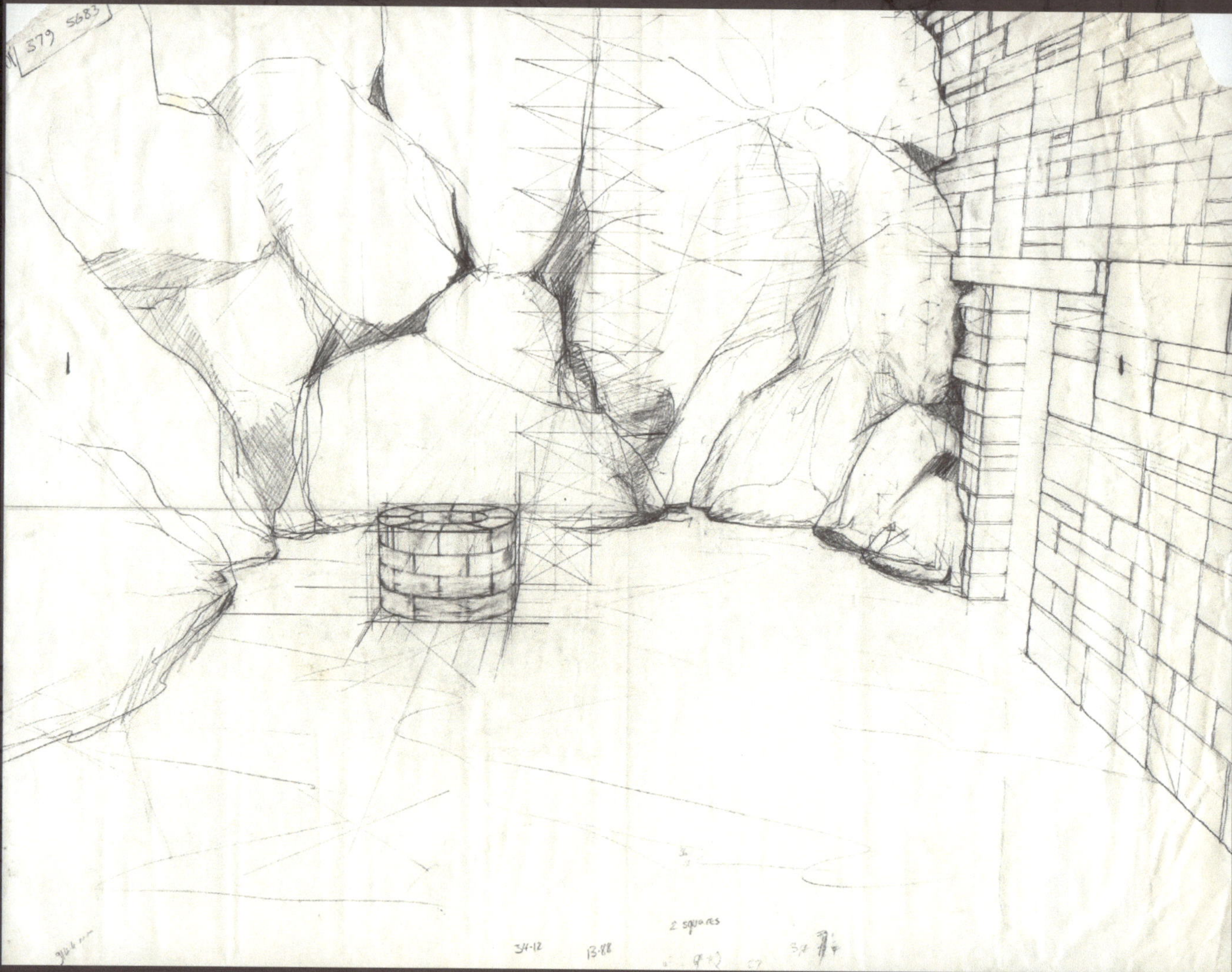

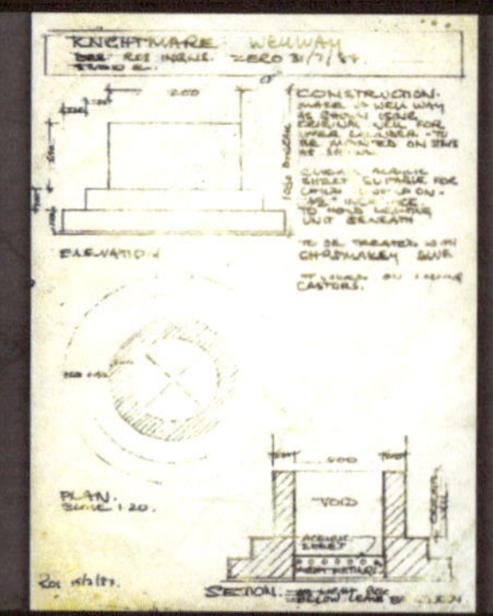

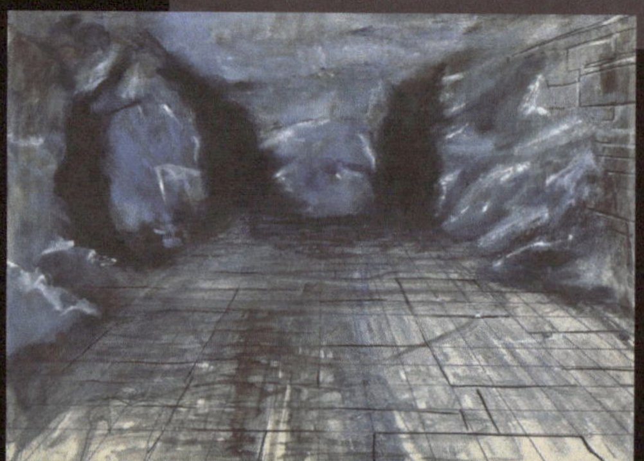

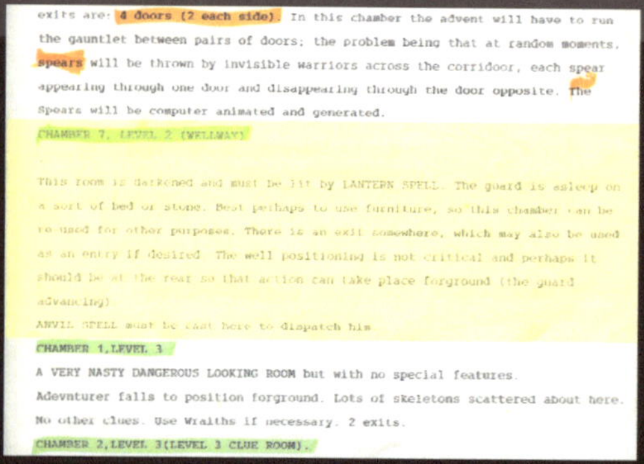

exits are: 4 doors (2 each side). In this chamber the advent will have to run the gauntlet between pairs of doors; the problem being that at random moments, spears will be thrown by invisible warriors across the corridoor, each spear appearing through one door and disappearing through the door opposite. The Spears will be computer animated and generated.

CHAMBER 7, LEVEL 2 (WELLWAY)

This room is darkened and must be lit by LANTERN SPELL. The guard is asleep on a sort of bed or stone. Best perhaps to use furniture, so this chamber can be re-used for other purposes. There is an exit somewhere, which may also be used as an entry if desired. The well positioning is not critical and perhaps it should be at the rear so that action can take place forground (the guard advancing)

ANVIL SPELL must be cast here to dispatch him.

CHAMBER 1, LEVEL 3

A VERY NASTY DANGEROUS LOOKING ROOM but with no special features. Adevnturer falls to position forground. Lots of skeletons scattered about here. No other clues. Use Wralths if necessary. 2 exits.

CHAMBER 2, LEVEL 3 (LEVEL 3 CLUE ROOM).

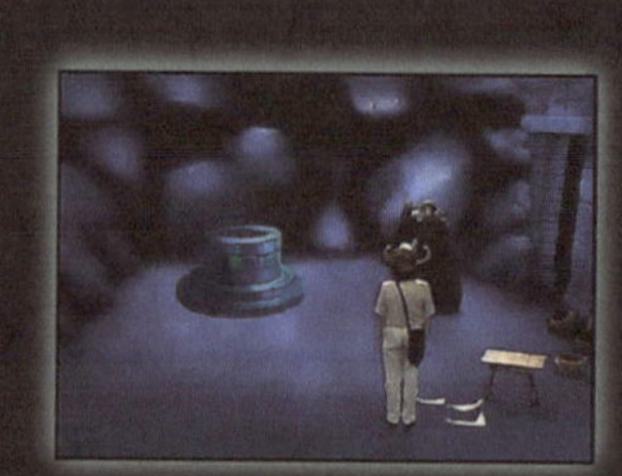

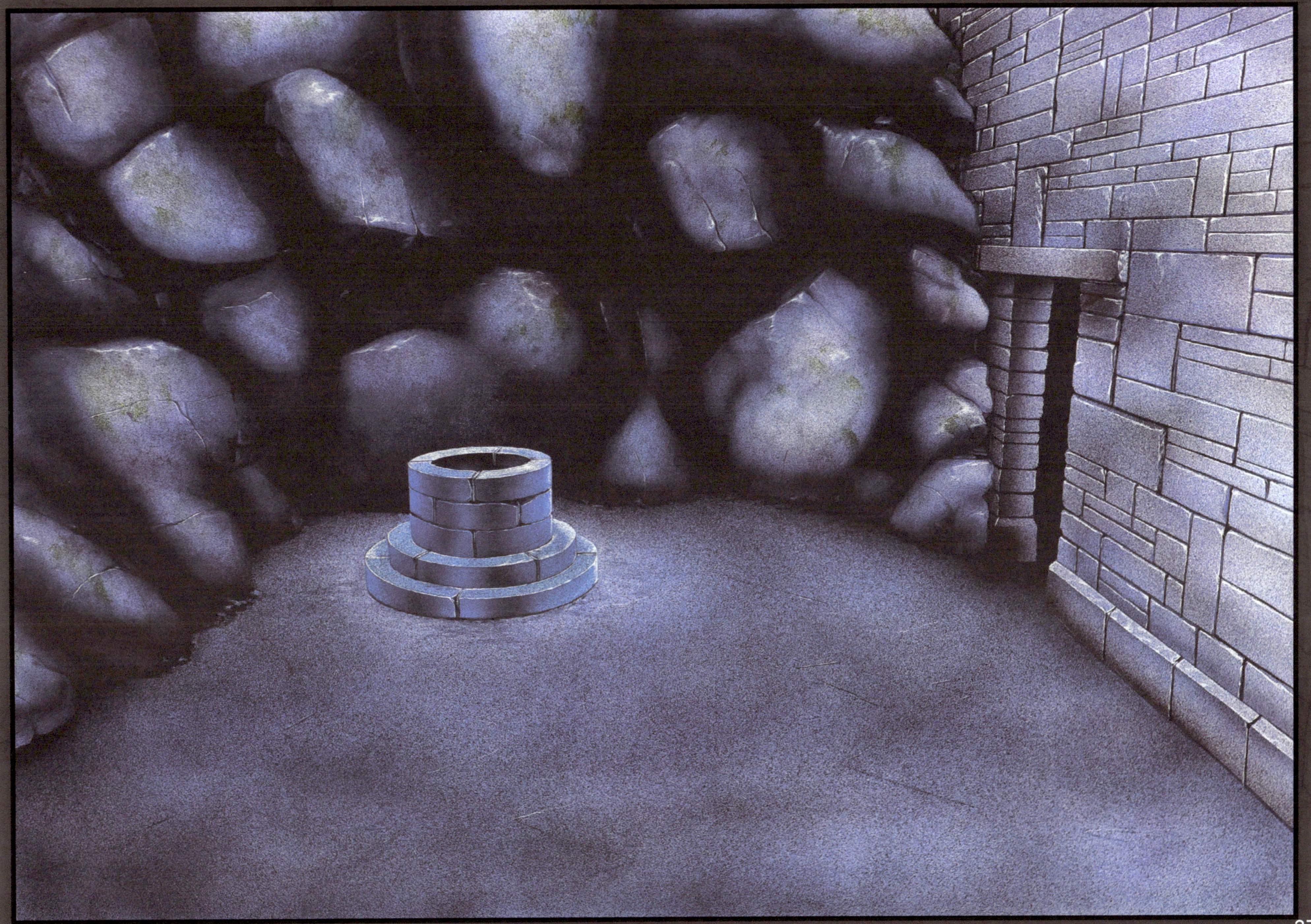

Crossing Room 1
1.11a

The general idea was sent as a faxed drawing and typed description. Crossing Rooms provided an alternative to exploring the familiar 'box' room and offered a different challenge.

The artwork shows the stone texture technique explained earlier as a build up of brightly coloured layers of spatter and 'printed' transfer of inks. It also shows the highlighting achieved by gentle rubbing with a typewriter eraser pencil.

Right: *This rough was faxed to the Knightmare office for approval and to show that I understood what was required before I committed it to the illustration board.*

Below: *The original faxed brief notes;The tracing key line drawing; Broadcast composite showing half of the background as part of a two-stage scene; Alternative lighting on a full background composite.*

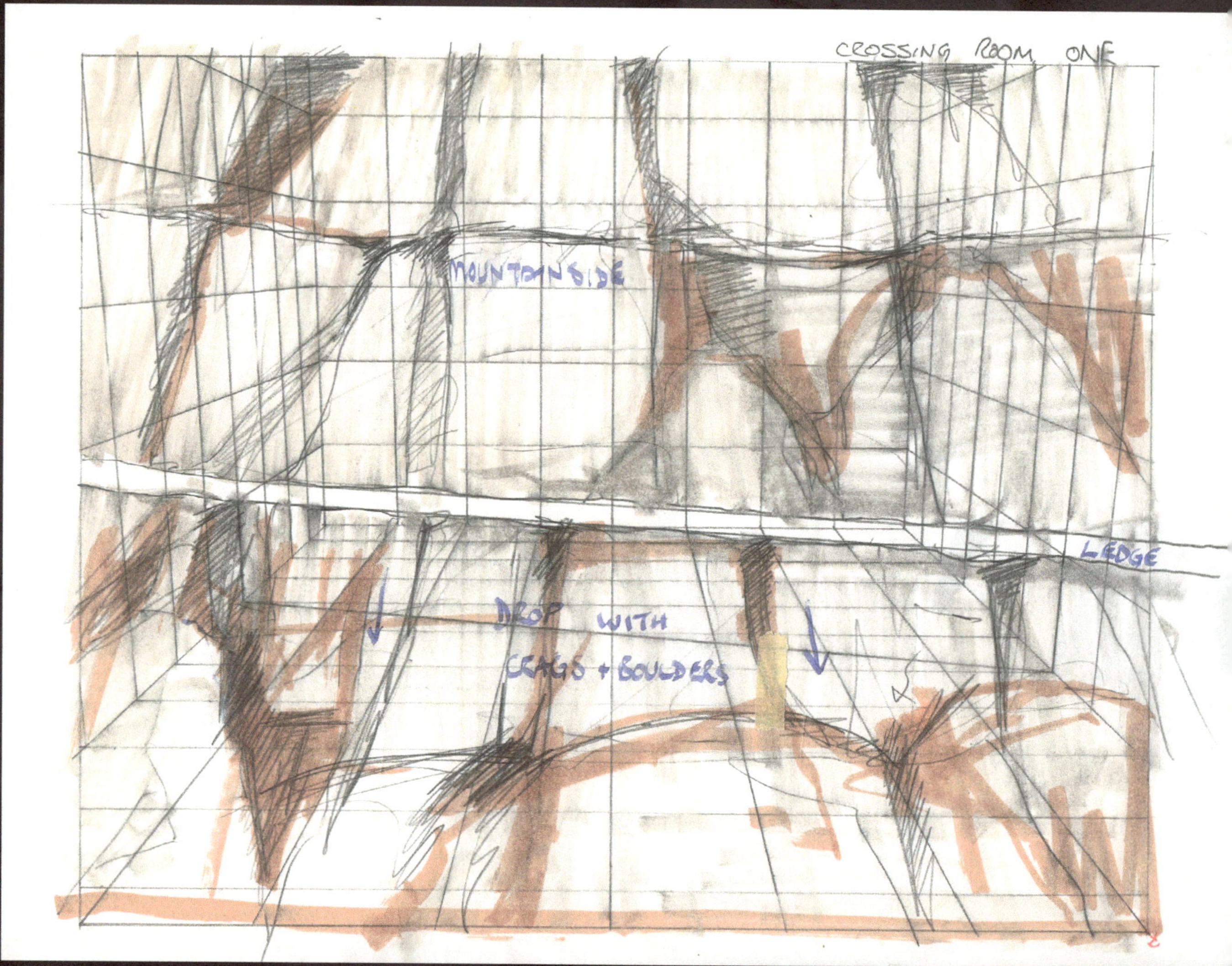

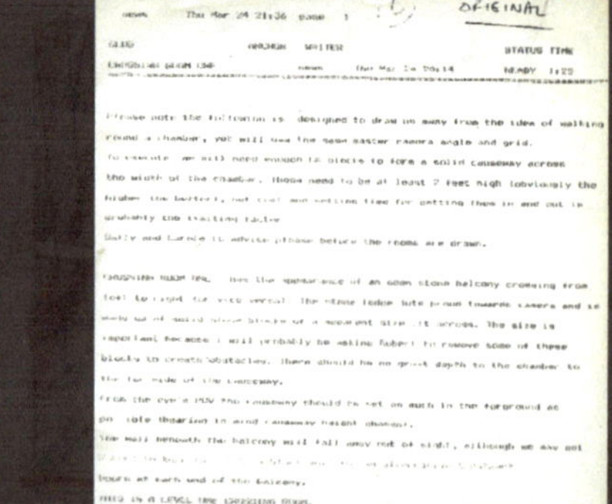

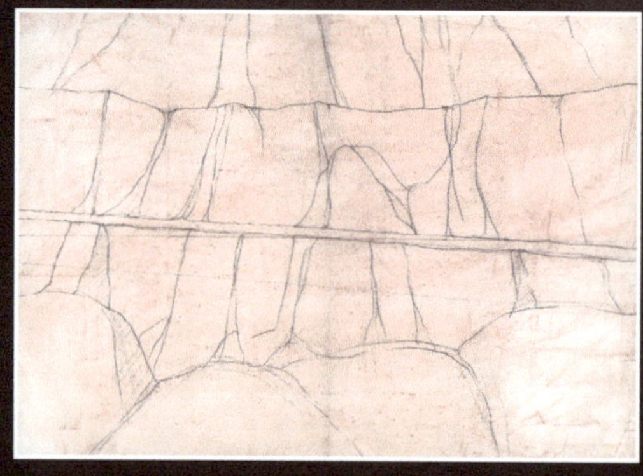

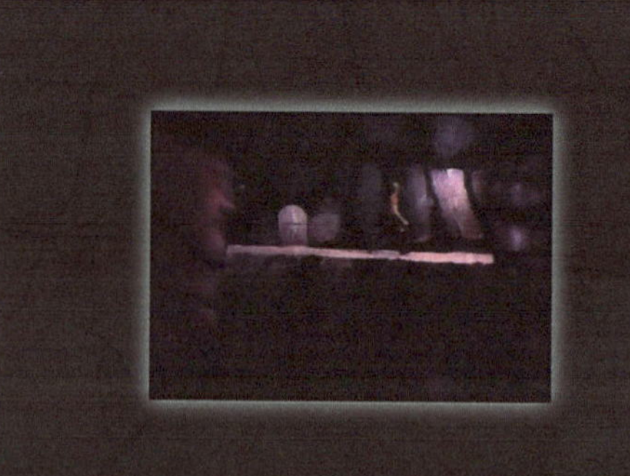

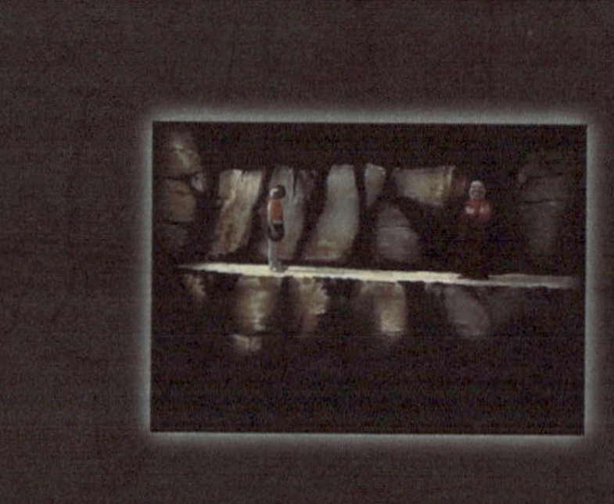

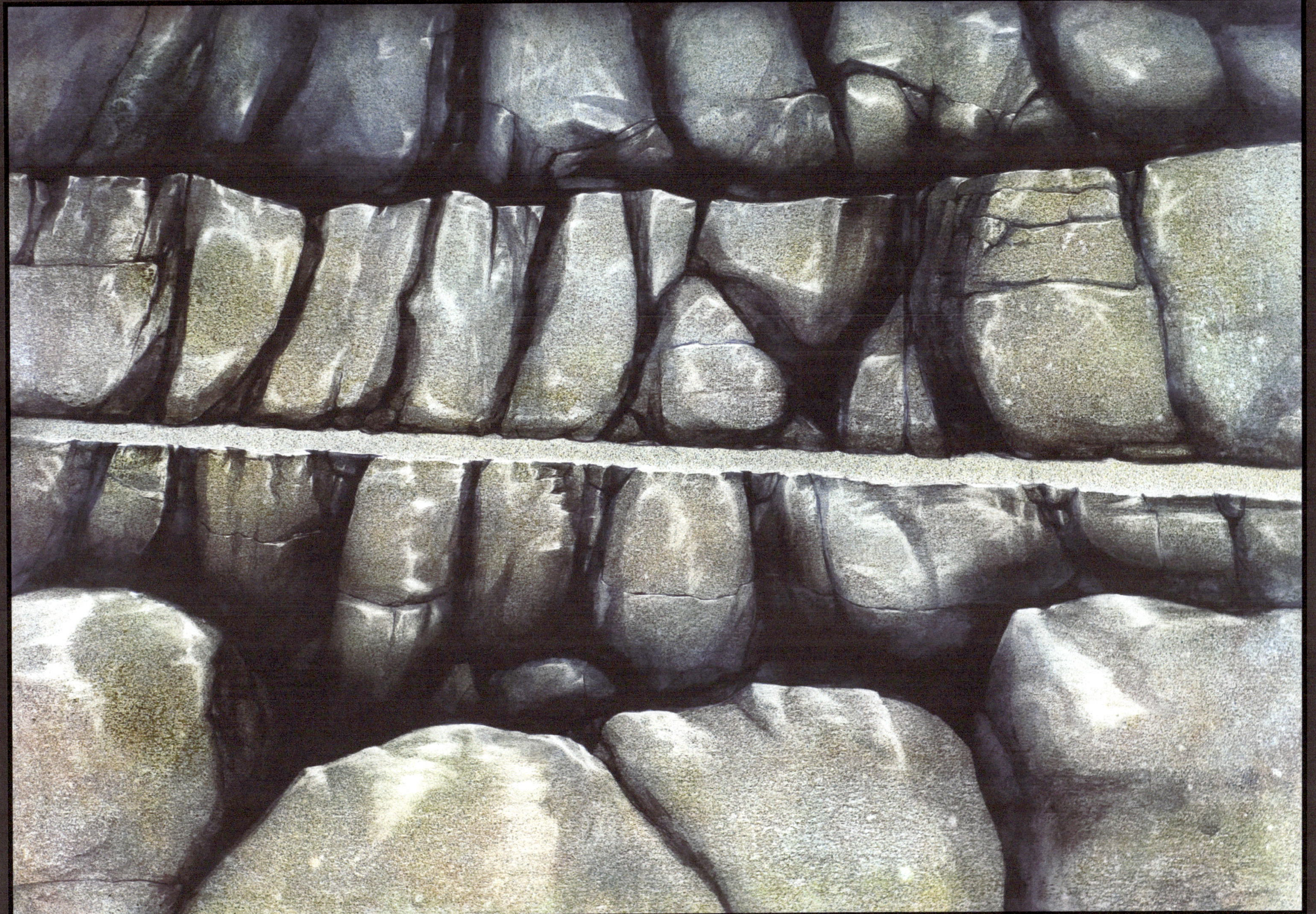

2nd. Wall Monster Room 1.14a

The rough sketch shows a good indication of the communication necessary to get all those involved on the same page. It is also a visual demonstration that the brief was understood and that there would be no alarming mistakes in the final artwork.
The wall was cheated forward to allow a larger manifestation of the wall monster. Modifications that were required were noted on the sketch and implemented in the colour rough.

Left to Right:
Faxed Brief. *Cropped by the machine.*

My thumbnails and notes.

Rough. *This that was sent to show how I intended to put the room together.*

Colour Rough. *The arrow at the base of the wall indicated a requirement that the wall had to be cheated forward to allow for a larger manifestation of the wall monster. Consequently, the doors were widened and stones removed.*

Tracing. *The approved rough was developed to produce the room drawing straight onto tracing paper and rubbed with brown pastel ready for the transfer.*

The final broadcast composite.

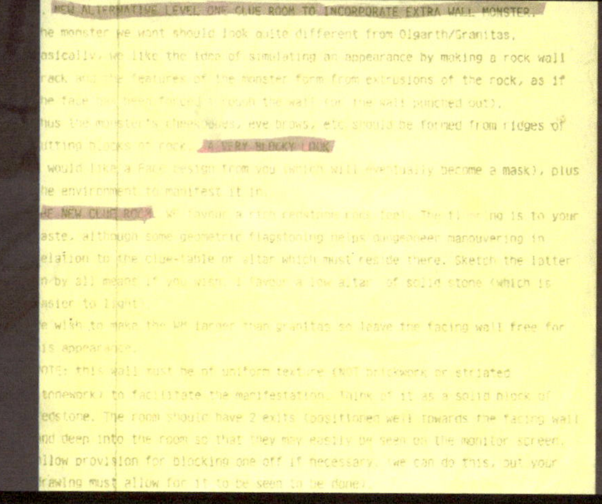

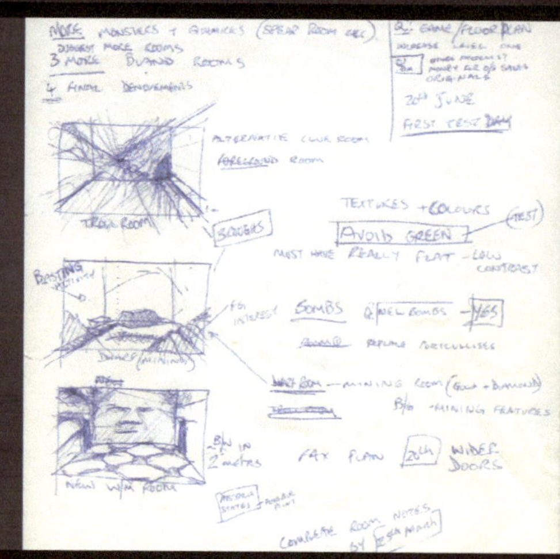

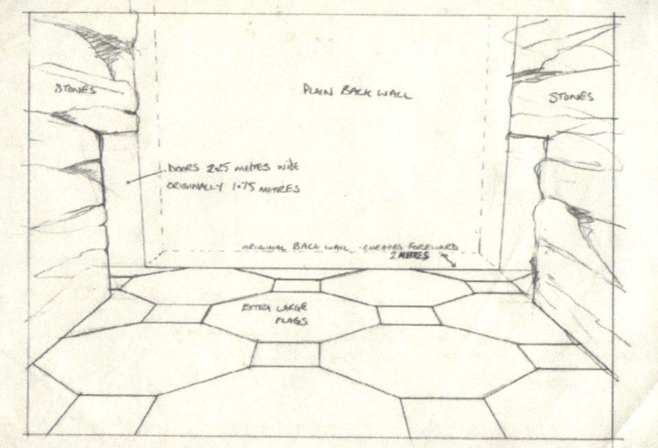

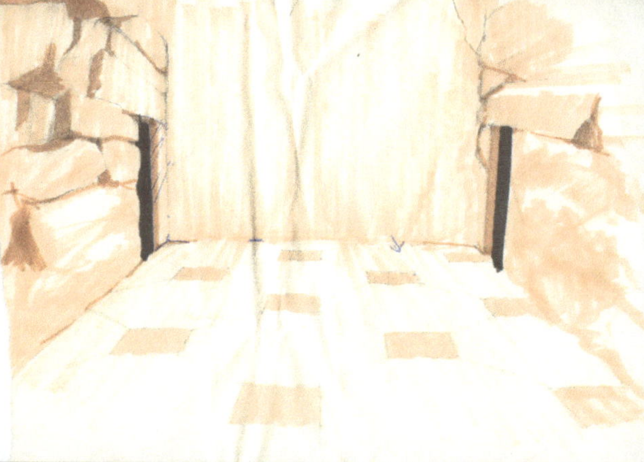

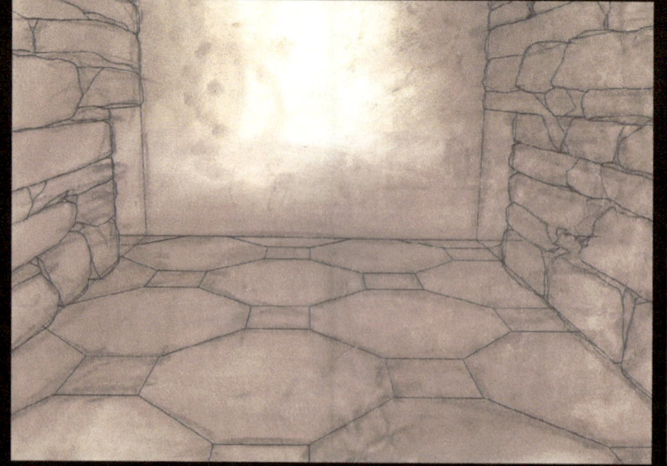

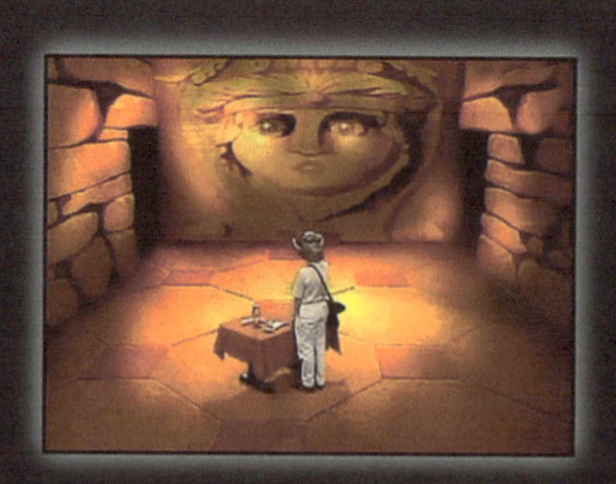

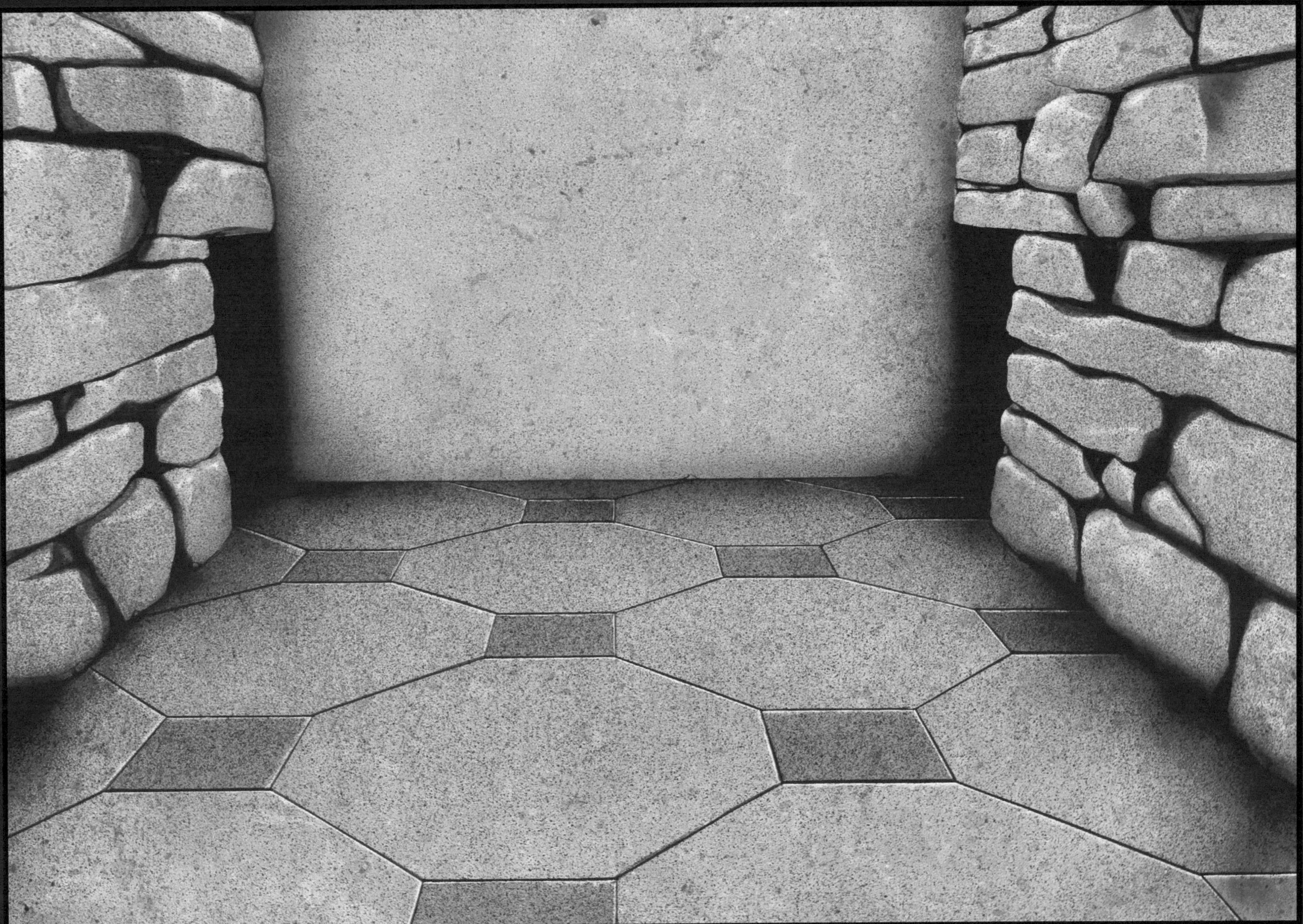

Troll Room 1.15a

The Troll Room was commissioned as a second giant's room.
The brief was very clear and had covered any potential problems.
Drawing straight onto the tracing paper sped the process up considerably.

Right: *This is the rough for the Troll room. The note to ring Robert Harris was made during a phone call which was a typical occurrence. The dragon was featured in the Level 3 Crossing room, 3/7c.*

Below: *Original Meeting notes describing room details for my reference. The fax roll misbehaved and the left edge was cropped;*

The Troll Room tracing ready for transfer, backed with red pastel;

Hints of computer graphic landscape were added to provide an alternative scenario;

The broadcast composite with Troll.

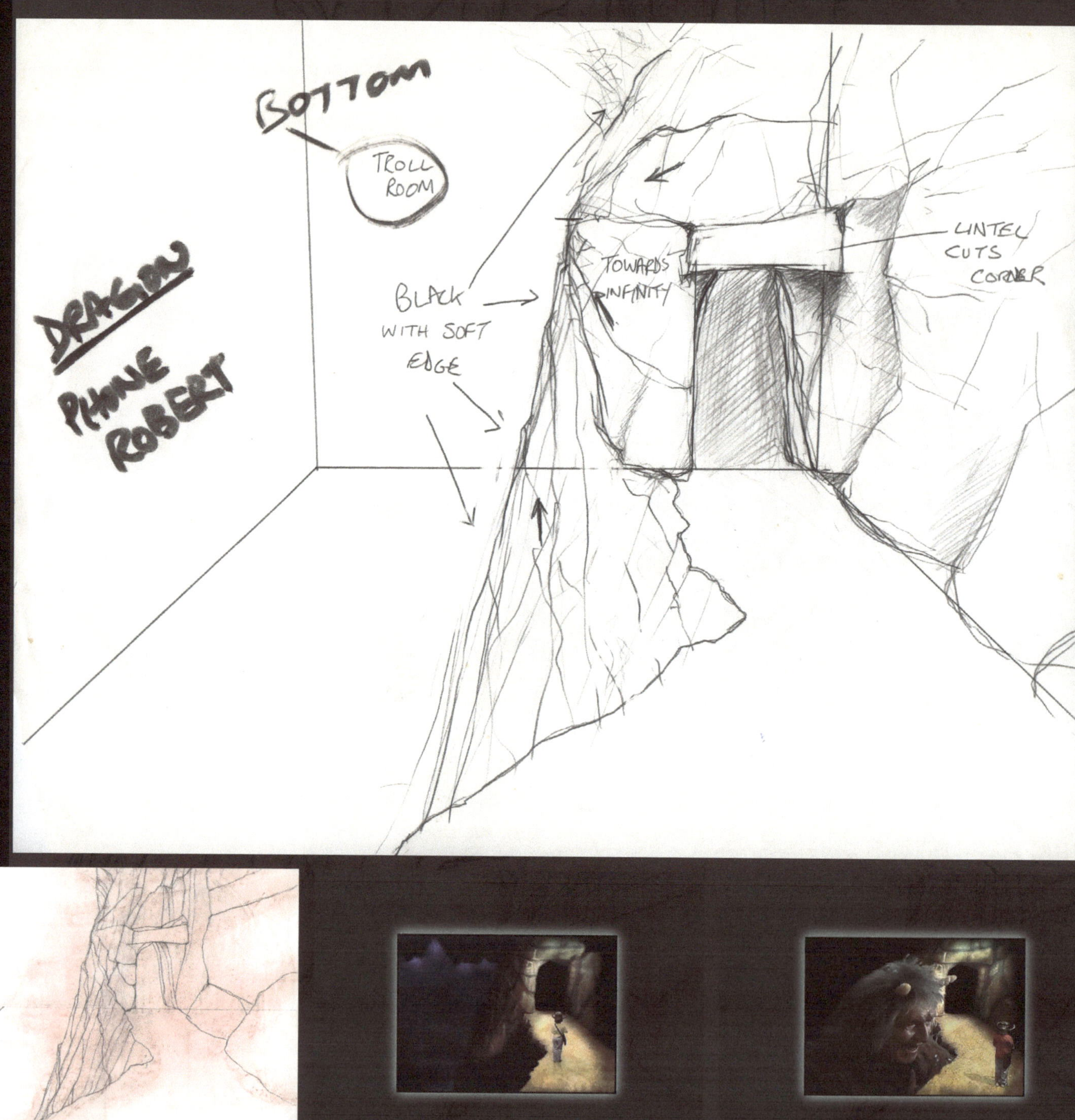

nd deep into the room so that they may easily be seen on the monitor screen.
llow provision for blocking one off if necessary. (we can do this, but your
rawing must allow for it to be seen to be done).
e also need a new giant room, only this time it will hold a troll. Please
everse your approach to the old one and allow entry onto a causeway running
along the right hand wall. Dispense with the left hand wall altogether, as if
the chamber is enormous and stretches away screen-left out of sight.
On confrontation with the Troll, our little victim will see only his upper
chest (if he could see it at all), and the troll will then bend down bringing
his whole face to bear directly in front of the dungeoneer. A VERY BIG FACE-TO
FACE if you see what I mean. Please blanket-light the chamber (as bland rooms)
and Roberto will do the necessary mood lighting. Avoid greens as in the old
Giant room please. Consult on colour scheme before commencing final, as Troll
may have either Blue or Green Face.
More outlines soon.
Regards Tim.
PS sketches for Wallmonster & room soonest please as it holds up Mask making.

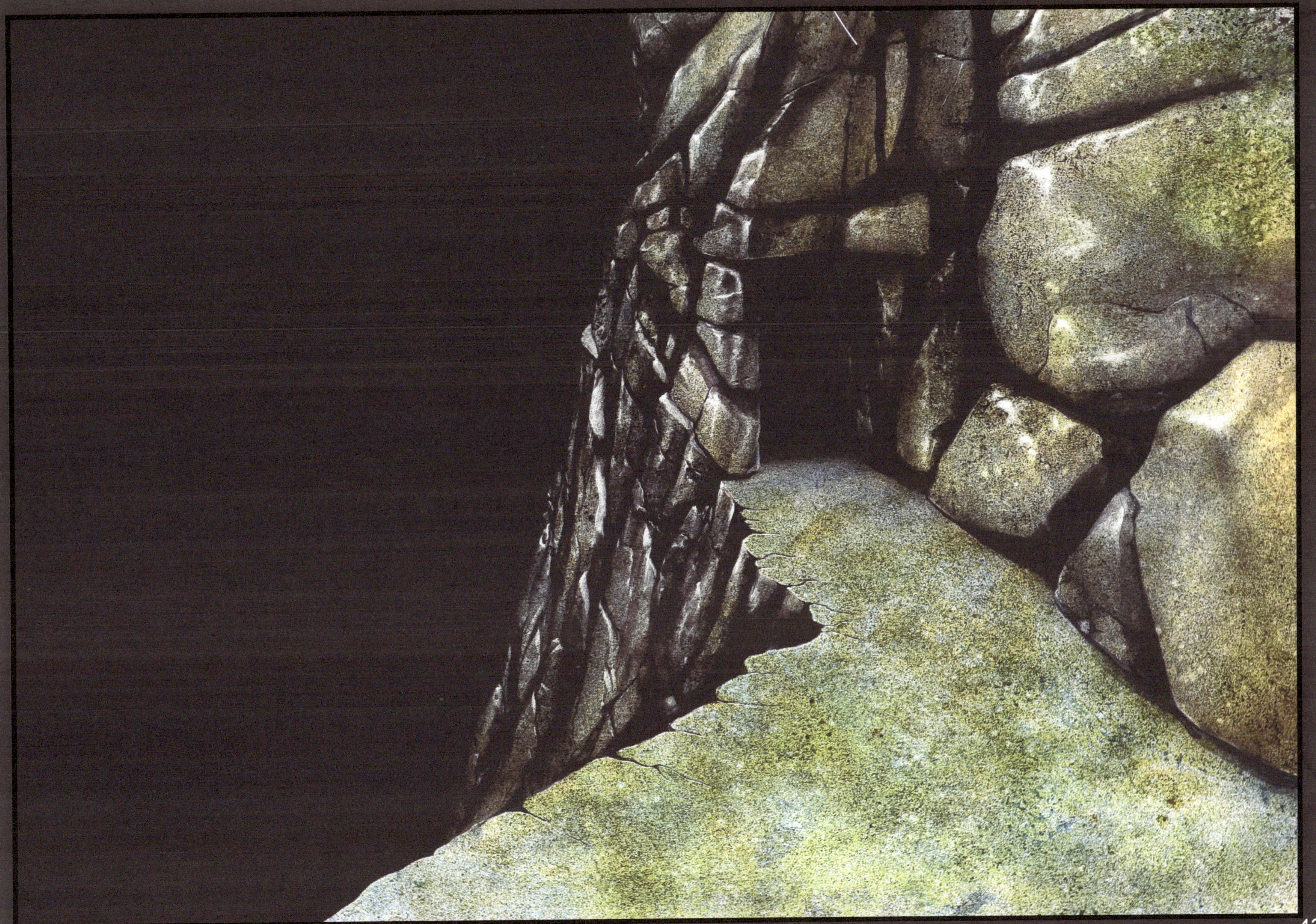

Spider Room 1.18a

The Spider Room brief indicated no tiling as it was felt that it might compete with a proposed spider's web computer graphic. The stone effect texture for the floor, however, did demand some features in order to confirm the perspective. Random cracks and flaws were included to achieve this goal.

Apart from the original painting, no drawings or roughs have survived.

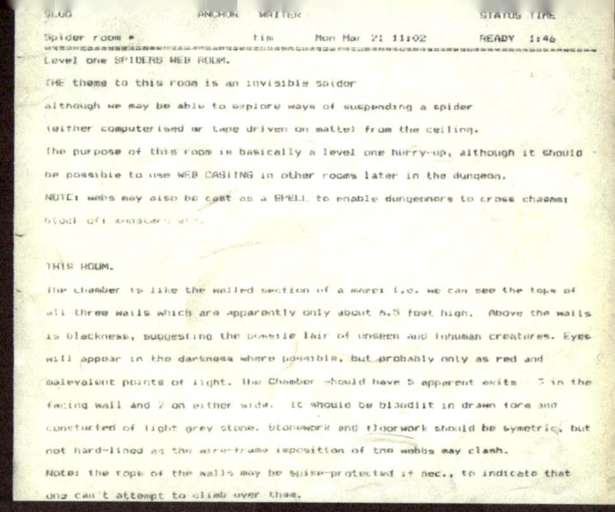

SLUG   ANCHOR   WRITER   STATUS TIME
Spider room *   tim   Mon Mar 21 11:02   READY 1:46
===
Level one SPIDERS WEB ROOM.

THE theme to this room is an invisible spider

although we may be able to explore ways of suspending a spider

(either computerised or tape driven on matte) from the ceiling.

The purpose of this room is basically a level one hurry-up, although it should

be possible to use WEB CASTING in other rooms later in the dungeon.

NOTE: webs may also be cast as a SPELL to enable dungeoners to cross chasms:

block off corridors etc.

THIS ROOM.

The chamber is like the walled section of a maze: i.e. we can see the tops of

all three walls which are apparently only about 6.5 feet high.   Above the walls

is blackness, suggesting the possible lair of unseen and inhuman creatures. Eyes

will appear in the darkness where possible, but probably only as red and

malevalent points of light. The Chamber should have 5 apparent exits - 3 in the

facing wall and 2 on either side.   It should be blandlit in drawn form and

constructed of light grey stone. Stonework and floorwork should be symetric, but

not hard-lined as the wire-frame imposition of the webbs may clash.

Note: the tops of the walls may be spike-protected if nec., to indicate that

one can't attempt to climb over them.

The original faxed brief notes from Tim Child.

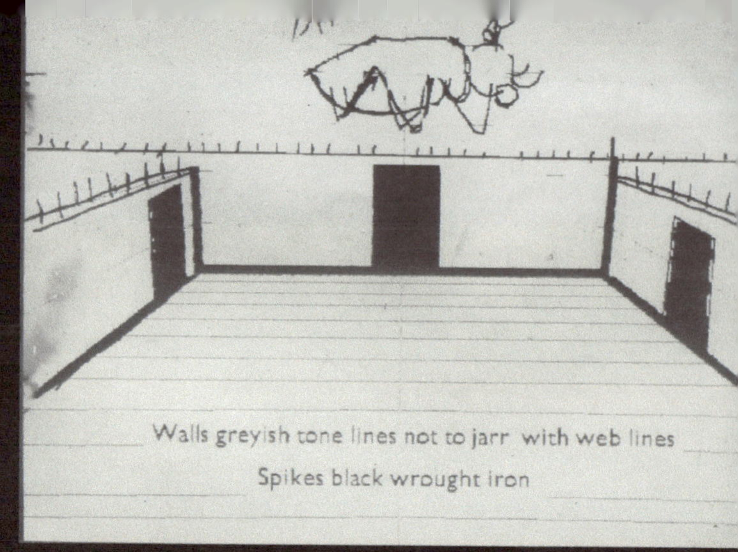

This is the rough sketch sent from the Travelling Matt Company.

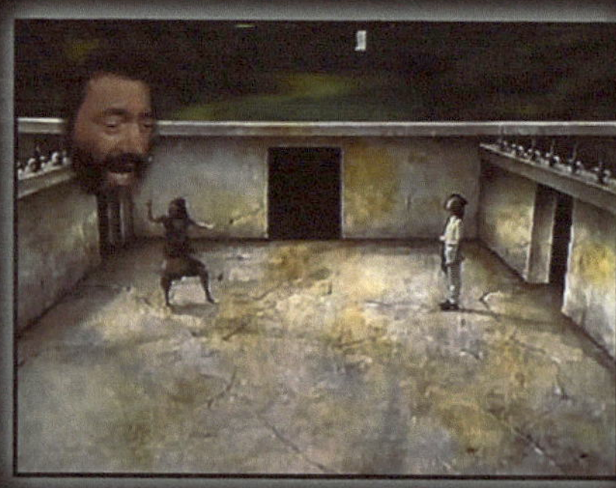

A Broadcast composite with a 'Vale of Banburn' room cut into the background.

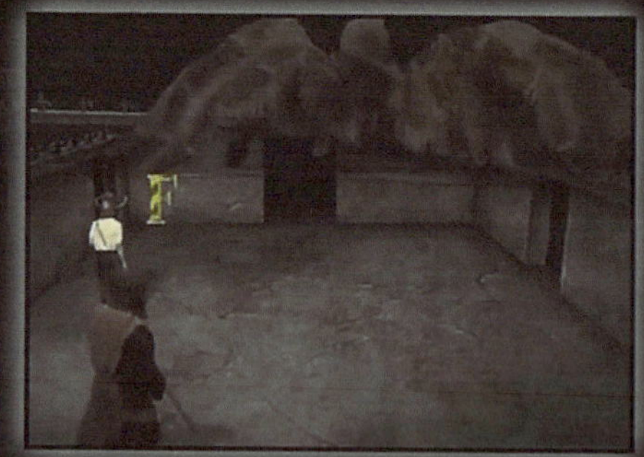

The composite view complete with a big, hairy spider.

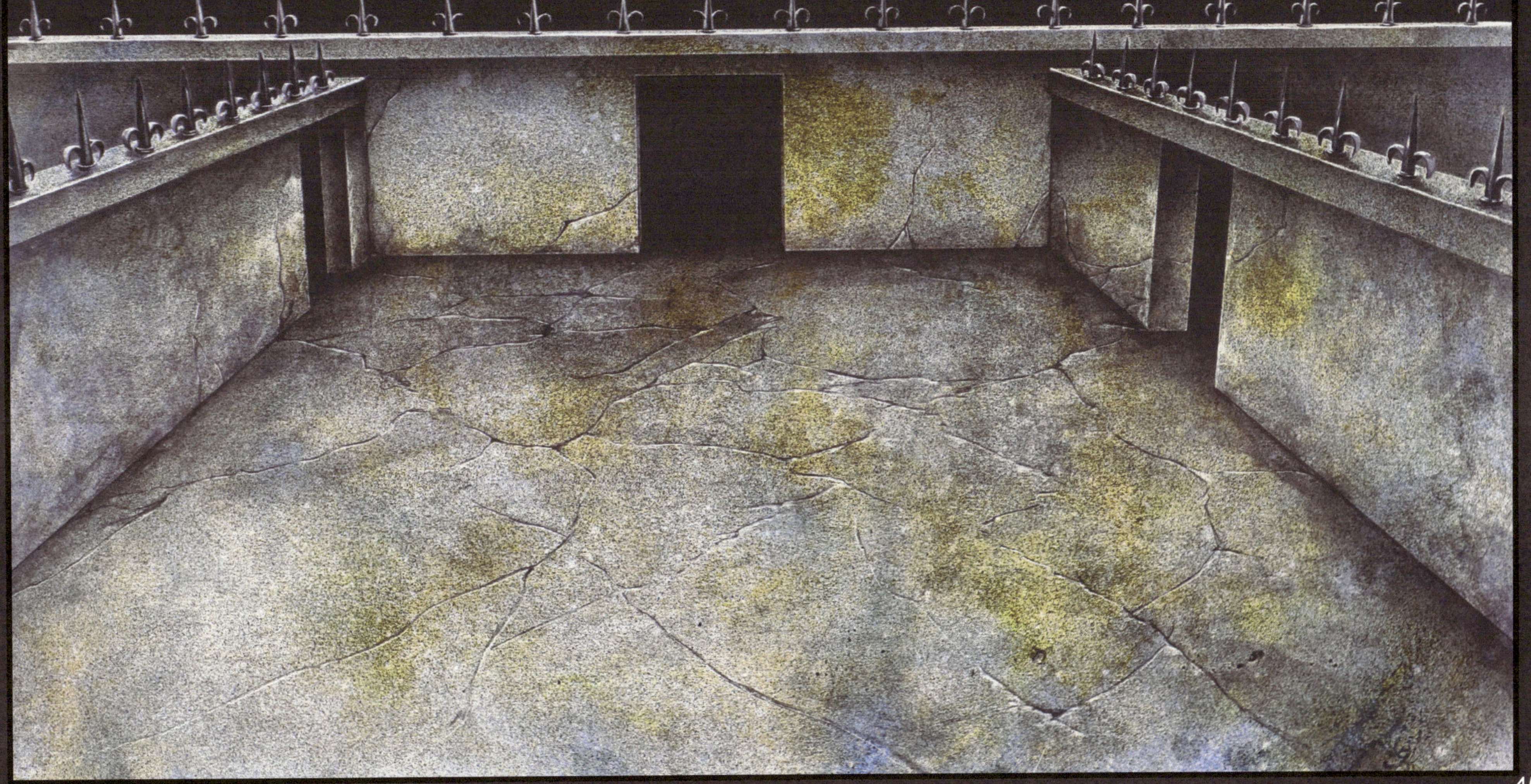

Kitchen Room 1.19a

The computer generated component in the final composite was added by The Travelling Matte Company using a Spaceward Supernova computer graphics system.

They were able to make adjustments and additions to the original paintings as well as add the atmospheric lighting to suit any particular situation. This added a lot of flexibility to the creation of the final broadcast composites.

The lighting was achieved by overlaying the scanned original image with a layer of black and then applying a semi transparent eraser to reveal the original beneath. Soft edges and varying the level of transparency achieved the desired effect. This method allowed the room to be relit in any way required.

Variations to the rooms could also be made with the computer. Sampling sections and applying them over the original scan allowed the stack of logs and the dresser to be removed in one variation of the Kitchen Room.

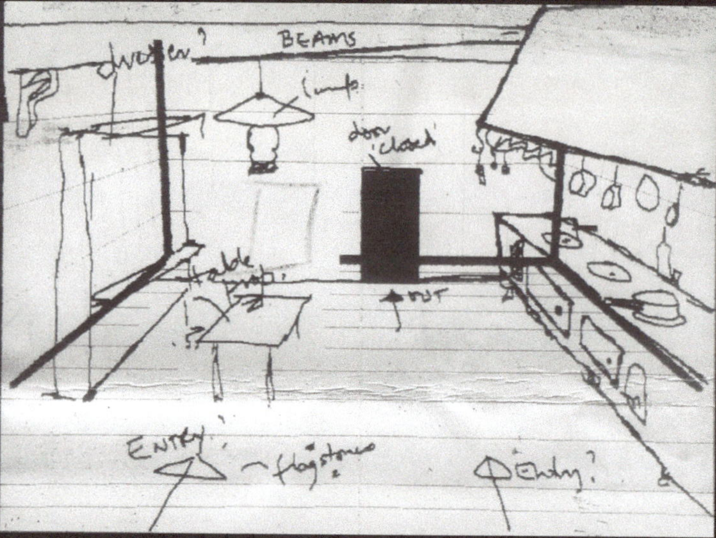

A rough sketch that was sent to me by the Travelling Matte Co. No other preparatory drawings survives.

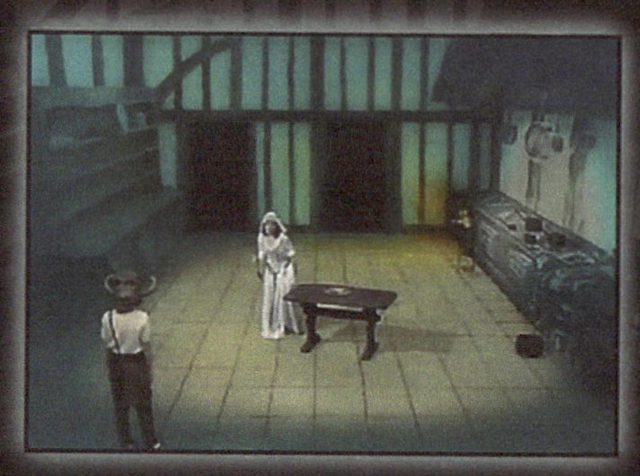

A broadcast composite with mood lighting added.

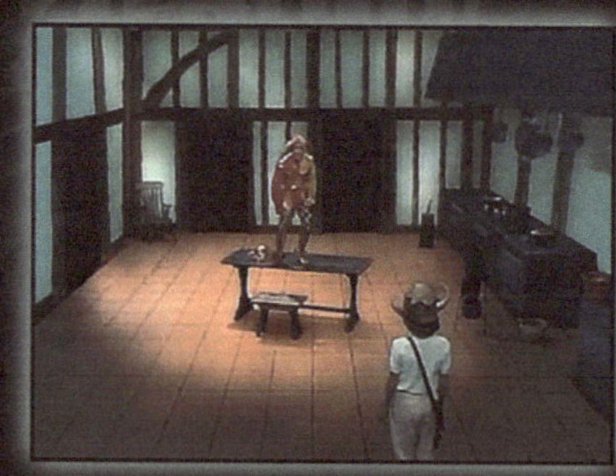

The artwork was manipulated and altered to suit the current quest. Spot the difference!

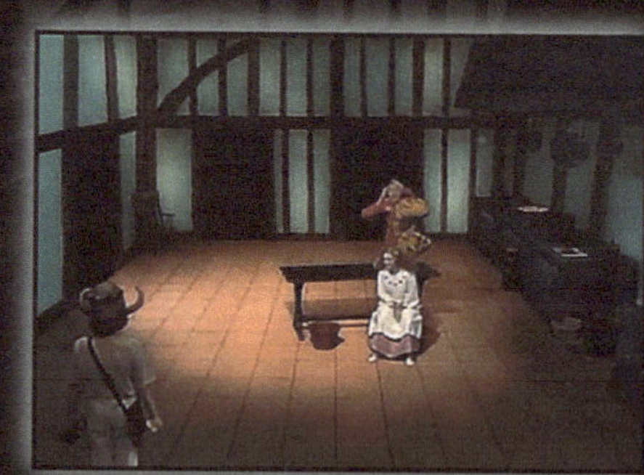

Another quest and items have been repositioned to show recent activity.

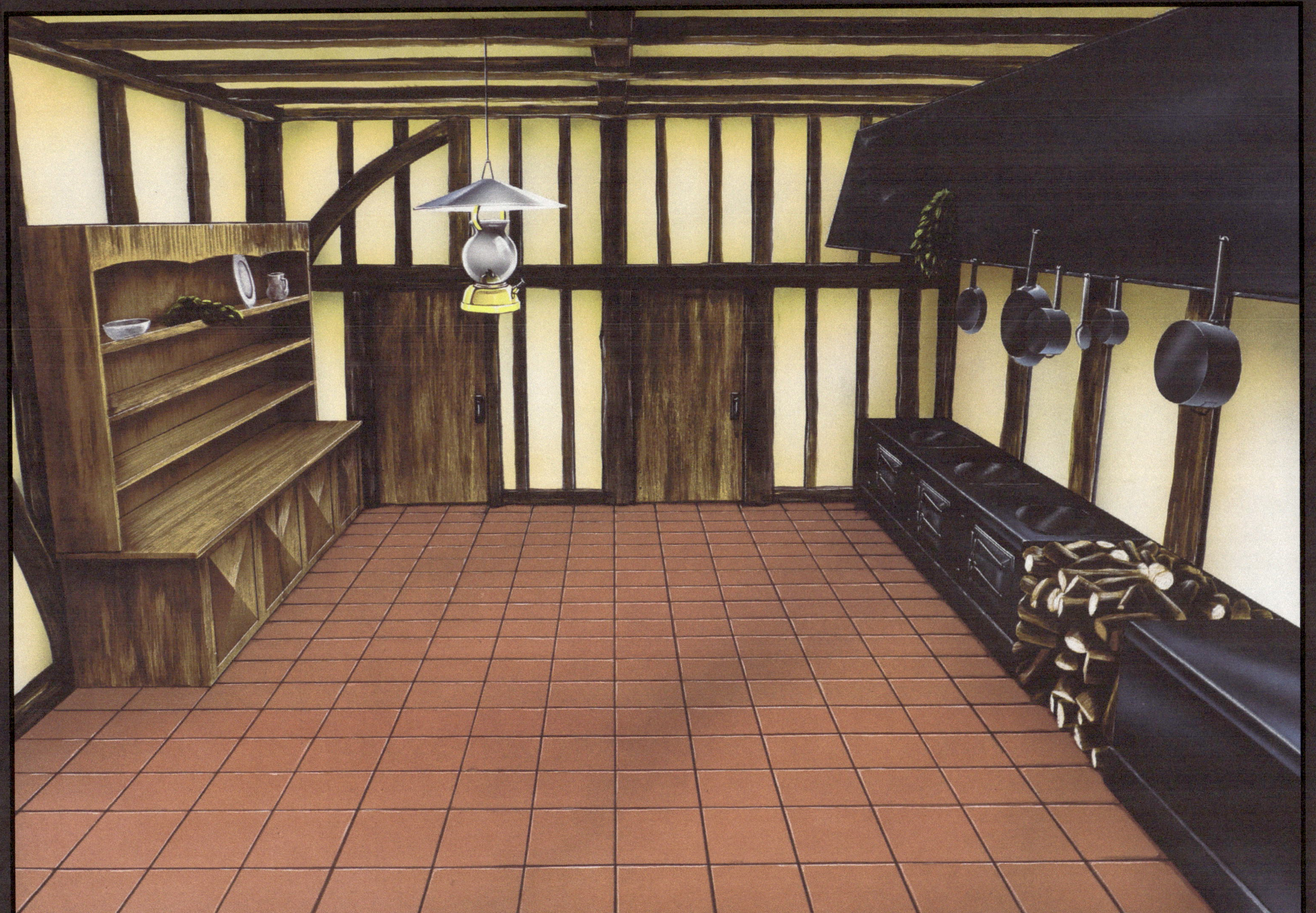

Books

These illustrations are for the The Knightmare Books, published by Transworld/Corgi and written by Dave Morris. They show the evolution from rough sketched designs to finished artwork.

As there is a lot of space left clear for the title and logo, I have mocked up the appearance by including the Knightmare logo on each.

Clockwise from top left:

Can you beat the challenge?

The Labyrinths of Fear.

The Sorcerer's Isle.

Fortress of Assassins.

The Forbidden Gate

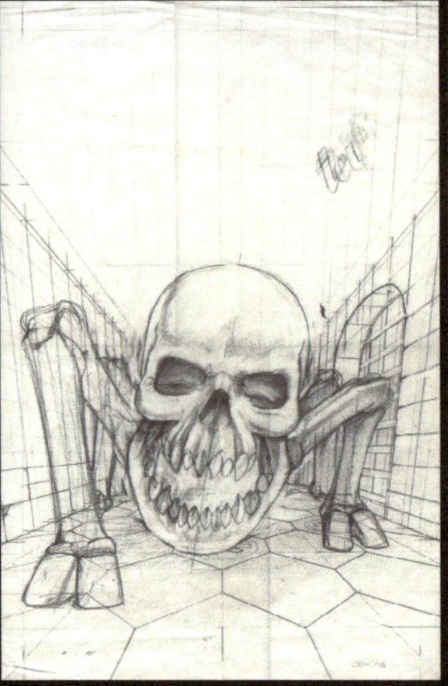
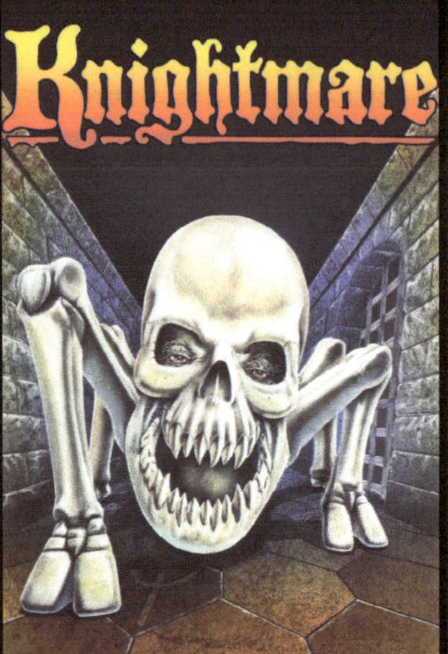
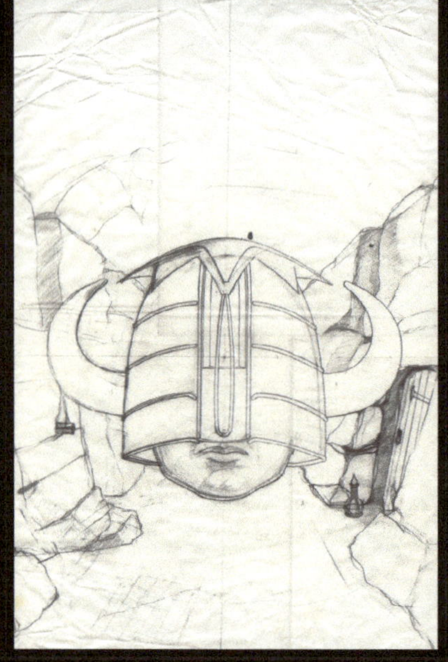
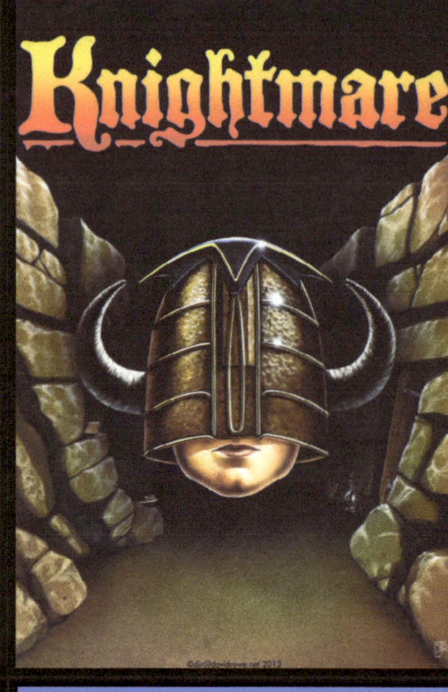
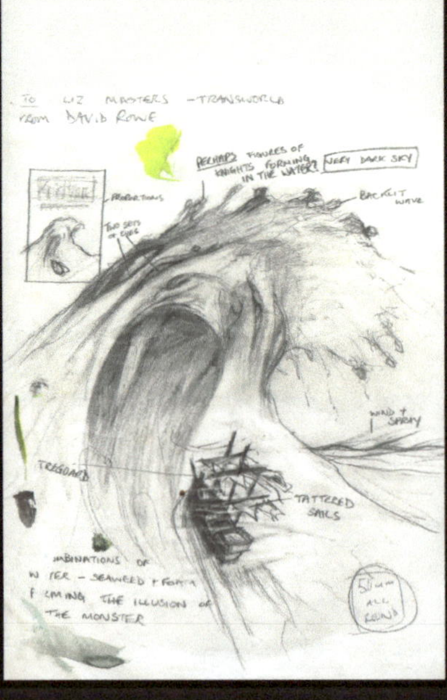
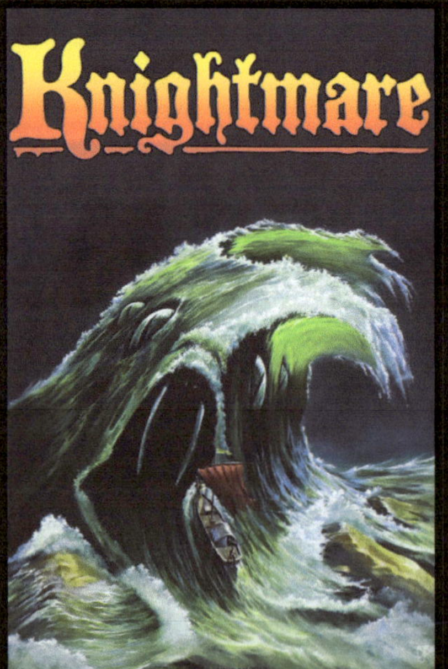
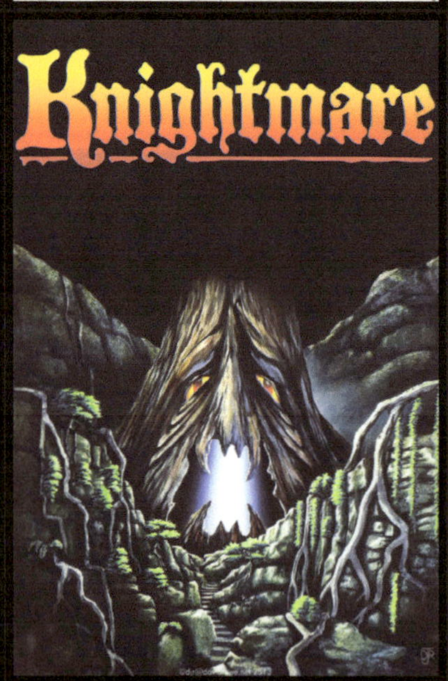
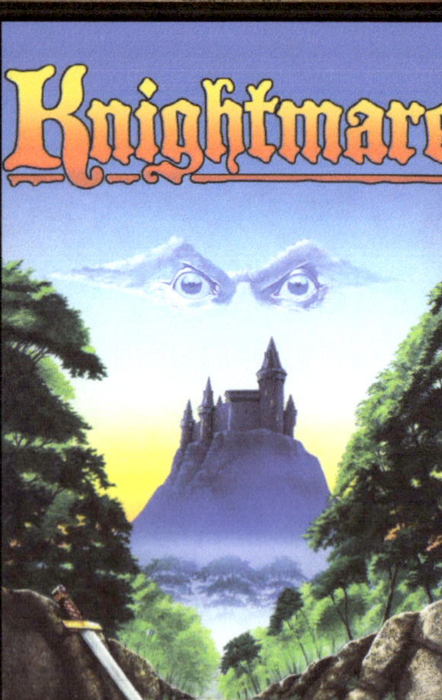

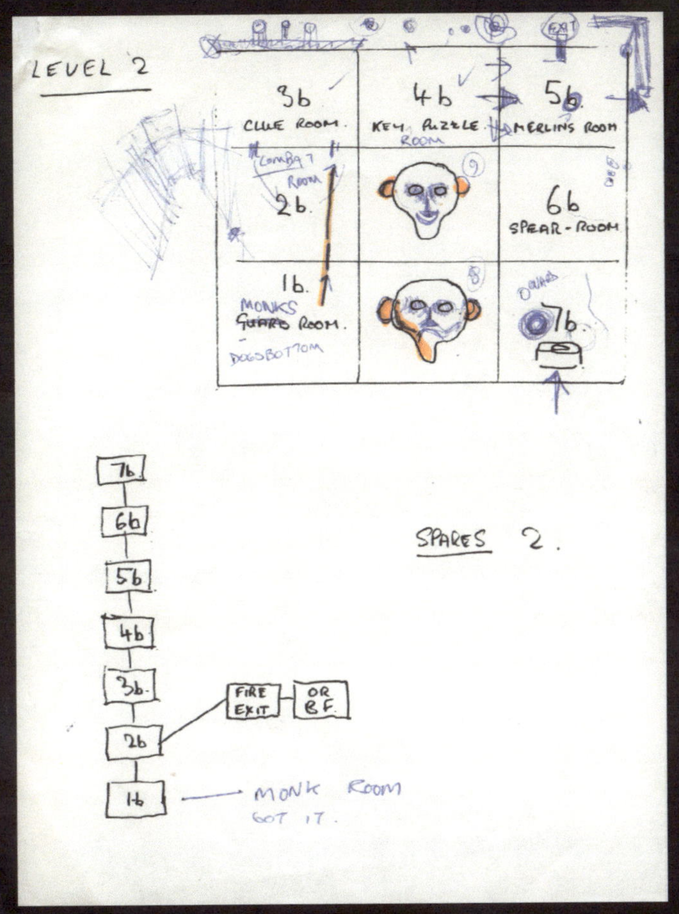

<u>Level 2</u>

2/1b   Monk Rm
2/2b   Combat Rm
2/3b   2nd Level Clue Rm
2/4b   Key Puzzle Rm ———— S Dor
2/5b   Merlin Rm
2/6b   Spear Rm
2/7b   2nd Wellway Rm
2/8b   Bland Rm
2/9b   Exploding Bomb Rm
2/10b Crossing Room Two
2/11b Roller Coaster Corrider
2/12b Mining Room

Note – 1/18a Crone Rm can be used in Level 2

2/13b   KITCHEN ROOM

Monk Room 2.1b

The original images were drawn in a 4:3 aspect ratio which was the standard format for televisions during the early series of Knightmare.
Wide screen TVs are now the norm and so the final composite screens tend to have the top portion cropped to fit the modern screen in recent re-runs.

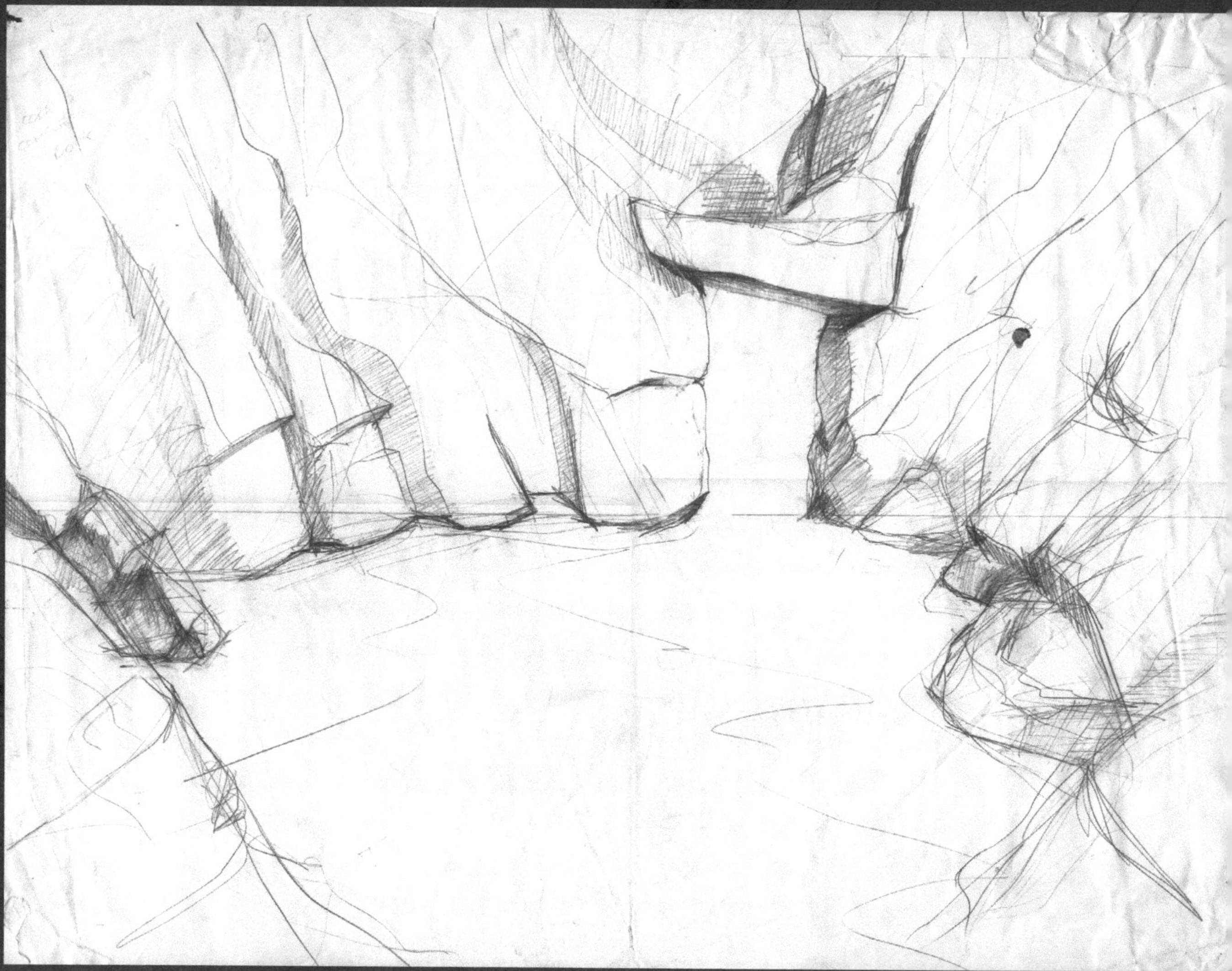

Right: *A rather crumpled and sorry looking Monk's Room drawing.*

Below:
The colour rough for the Monk's Room. It was painted onto an actual copy of the grid.

The floor plan fax showing the positions for the blue chromakey painted blocks.

The tracing.

The composite with strong mood lighting.

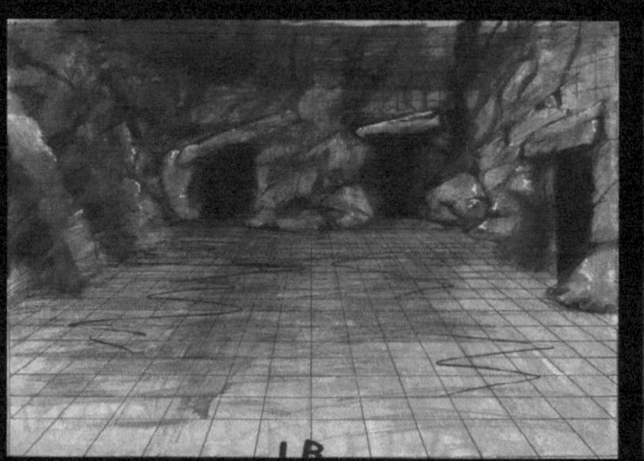

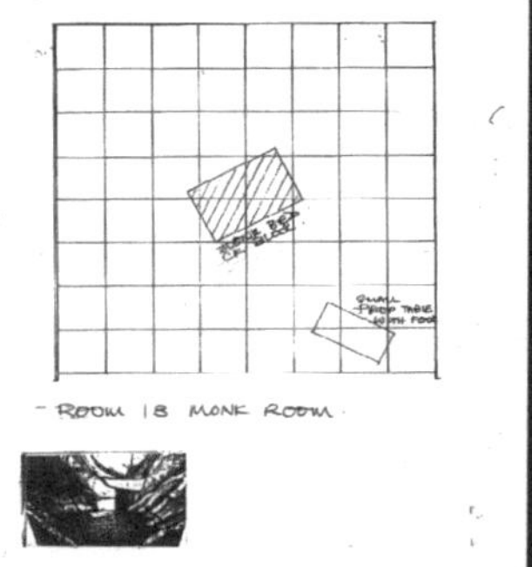

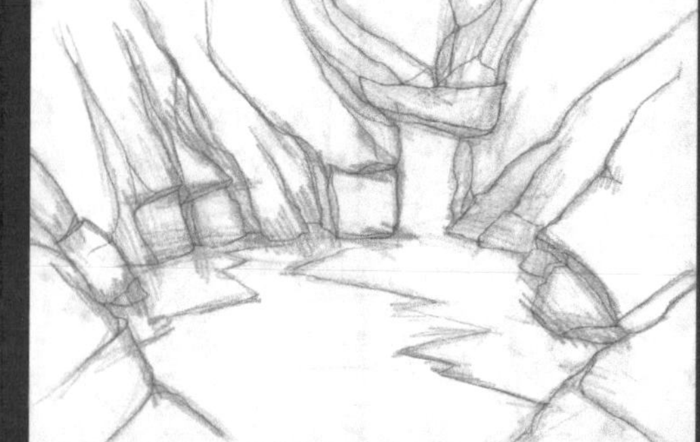

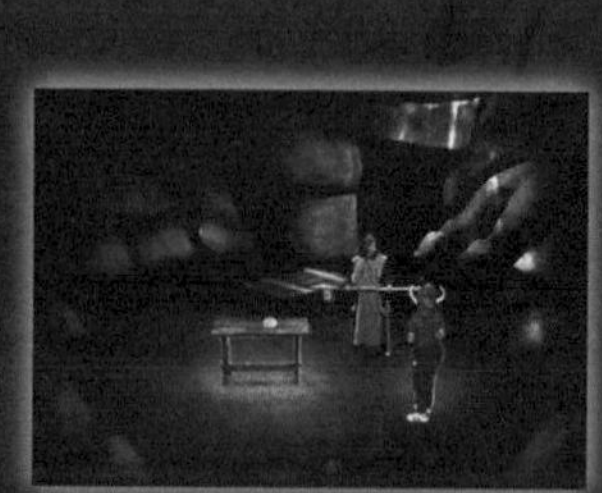

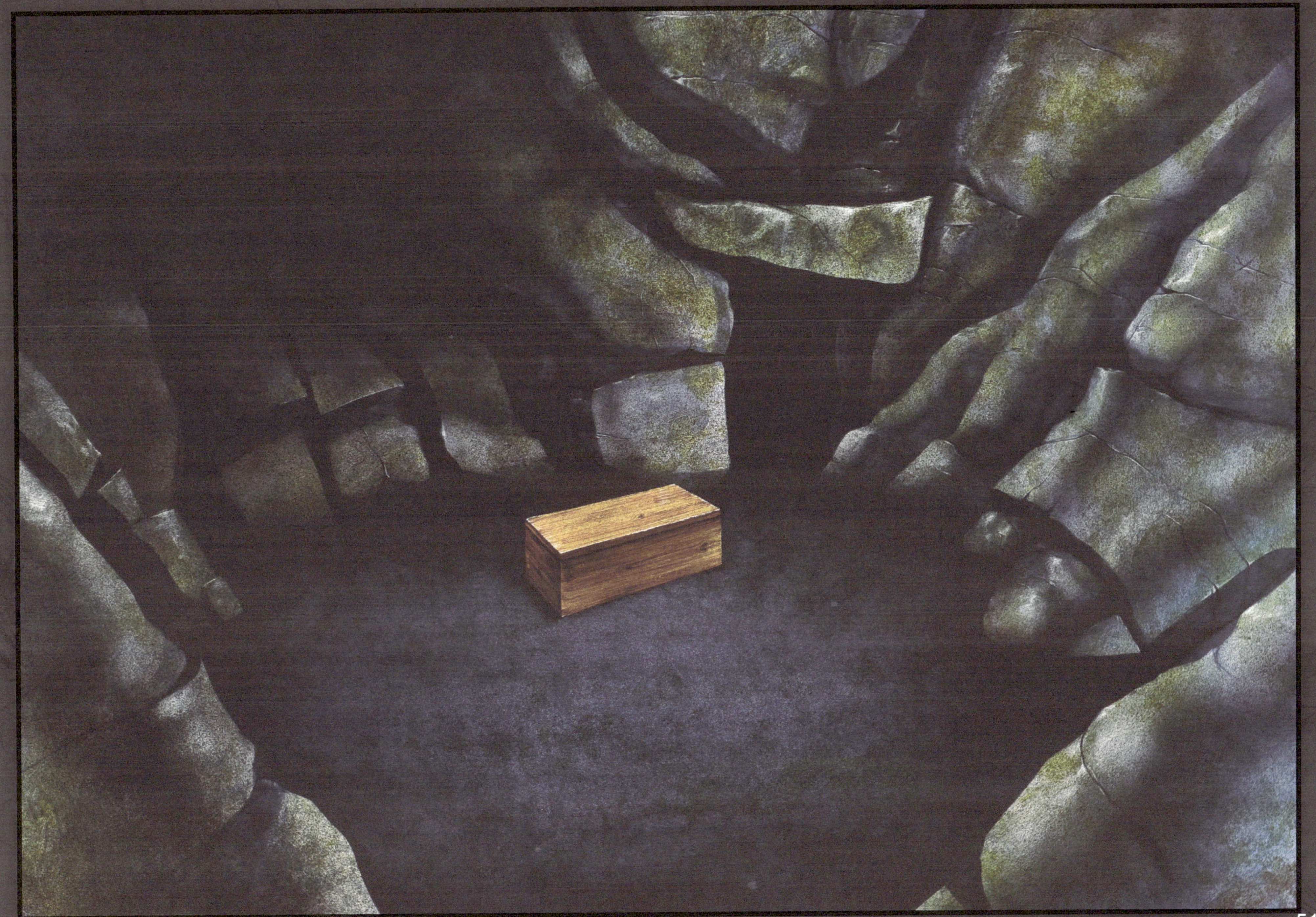

Combat Room 2.2b

The rather gory combat room was amended for the broadcast version. Some of the blood was cleaned up, the trunk was removed and the weaponry was moved out of reach. The weapons represented a selection opportunity which couldn't be offered to the Dungeoneers. The axe was sampled and four copies were placed higher up the wall whilst the originals were overwritten with sampled wall texture.

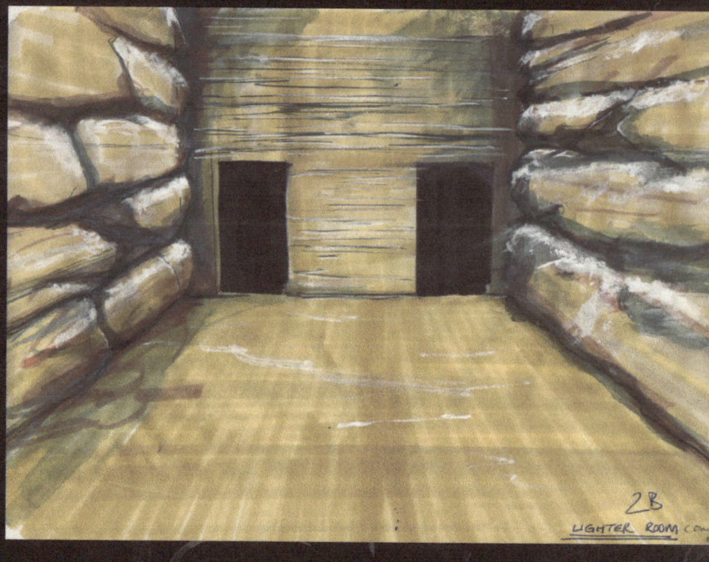

The colour rough for the Combat Room.

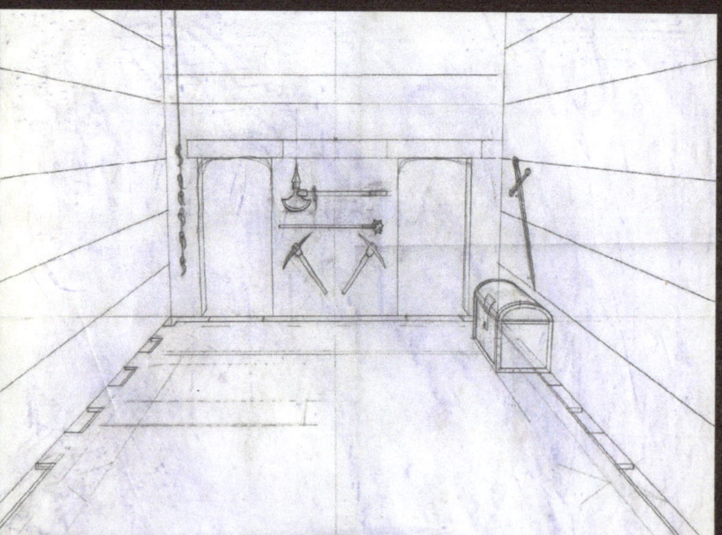

The Original faxed brief notes from Tim Child.

CHAMBER 2 LEVEL 2................. A full width room for combat. No forground objects. Needs full availabe floor space for Captive warrior scenario. One Door exit only. The other Door is locked. This denoted by large yellow keyhole (x10 normal size).

CHAMBER 3 LEVEL 2.................This is Level 2 Clue room. Advent needs to be found screen right at least mid-depth into the room (from Camera POV). Room designed to bring him down staircase and forward and into position behind stone (or wood table). Suggest this would work well if it looked like stylised altar with altar cloth. If room works properly it should bring adventurer to the front of the room and facing the camera and the Clue Table Objects. The table should be raised to an abnormal height so the top is level with the adventurer's chin. The exit door is on ground floor level to the left. Clues found here: Food. Potion. Caspar the Key, dagger.

CHAMBER 4. LEVEL 2...............This is a single level room. Full width, but with four (or even 5 doors) all unnaturally close together and all side by side in the wall facing cam. The room is full width, but only about half depth; the

Key lines were transferred to the illustration using blue pastel.

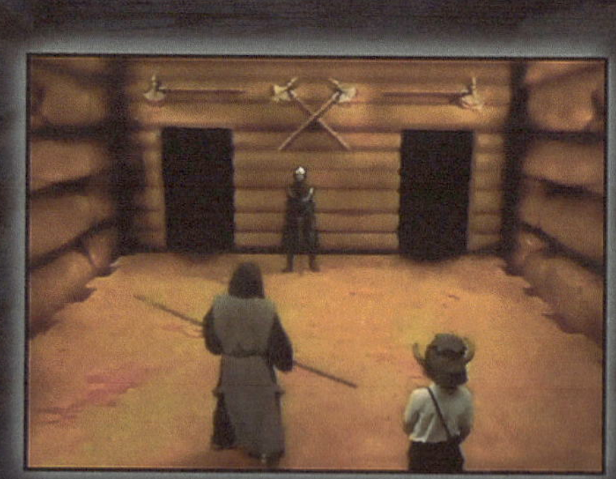

The final composite as broadcast.

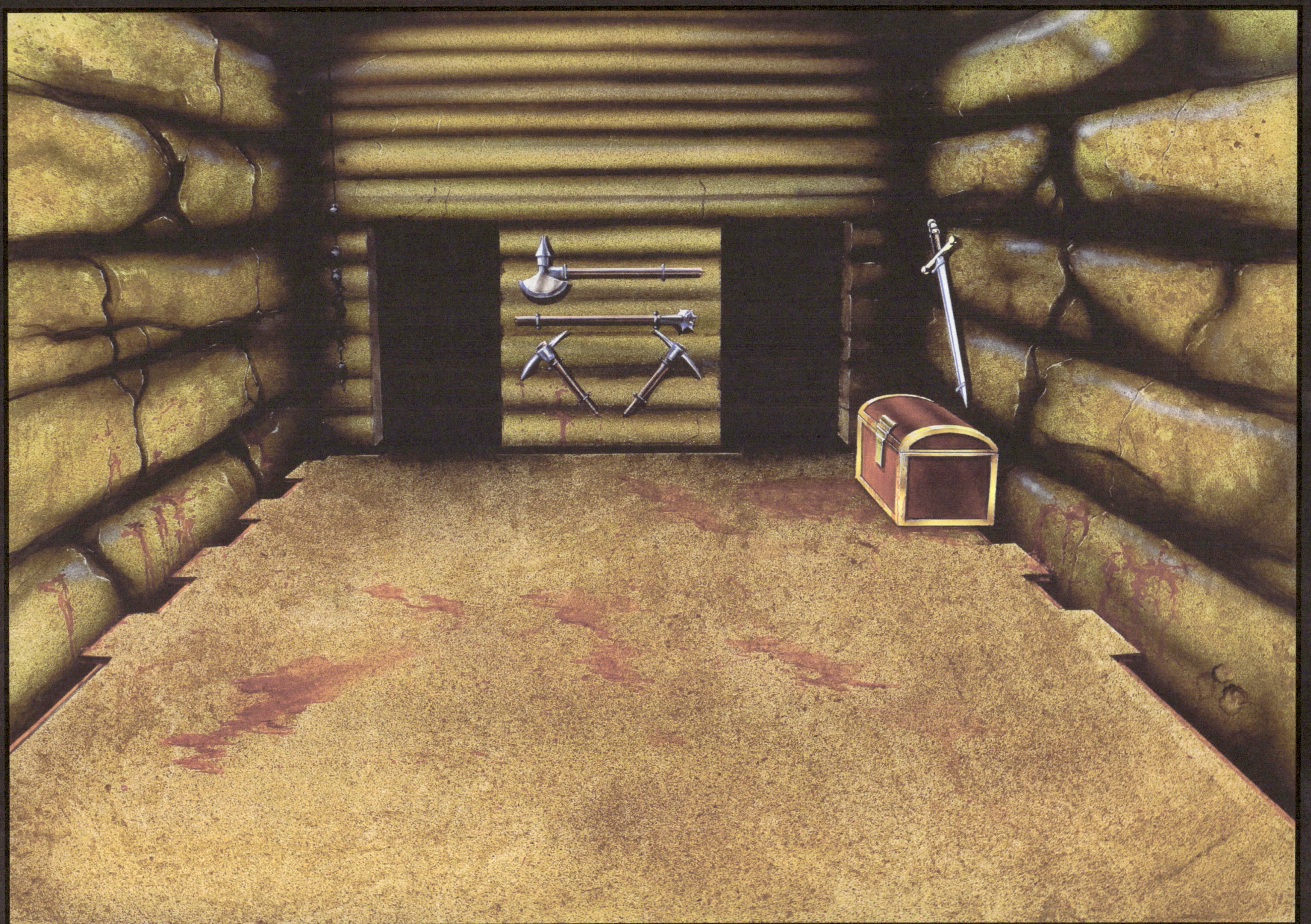

2nd. Level Clue Room 2.3b

The roughs for this room helped iron out quite a few problems. The curved staircase would have posed a (K)nightmare to produce not to mention the health and safety issues for the poor Dungeoneer who would have had to negotiate them. Directions from the rest of the team would have been over complicated too. Straight stairs offered the solution.

Note the omission of the shield that was in the rough as it was within reach of a Dungeoneer.

The keyhole in the drawing was drawn and painted separately for the key puzzle room.

Right: *At the time, the drawings were never meant to be more than working drawings. I would think nothing of making notes over a phone conversation as I worked. They served to jog my memory.*

Below: *Original faxed brief; Colour rough; Floor plan for props; Dramatically lit broadcast composite.*

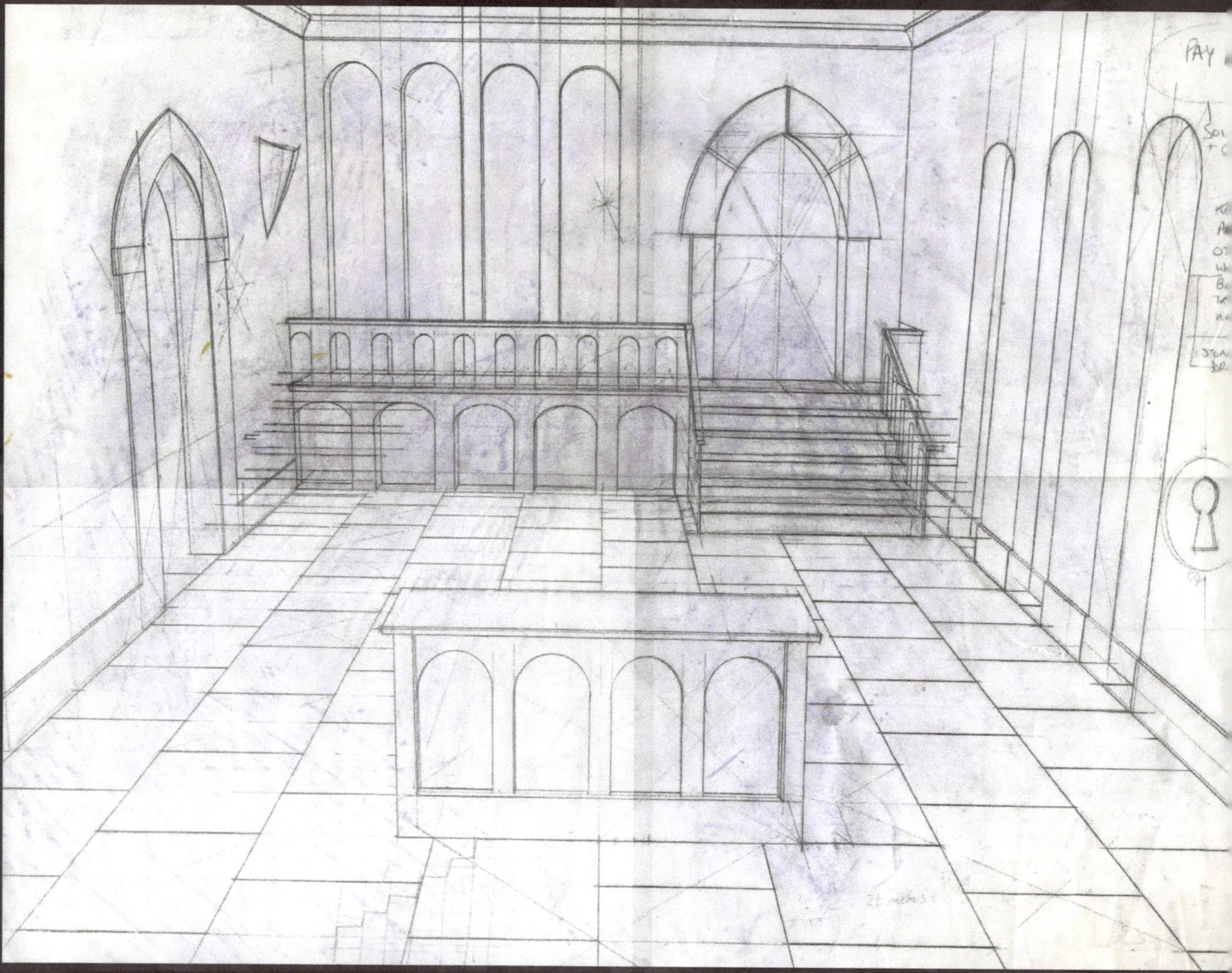

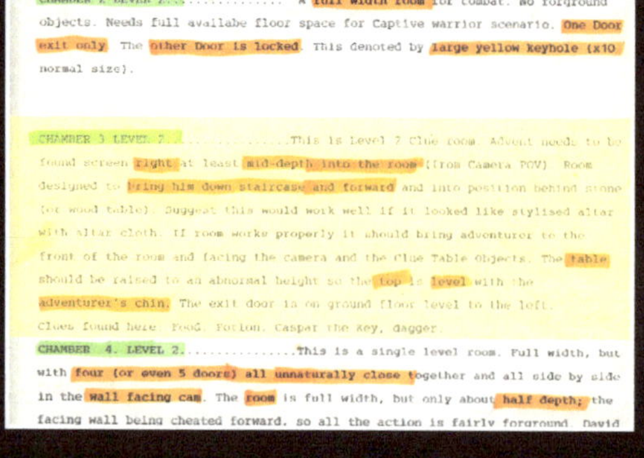

CHAMBER 2 LEVEL. 2................ A full width room for combat. No forground objects. Needs full availabe floor space for Captive warrior scenario. One Door exit only. The other Door is locked. This denoted by large yellow keyhole (x10 normal size).

CHAMBER 3 LEVEL 2...............This is Level 2 Clue room. Advent needs to be found screen right at least mid-depth into the room (from Camera POV). Room designed to bring him down staircase and forward and into position behind stone (or wood table). Suggest this would work well if it looked like stylised altar with altar cloth. If room works properly it should bring adventurer to the front of the room and facing the camera and the Clue Table objects. The table should be raised to an abnormal height so the top is level with the adventurer's chin. The exit door is on ground floor level to the left. Clues found here: Frog, Potion, Caspar the key, dagger.

CHAMBER 4. LEVEL 2................This is a single level room. Full width, but with four (or even 5 doors) all unnaturally close together and all side by side in the wall facing cam. The room is full width, but only about half depth; the facing wall being cheated forward, so all the action is fairly forground. David

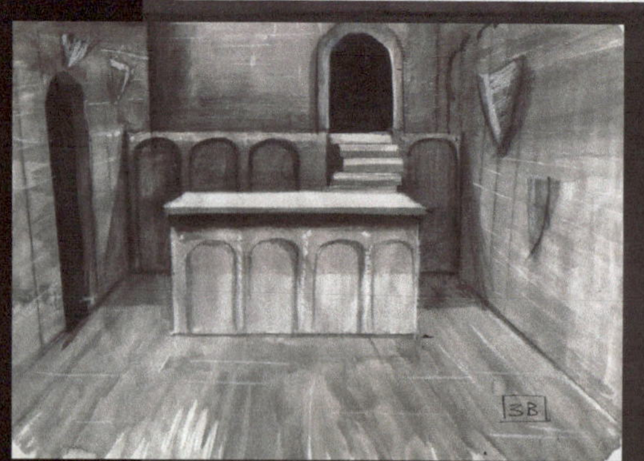

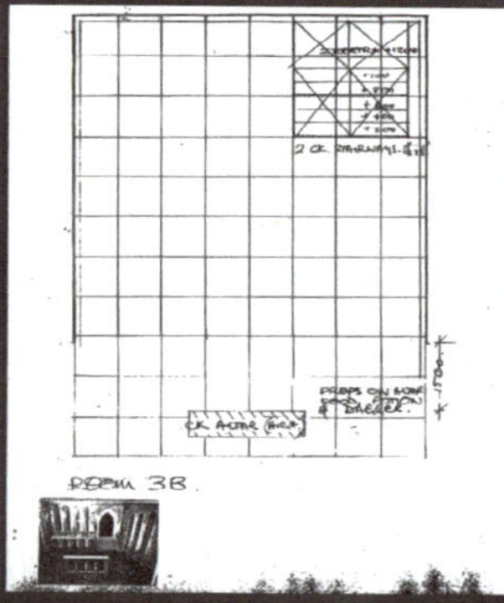

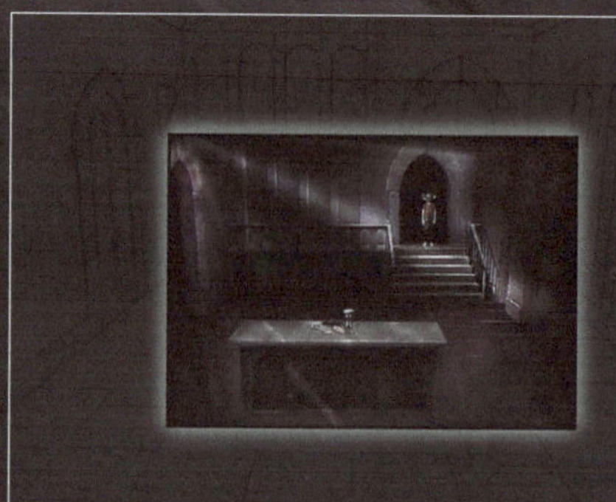

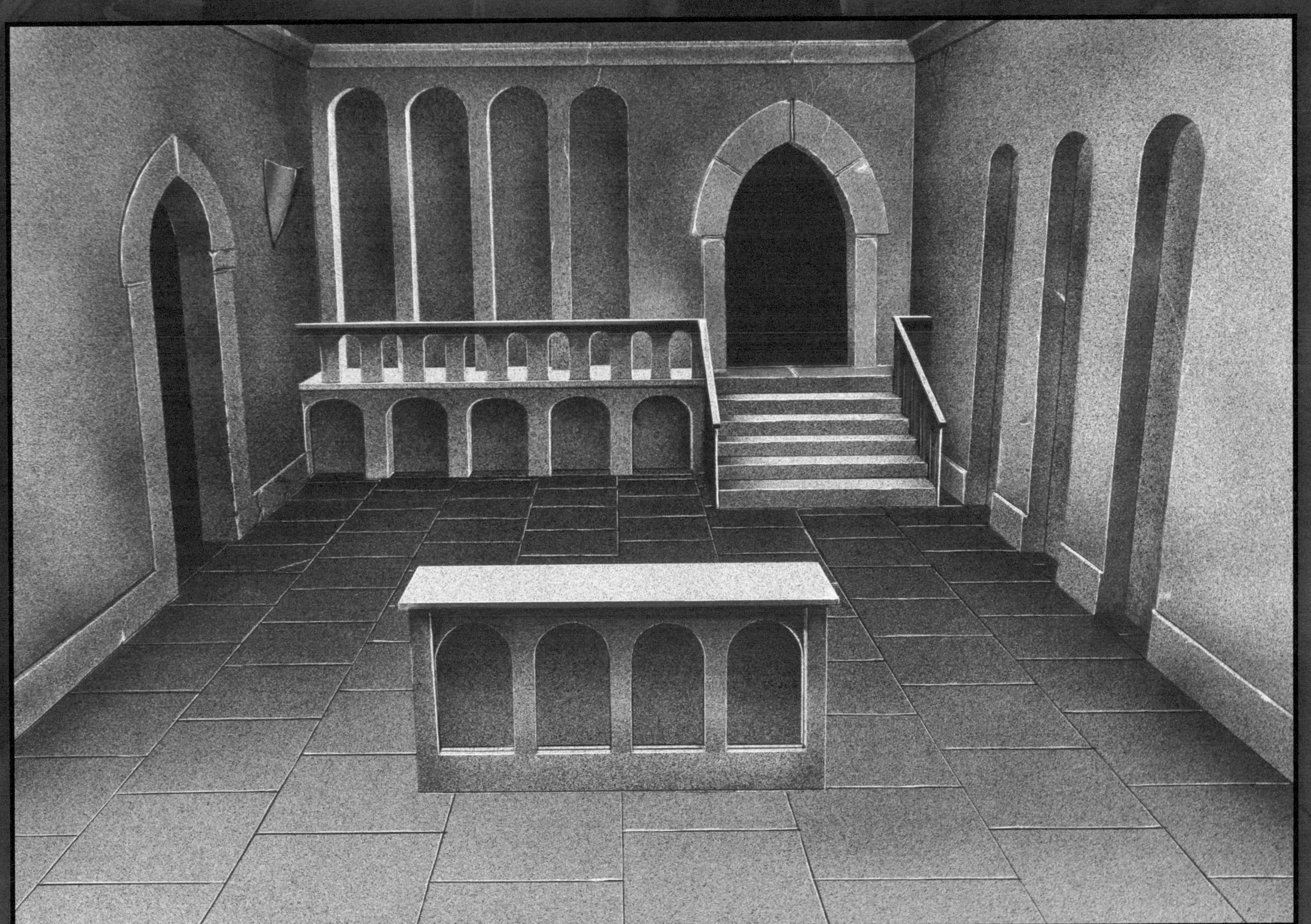

Key Puzzle Room 2.4b

The drawing for this room was made straight onto the tracing paper. There are construction lines which show the way that the underlying grid lines were subdivided with diagonal lines. This helped place brick and flagstone lines in correct perspective. The subdivisions were further subdivided when more intricate detail was required. Construction lines for the doors were made to find their position in that part of the grid and to find their centres so that the arch ellipses could be drawn in accurately.

Right: *The colour roughs were made very quickly and spontaneously.*

Below:
The faxed brief notes;
The floor plan for props;
The tracing showing the back wall brought forward;
The fully lit broadcast composite.

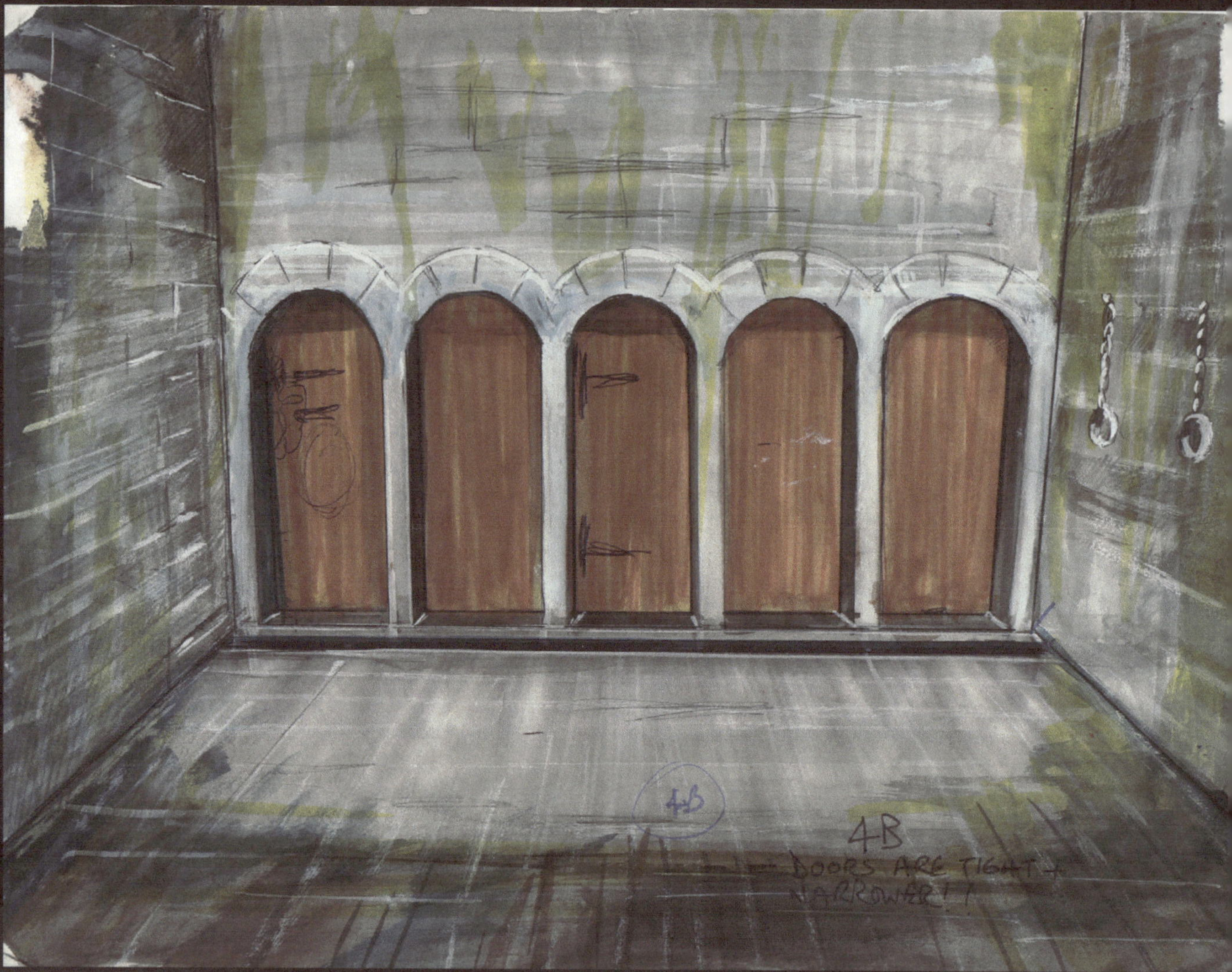

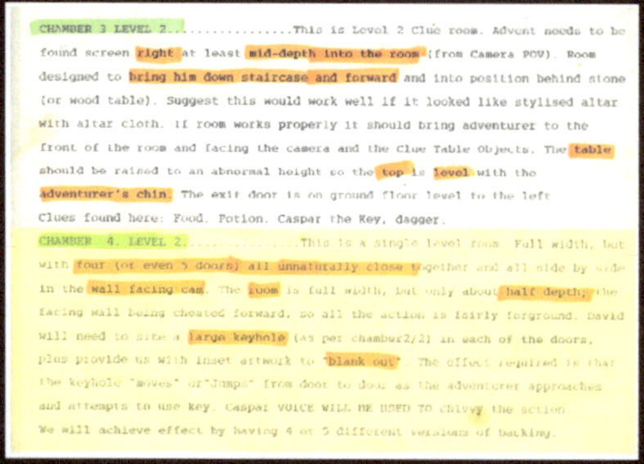

CHAMBER 3 LEVEL 2....................This is Level 2 Clue room. Advent needs to be found screen right at least mid-depth into the room (from Camera POV). Room designed to bring him down staircase and forward and into position behind stone (or wood table). Suggest this would work well if it looked like stylised altar with altar cloth. If room works properly it should bring adventurer to the front of the room and facing the camera and the Clue Table Objects. The table should be raised to an abnormal height so the top is level with the adventurer's chin. The exit door is on ground floor level to the left Clues found here: Food. Potion. Caspar the Key, dagger.

CHAMBER 4. LEVEL 2....................This is a single level room. Full width, but with four (or even 5 doors) all unnaturally close together and all side by side in the wall facing cam. The room is full width, but only about half depth; the facing wall being cheated forward, so all the action is fairly foreground. David will need to site a large keyhole (as per chamber2/2) in each of the doors, plus provide us with inset artwork to "blank out". The effect required is that the keyhole "moves" or "jumps" from door to door as the adventurer approaches and attempts to use key. Caspar VOICE WILL BE USED TO chivvy the action. We will achieve effect by having 4 or 5 different versions of backing.

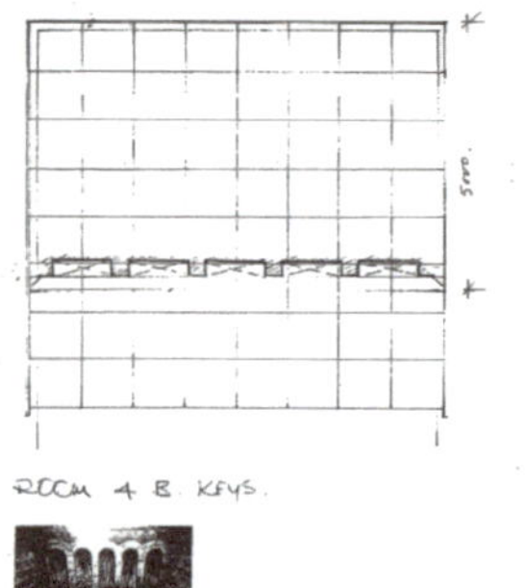

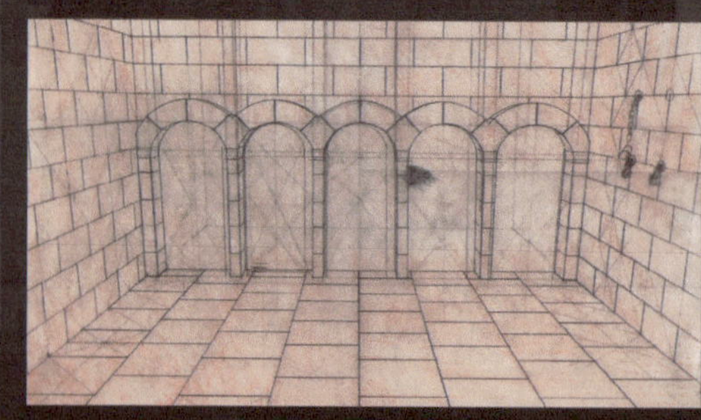

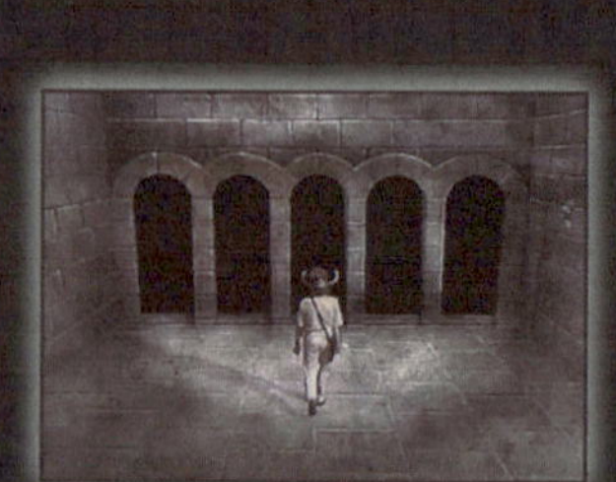

">

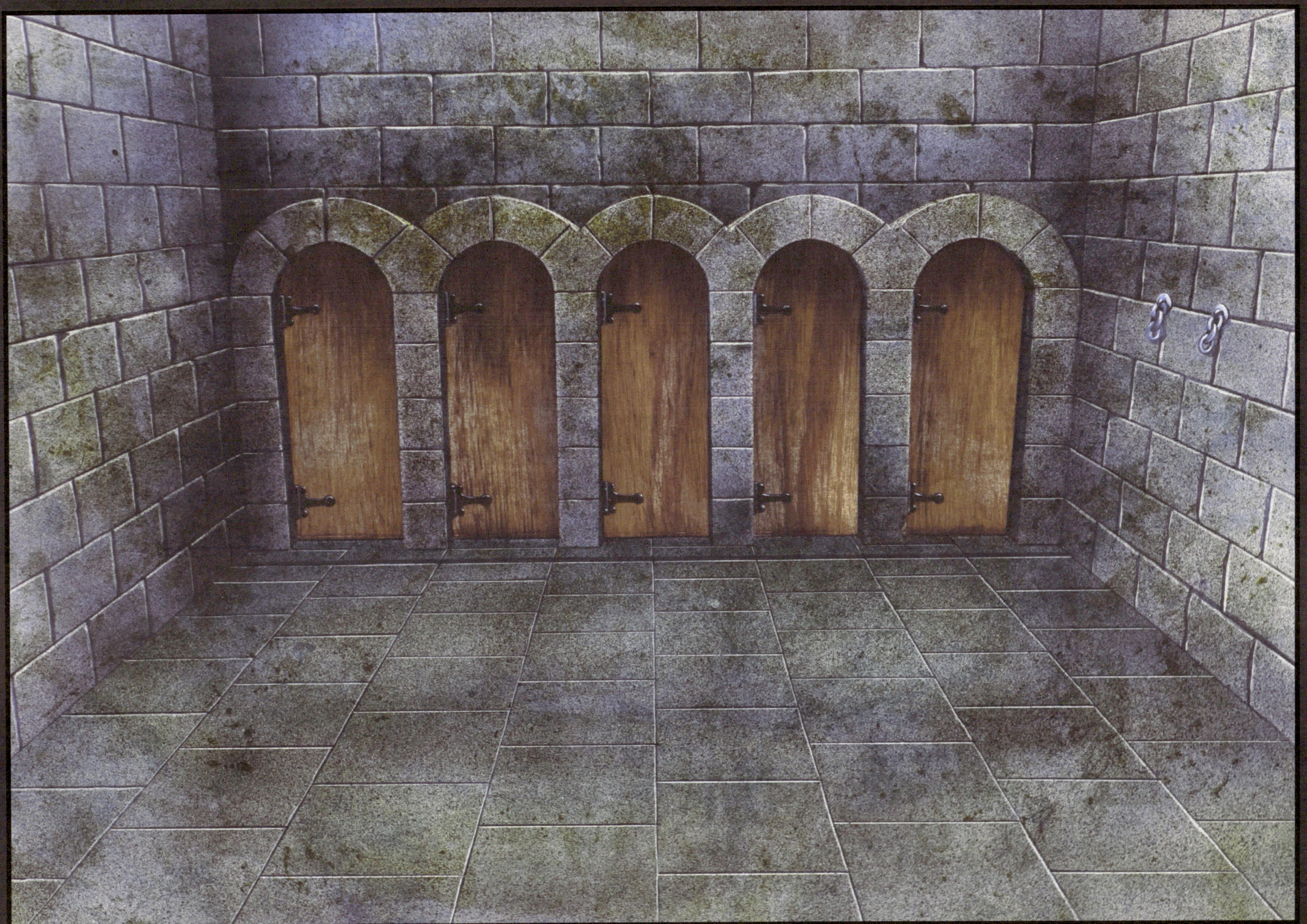

Merlin Room 2.5b

The drawing for the first Merlin Room shows once more how the detail was achieved by breaking down the grid with subdivisions to achieve the detail. The single perspective vanishing point is shown on the eye level which corresponded to about 3 metres up in the chromakey studio. The chair and dais required a two point perspective. The vanishing points were added to the left and right of the drawing on my drawing board. There are notes all over the place which refer to video game cover enquiries and a publishing proposal. The drawing was cut in two and faxed to the producer, Sally Freeman, at Anglia.

Right: *The drawing for the first Merlin Room. There are more phone notes jotted around the edge. The drawing is addressed to Sally Freeman, the producer.*

Below: Original faxed brief notes; Faxed prop floor plan; The lit final composite; An alternatively lit composite with puzzle solving in progress.

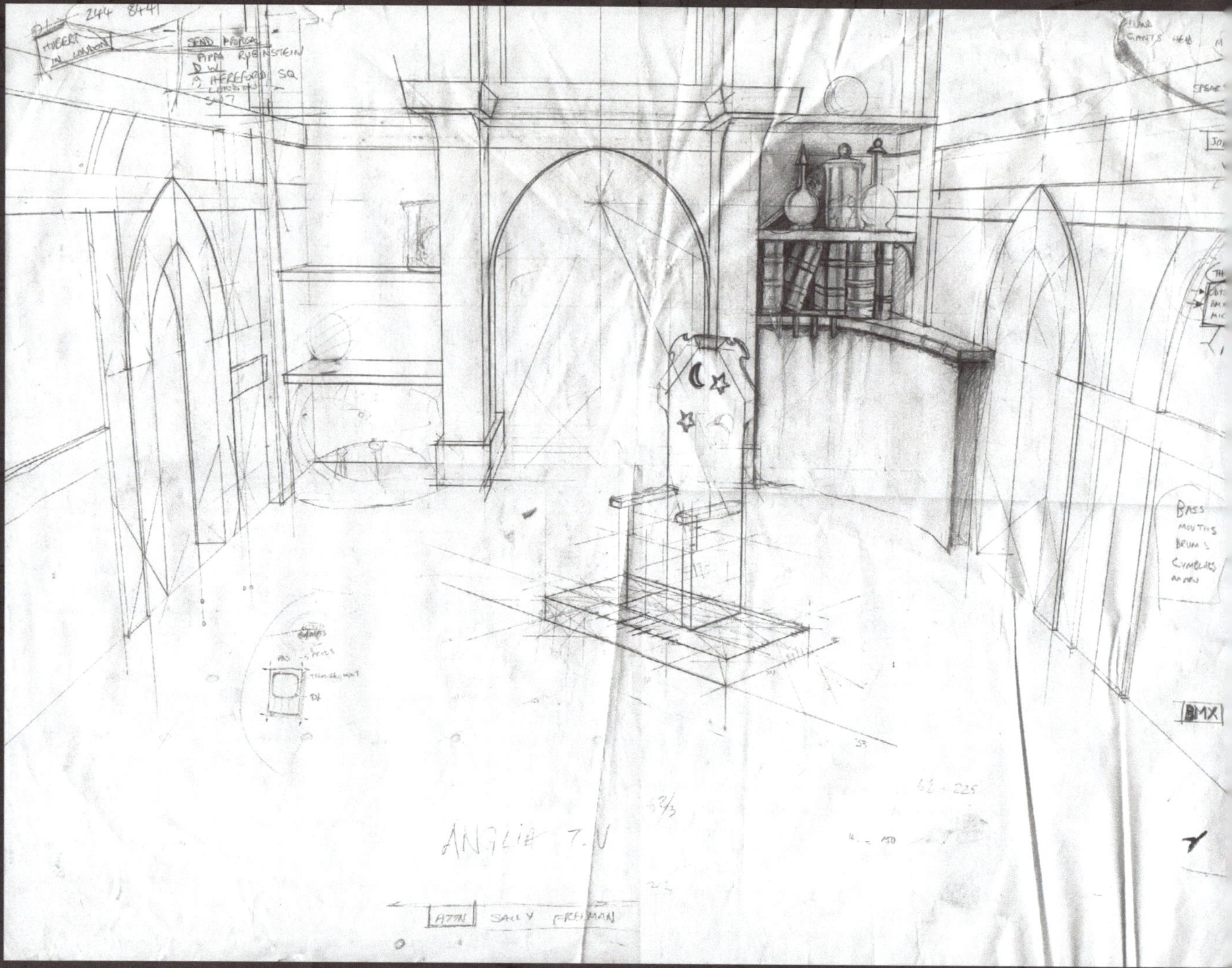

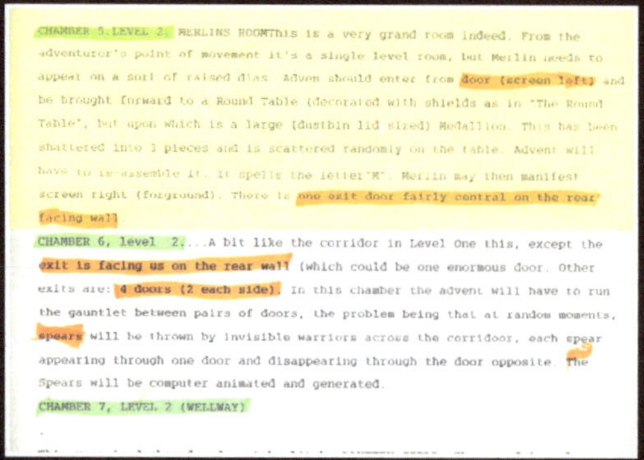

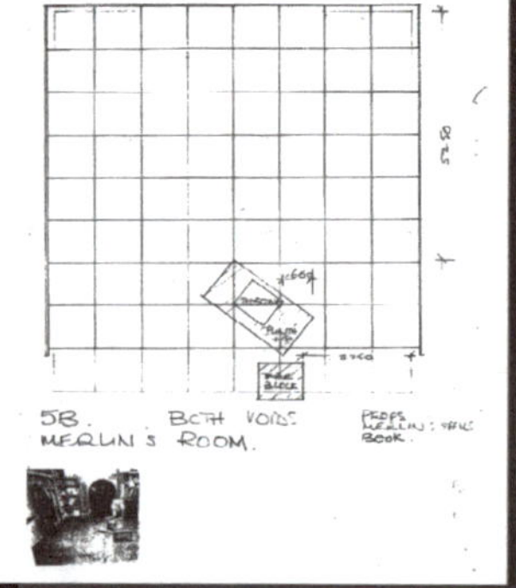

CHAMBER 5. LEVEL 2. MERLINS ROOMThis is a very grand room indeed. From the adventurer's point of movement it's a single level room, but Merlin needs to appear on a sort of raised dias. Adven should enter from door (screen left) and be brought forward to a Round Table (decorated with shields as in "The Round Table", but upon which is a large (dustbin lid sized) Medallion. This has been shattered into 3 pieces and is scattered randomly on the table. Adven will have to re-assemble it. It spells the letter 'M'. Merlin may then manifest screen right (forground). There is one exit door fairly central on the rear facing wall.

CHAMBER 6, level 2. ...A bit like the corridor in Level One this, except the exit is facing us on the rear wall (which could be one enormous door. Other exits are: 4 doors (2 each side). In this chamber the advent will have to run the gauntlet between pairs of doors, the problem being that at random moments, spears will be thrown by invisible warriors across the corridoor, each spear appearing through one door and disappearing through the door opposite. The Spears will be computer animated and generated.

CHAMBER 7, LEVEL 2 (WELLWAY)

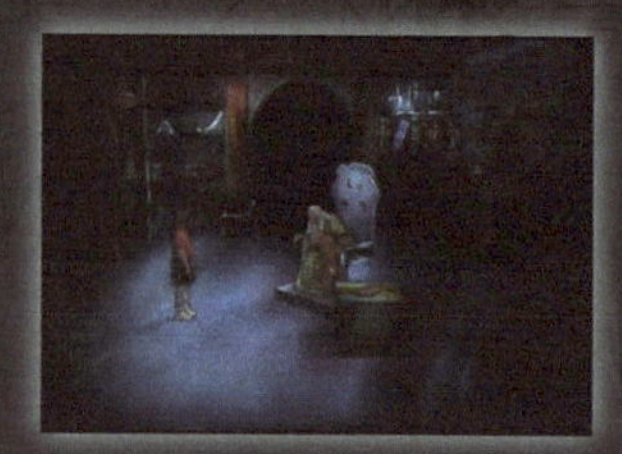

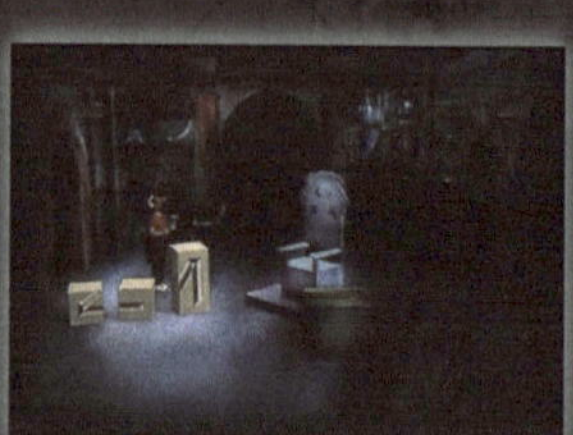

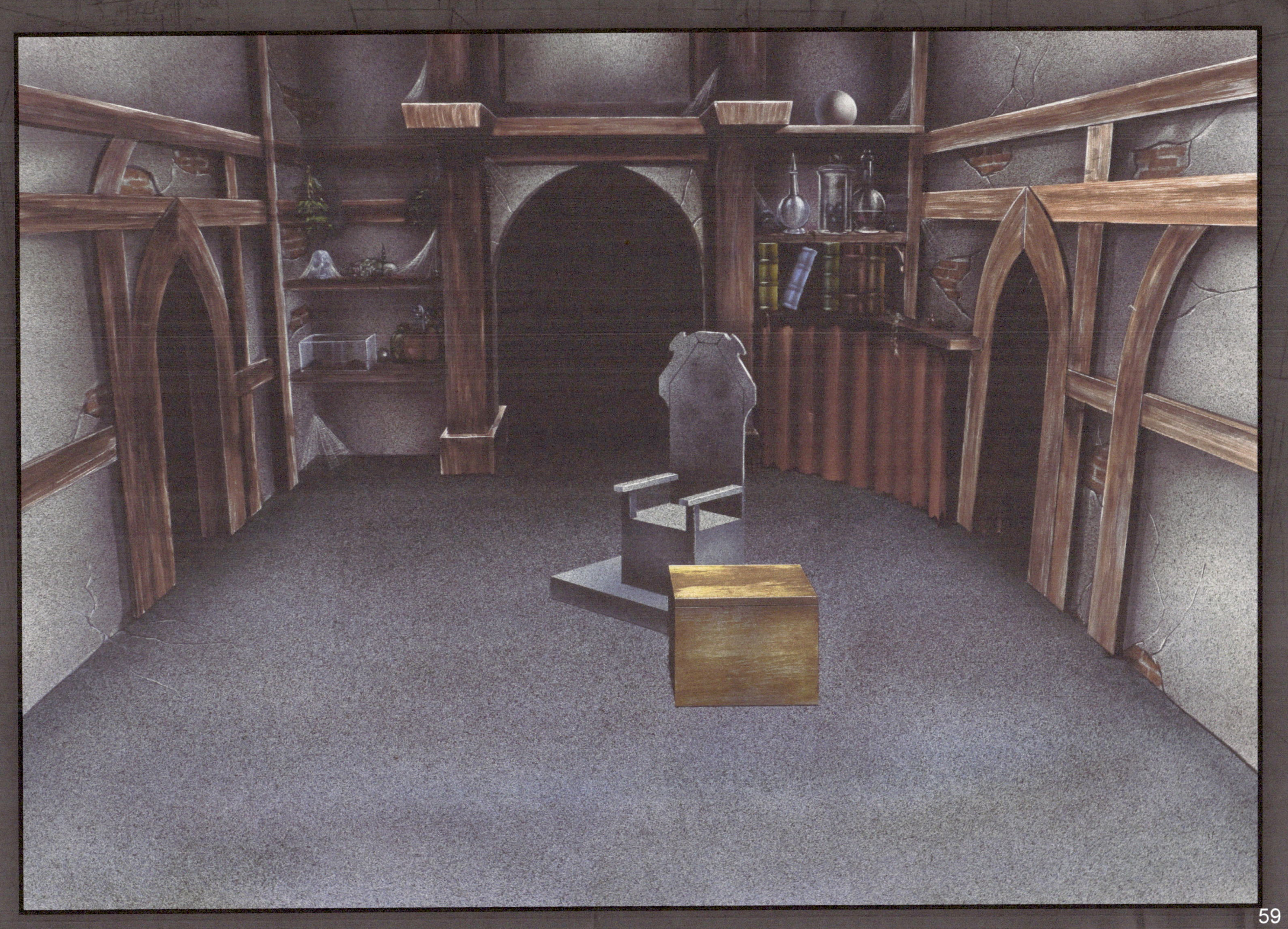

New Merlin Room 2.5b

The new Merlin Room was based upon the original Jean Peyre grid one. The fax from Tim indicated what was needed.

The drawing was very crumpled when it was discovered in storage.

Once the spatter and texture techniques were applied, the lines were inked in with a brush and liquid acrylic. Masking film was placed over the painting and cautiously cut with a scalpel being careful not to be so firm as to damage the board surface.

The floor holes and windows were sprayed in with their surrounds protected with masking film. The doorways were painted after masking the surrounding wall, but NOT the floor. Airbrushed spray was then applied being careful to leave some of the stone texture visible in the door depth. A hard edge was avoided against the floor by protecting it with the edge of a raised hand, piece of card or acetate.

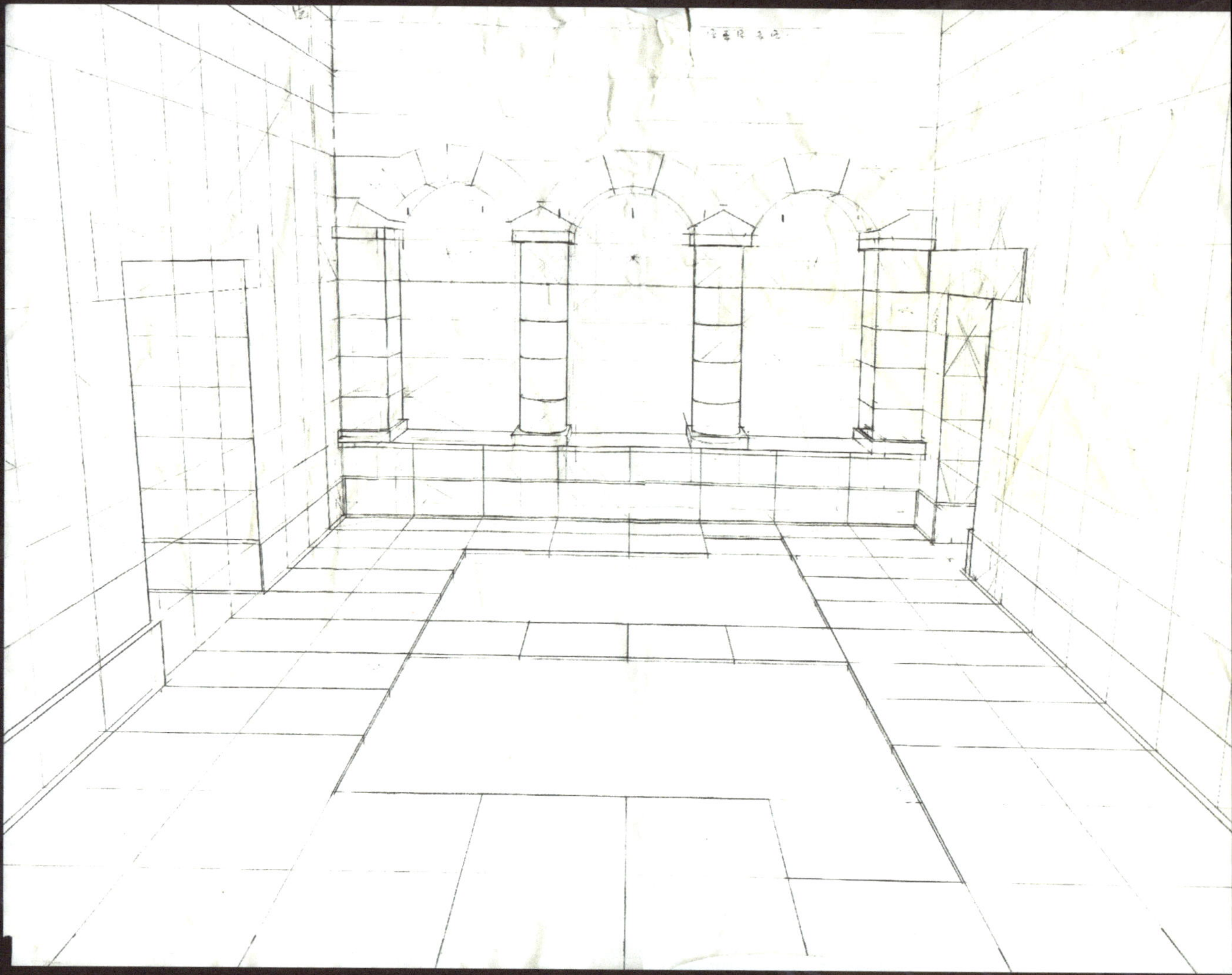

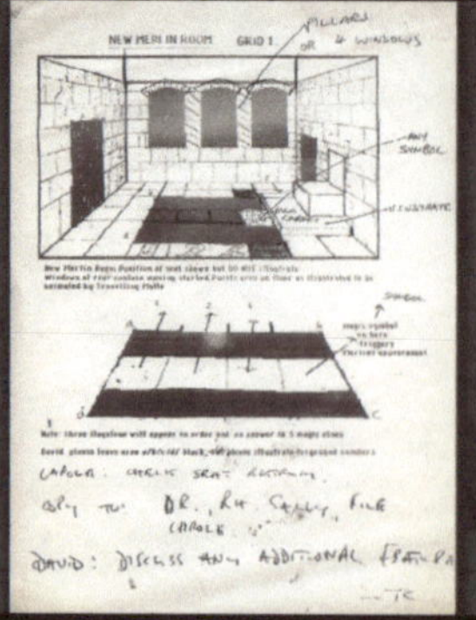

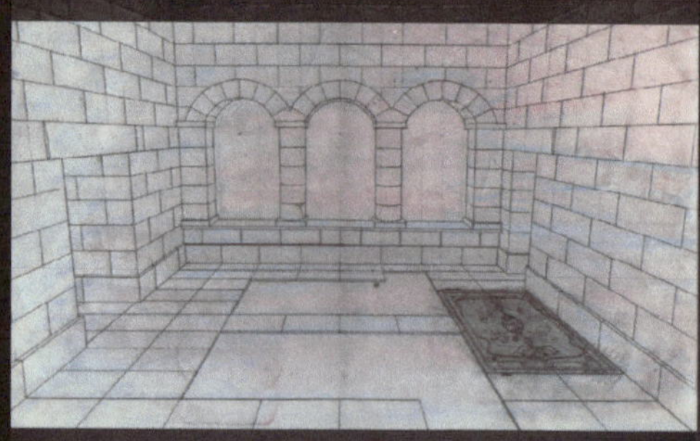

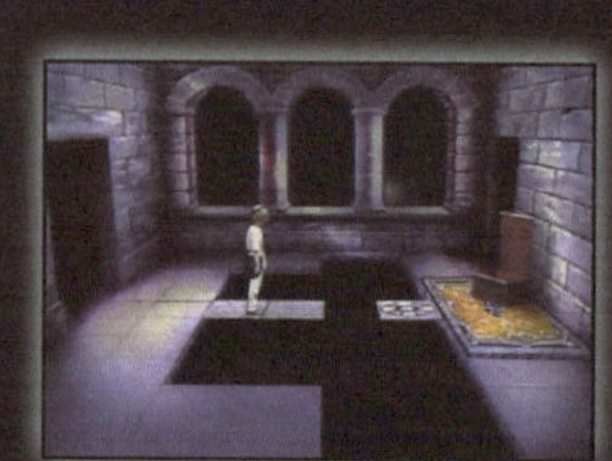

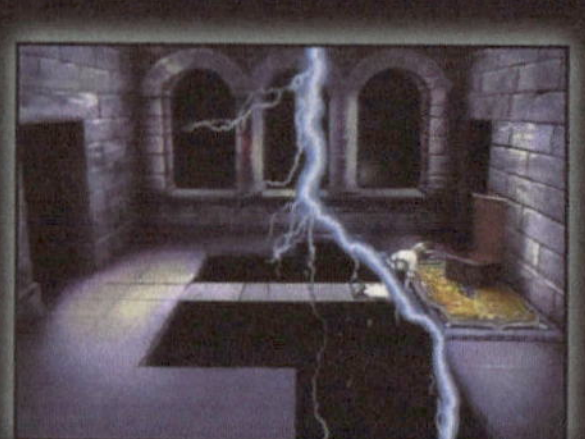

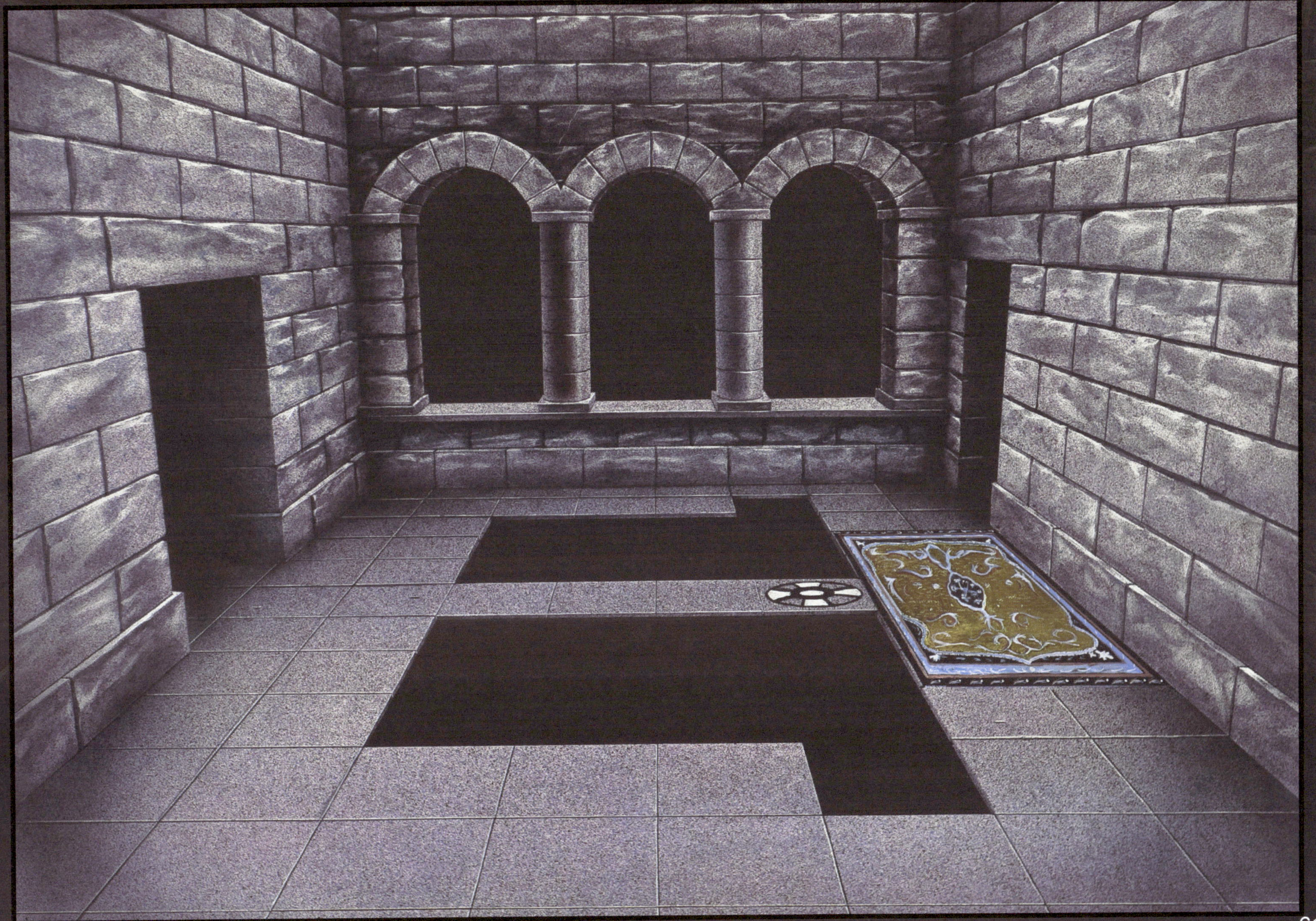

Spear Room 2.6b

Even though the view was narrower than the grid, there were no blue flats required for this room. This was presumably because the Dungeoneer entered form the centre front of the scene and had to make a beeline for the far door by running the gauntlet of spears being prodded towards him from the side doors.

The textures applied were airbrush spatter and drifts of mottled colour.

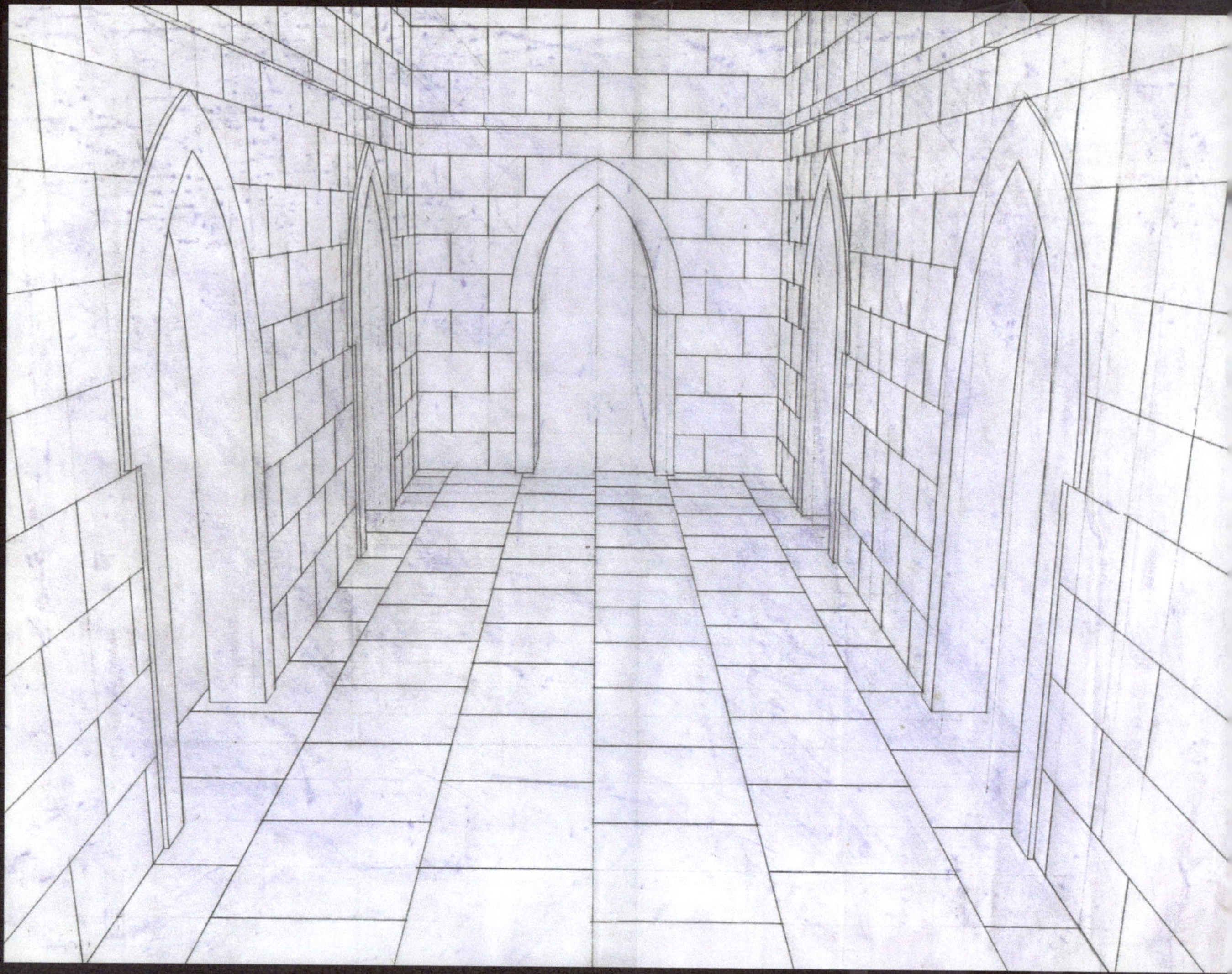

Right: The drawing, executed straight down onto tracing paper.

Below: *The original brief notes from Broadsword Television.*
The colour rough.
Two broadcast manifestations of the Spear room.

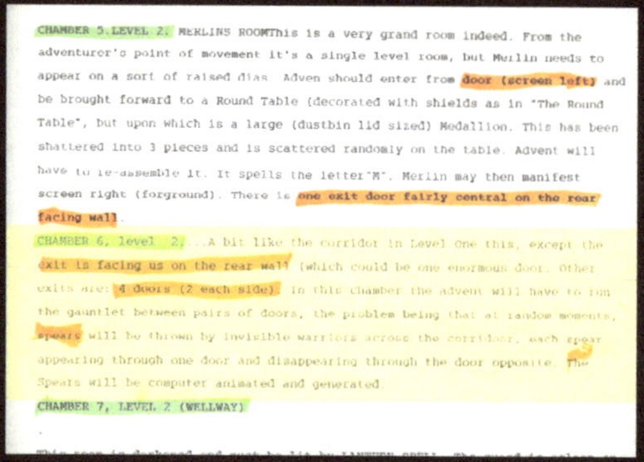

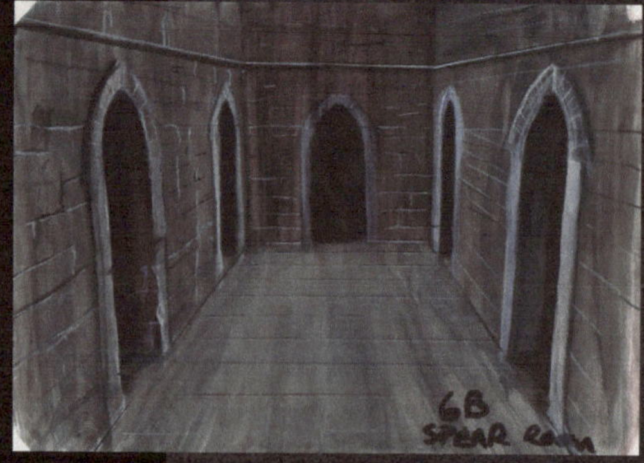

CHAMBER 5.LEVEL 2: MERLINS ROOMThis is a very grand room indeed. From the adventurer's point of movement it's a single level room, but Merlin needs to appear on a sort of raised dias Adven should enter from door (screen left) and be brought forward to a Round Table (decorated with shields as in "The Round Table", but upon which is a large (dustbin lid sized) Medallion. This has been shattered into 3 pieces and is scattered randomly on the table. Advent will have to re-assemble it. It spells the letter"M". Merlin may then manifest screen right (forground). There is one exit door fairly central on the rear facing wall.

CHAMBER 6, level 2:...A bit like the corridor in Level One this, except the exit is facing us on the rear wall (which could be one enormous door. Other exits are: 4 doors (2 each side). In this chamber the advent will have to run the gauntlet between pairs of doors, the problem being that at random moments, spears will be thrown by invisible warriors across the corridor, each spear appearing through one door and disappearing through the door opposite. The Spears will be computer animated and generated.

CHAMBER 7, LEVEL 2 (WELLWAY)

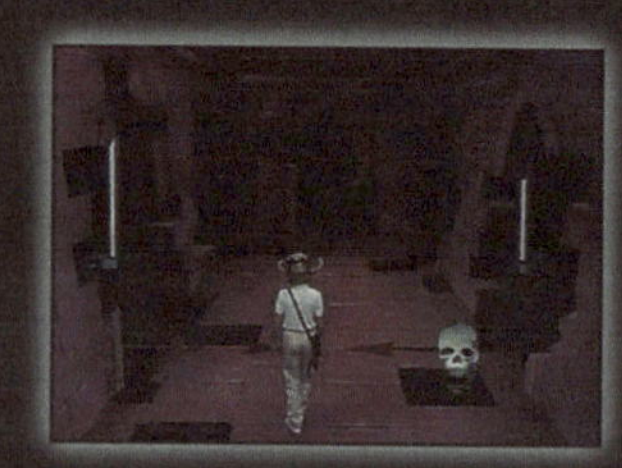

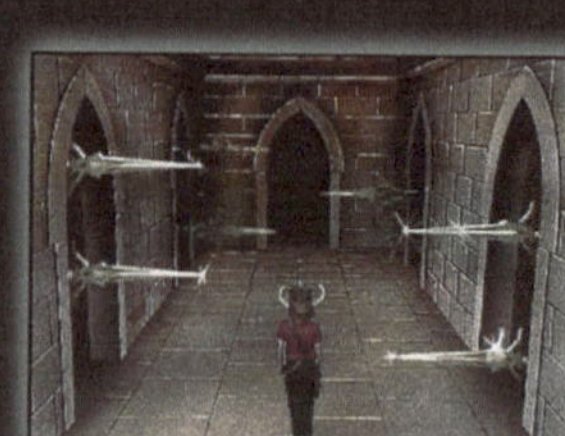

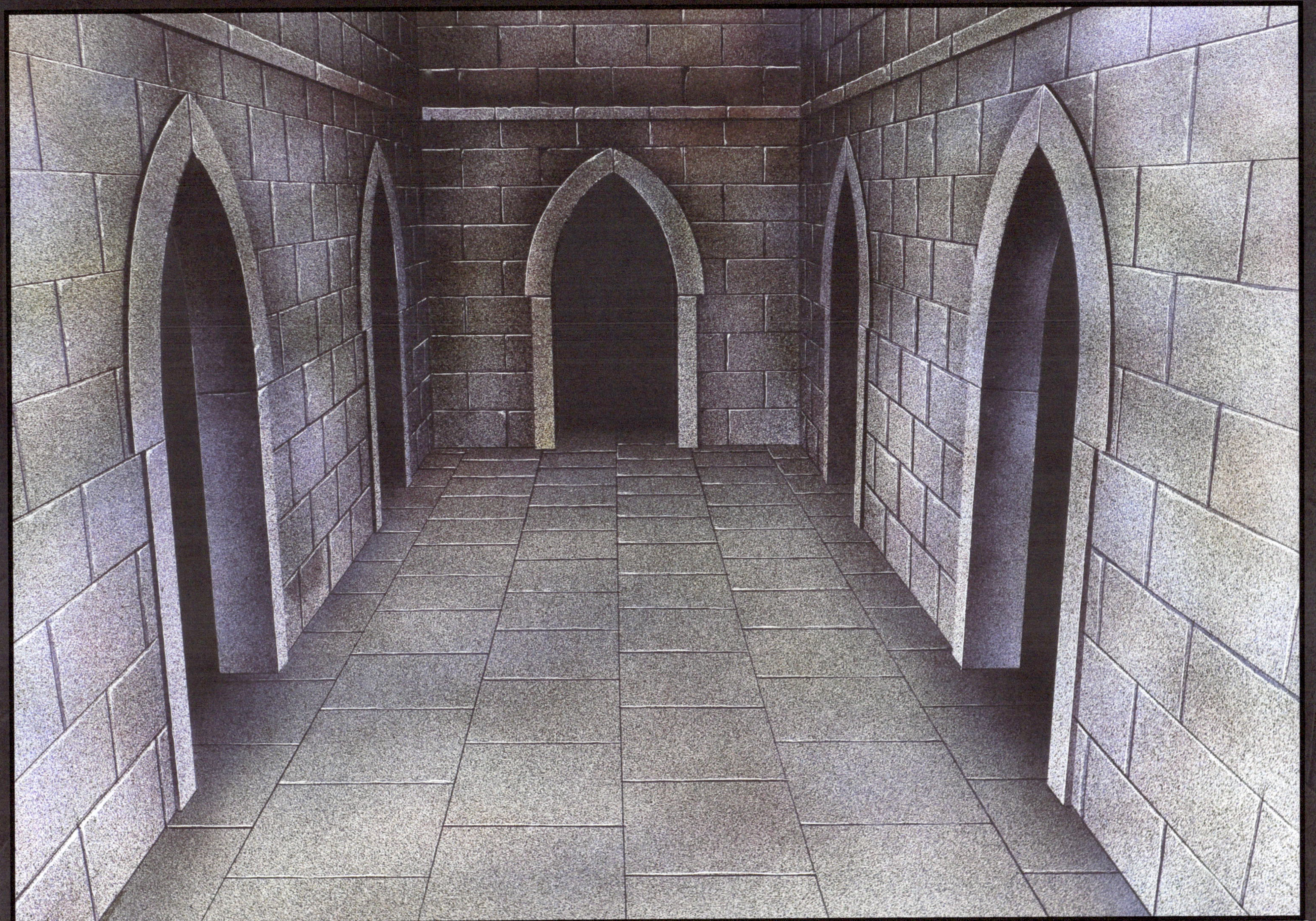

2nd. Well way Room 2.7b

The well drawing was not to the correct scale at the first attempt was and so was overdrawn in the correct proportions.
The chromakey props had to fit exactly in order for the Dungeoneer to make a convincing exit down the painted version of the well.
The props plan shows that the items were built and placed after the painting had been completed and delivered.
This was a complex scene to set up as it had to have the four prop elements working perfectly with the painting.

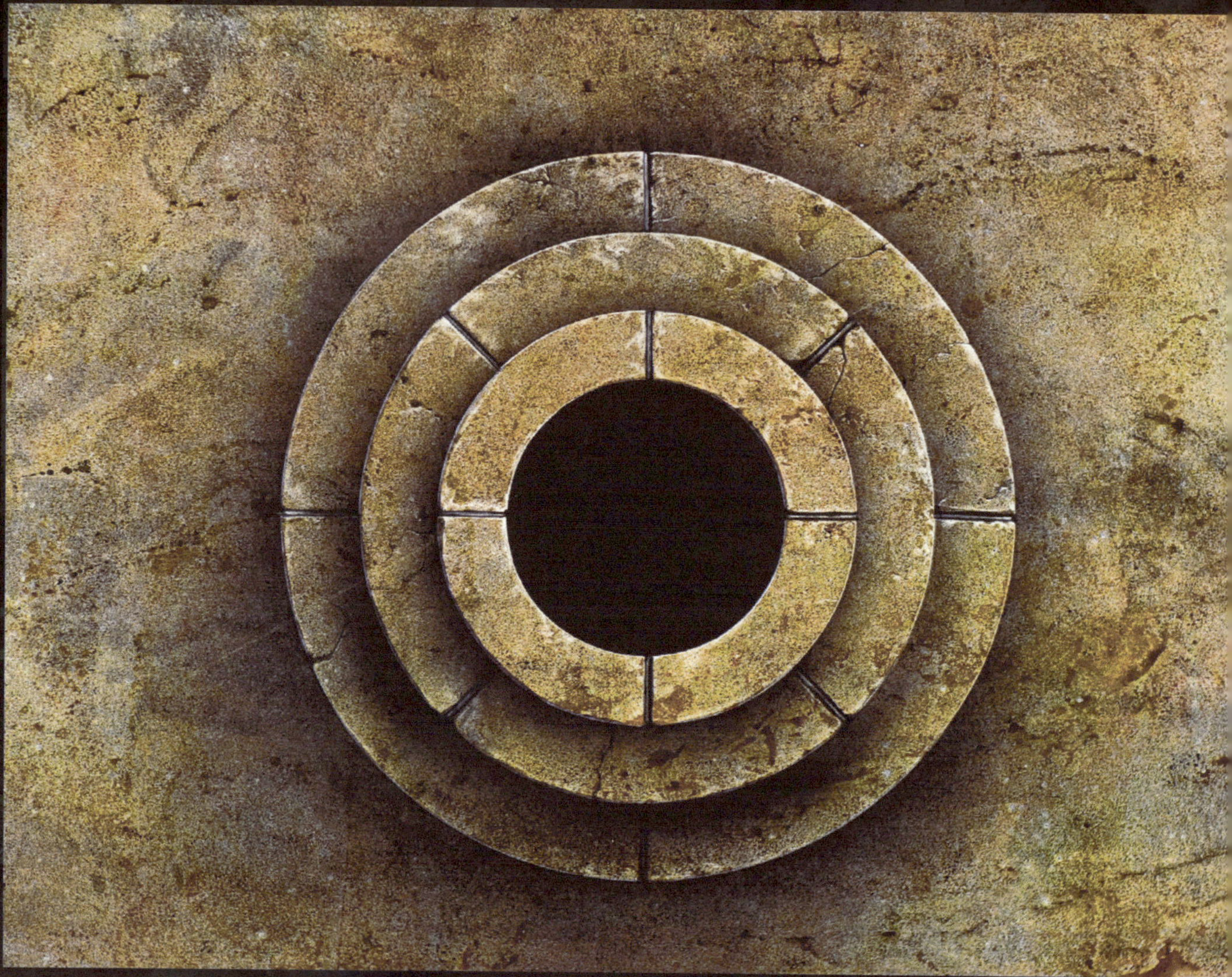

Right: *The top down view of the well as used in the series. Colour could be edited to suit the predominant colour of any of the well way rooms.*
Below: *My notes;*
Tracing with corrections;
Props floor plan;
Broadcast set showing the foreground boulder masking in operation.

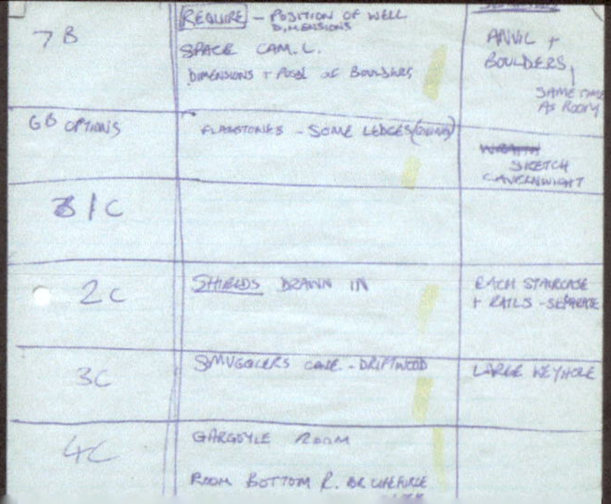

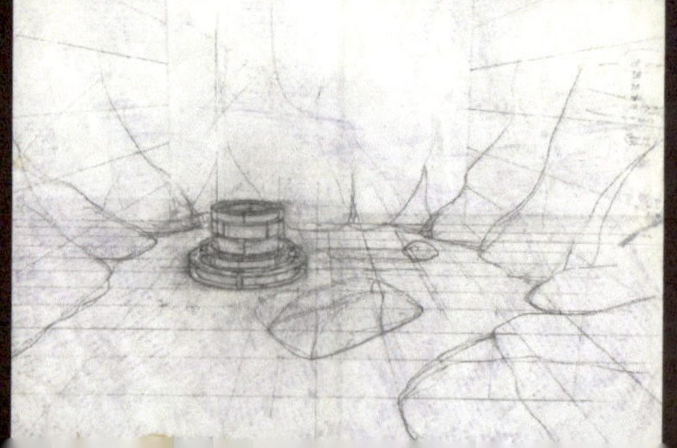

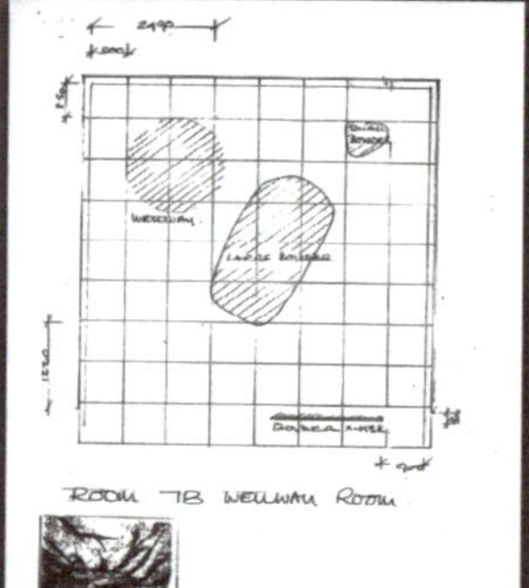

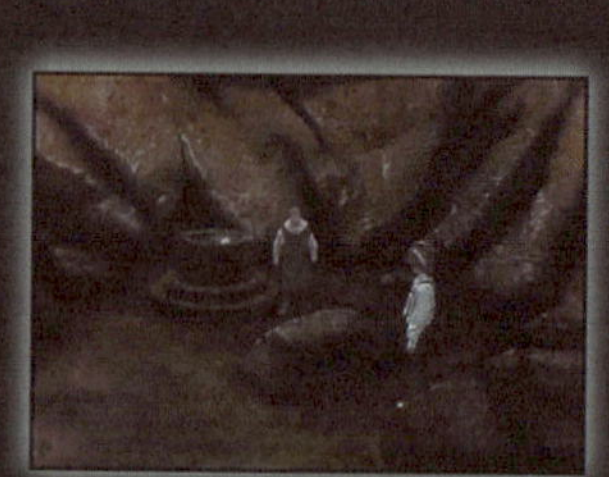

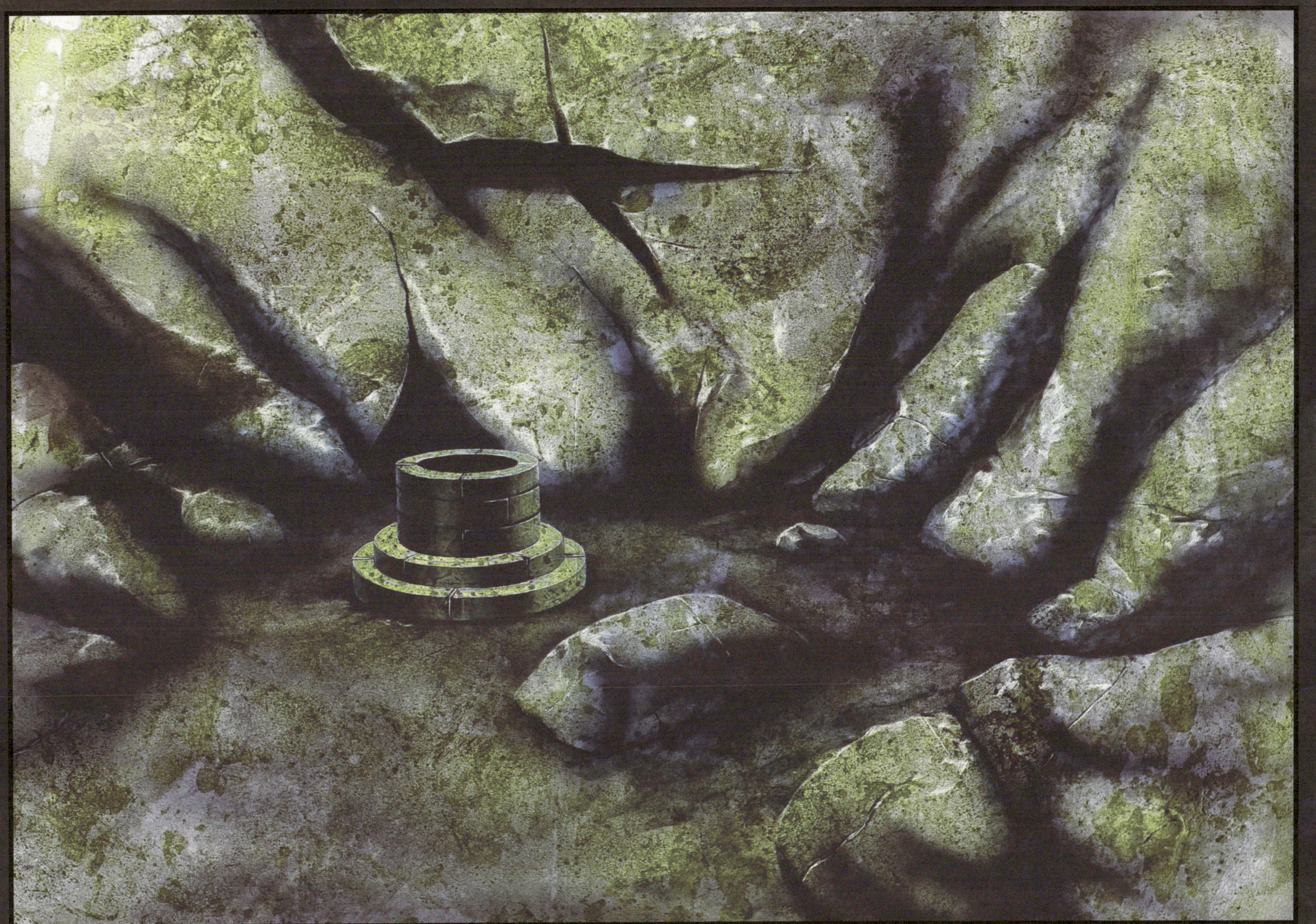

Bland Room 2.8b

Bland rooms were commissioned as a kind of stock item that could be adapted and used in a wide variety of ways as they didn't have inbuilt hazards or features that would limit their use.

The Bland Room painting was used many times as the underlying room. I have included four variations which show the depth and variety of different lighting and puzzles that were applied.

Top left: *Colour rough.*

Top Right: *Tracing for the final artwork, rather the worse for wear after 25 years.*

Bottom four: *Only some of the scenarios that used the bland room painting as a starting point.*

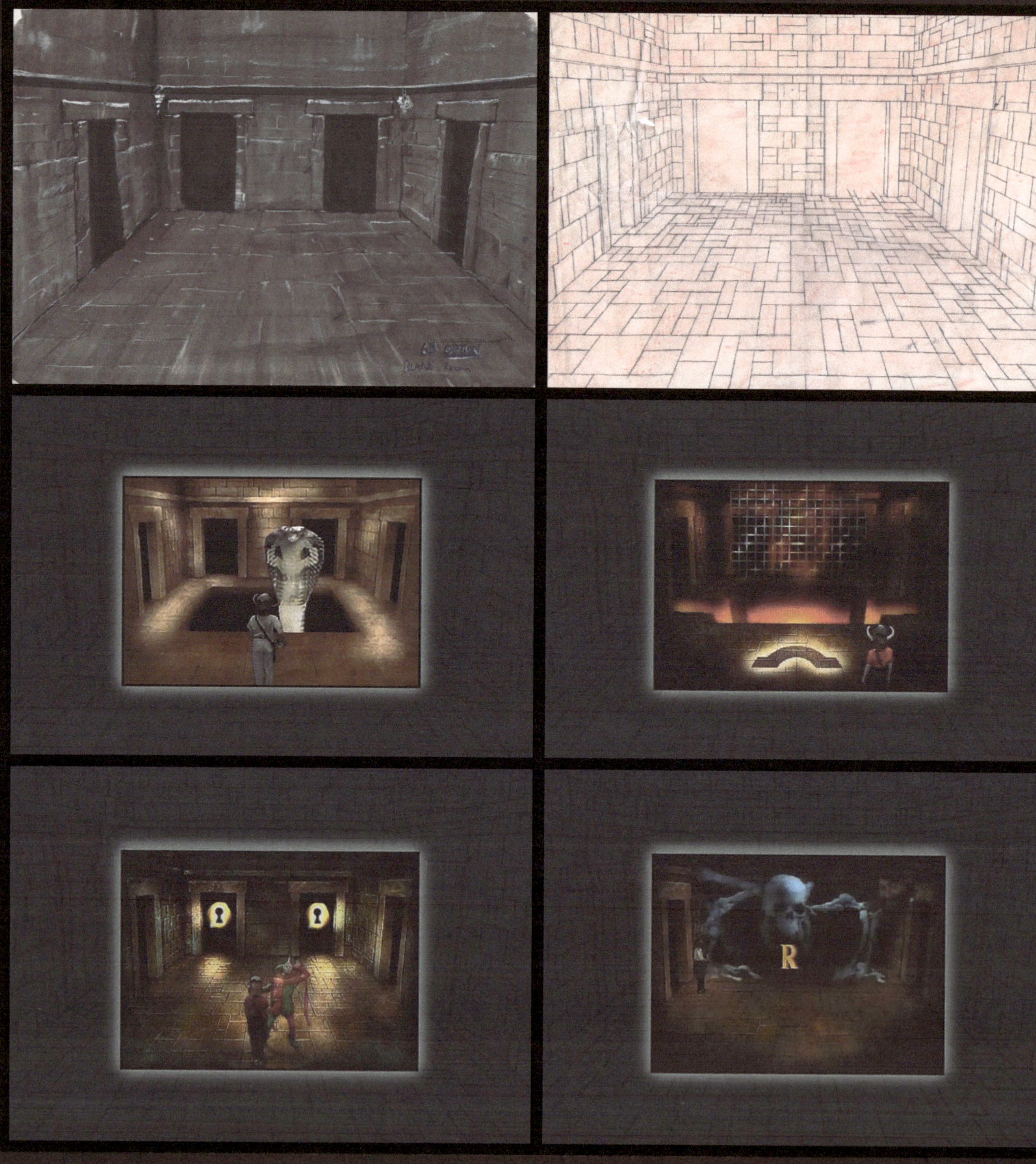

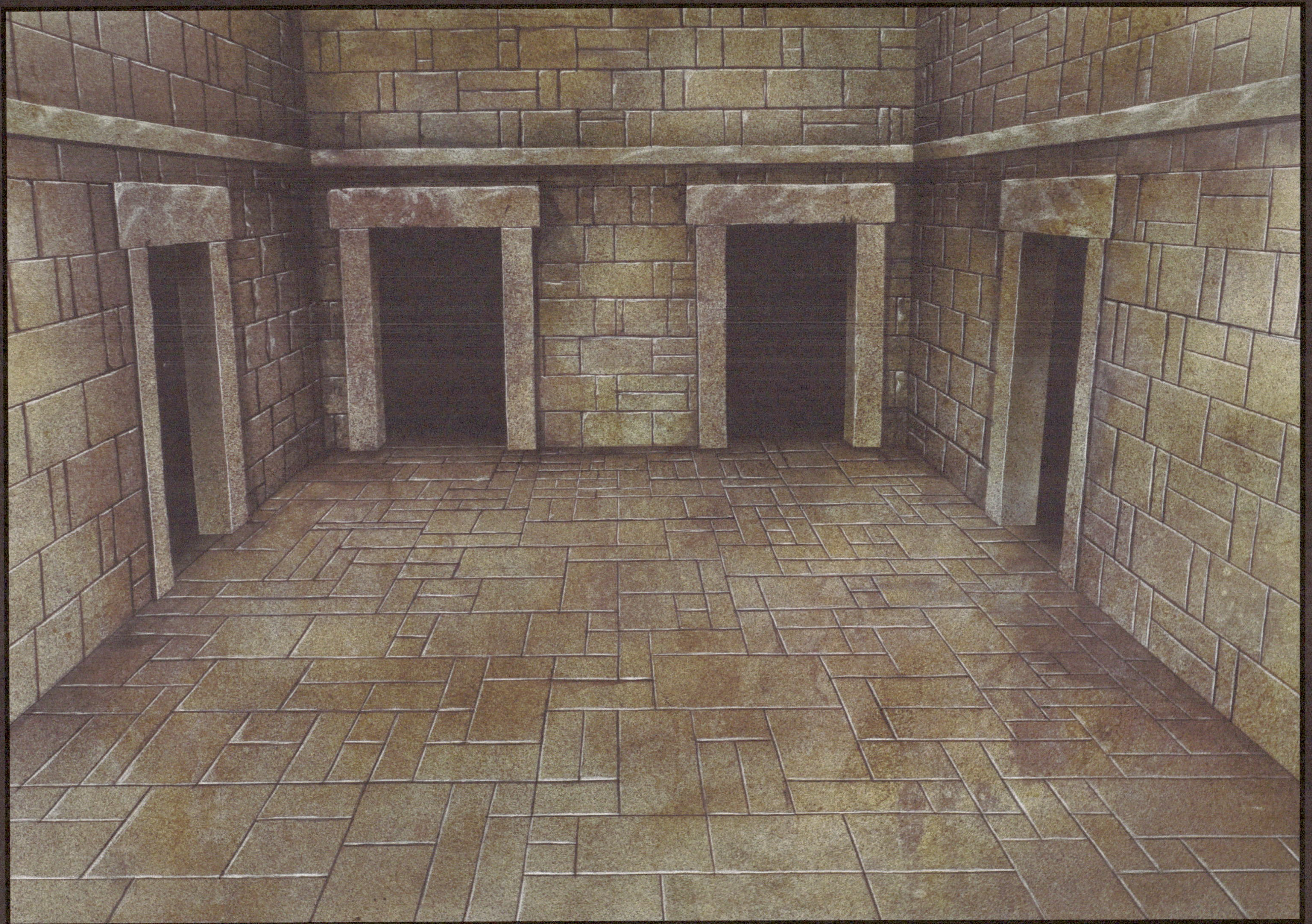

Crossing Room 2
2.10b

The second level Crossing Room was drawn with the bridge one metre up from the studio floor. This could then coincide with the metre high blue chromakey blocks that the performers would walk on.
The rough sketches were produced very quickly and spontaneously to give the overall impression of each room. Once approved, the execution of the final painting had to be measured and accurate as it had to conform to the grid that every contributor relied upon.

Right: *Picturing the requirements of the brief and putting that down as a rough sketch was an essential part of the process.*

Below: *Original faxed brief; Tracing produced overlaying a grid so that the walkway could be lined up for the blue blocks that formed it in the studio; Two final composite variations.*

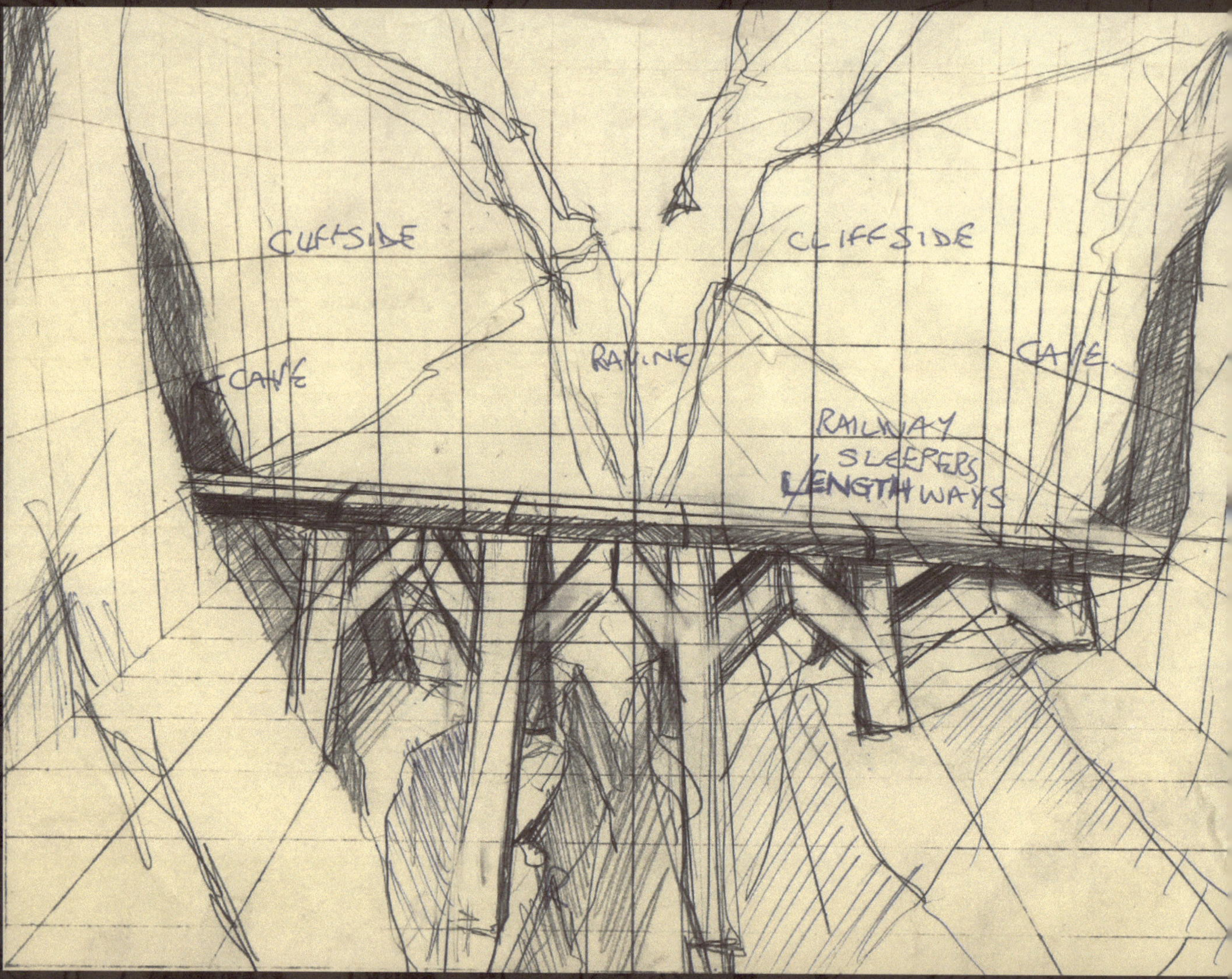

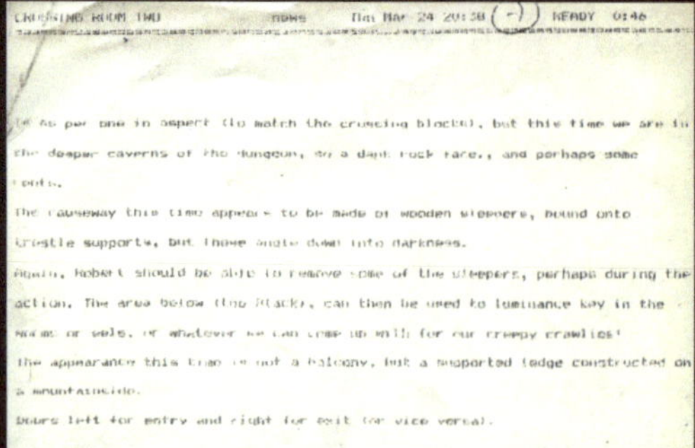

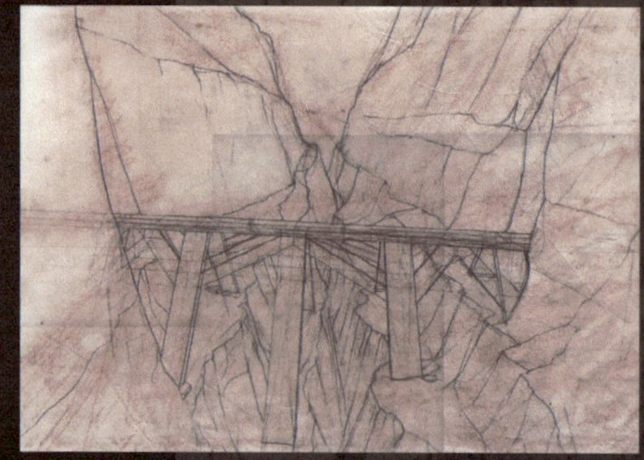

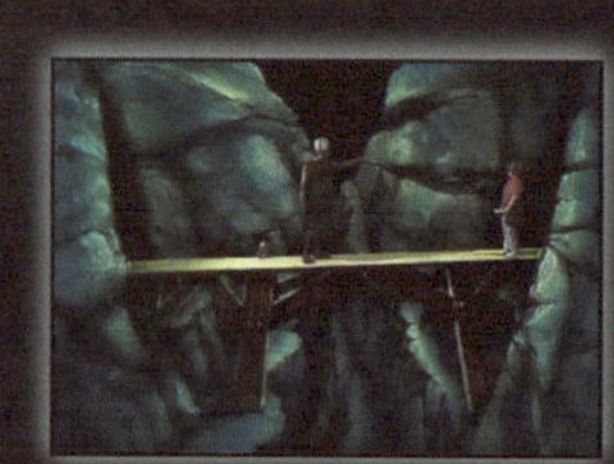

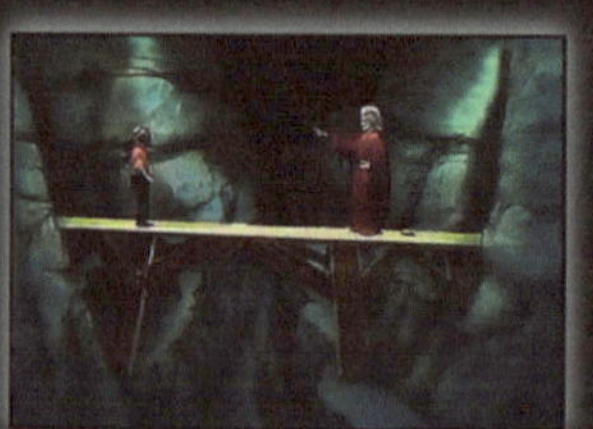

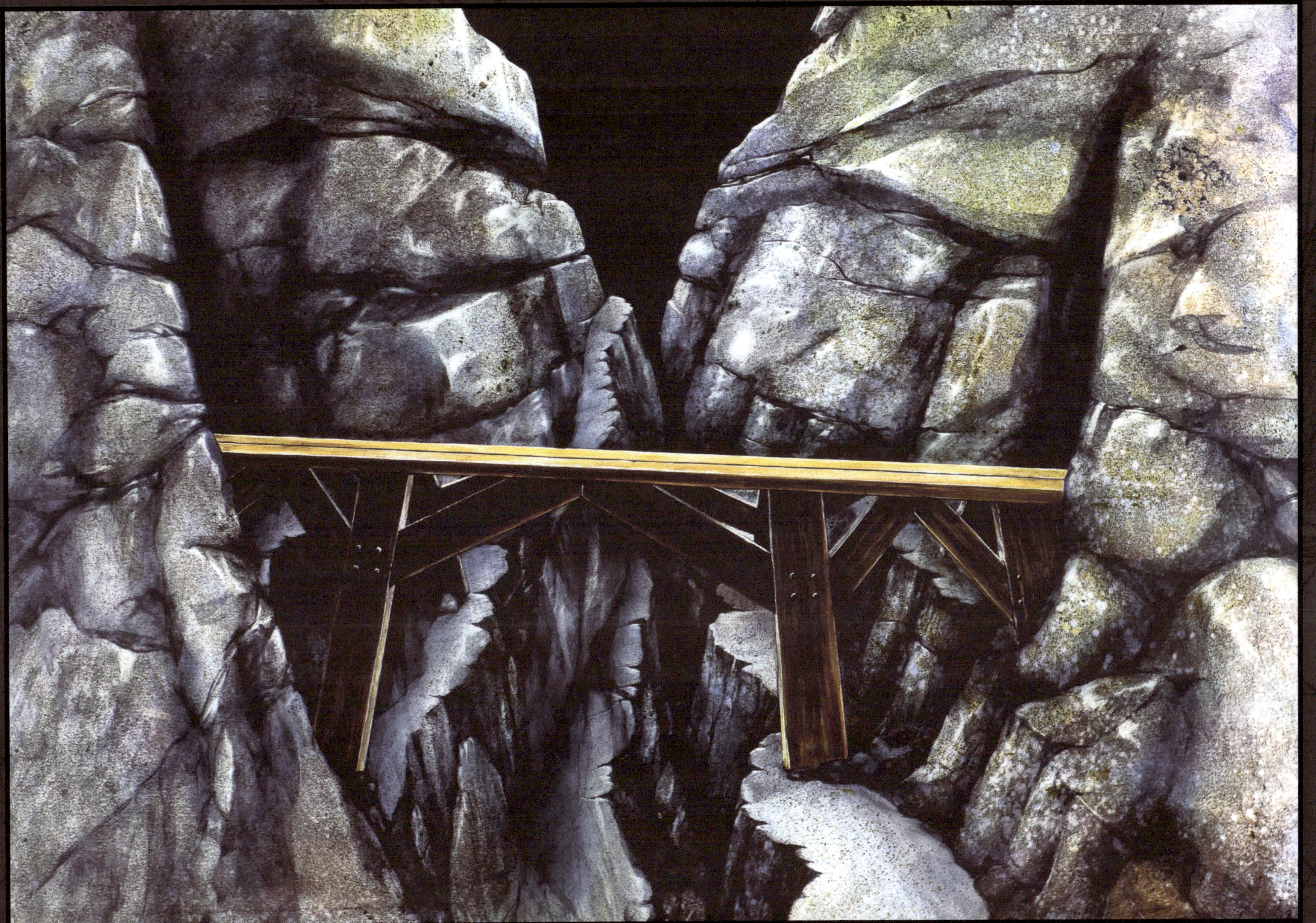

Mining Room
2.12b

The VP note refers to the vanishing point for the rail tracks which, as they are at an angle to the grid floor is situated one and a half squares to the right of the VP for the grid. The VP for the sleepers width was established on the eye level way over to the left of the drawing board and lines were drawn in with an extra long ruler.
The illustrations were made when the Indiana Jones films were current and more than a passing thought was given to them as the paintings progressed.

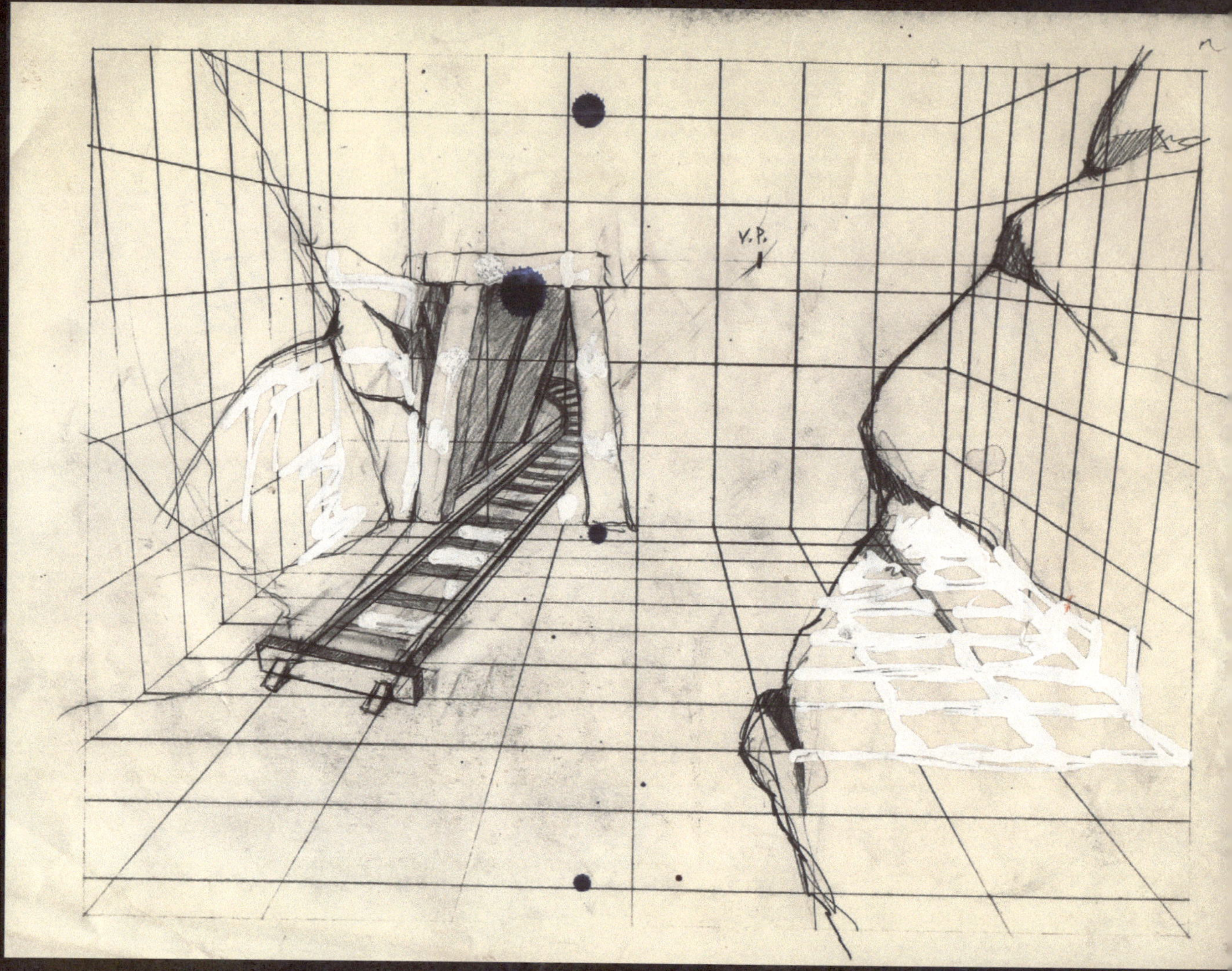

Right: *I made copies of the grid at A4 size to help with the production of the rough sketches. As you can see, the ink really flew when I was adding the texture to the final artworks. This rough got rather close!*

Below: *Original faxed brief notes; My quick thumbnail sketches; Tracing; Broadcast set with crashed roller coaster from the previous level.*

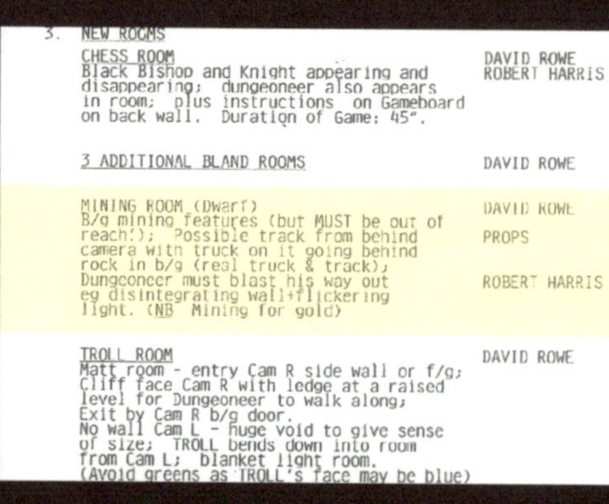

3. NEW ROOMS

CHESS ROOM — DAVID ROWE / ROBERT HARRIS
Black Bishop and Knight appearing and disappearing; dungeoneer also appears in room; plus instructions on Gameboard on back wall. Duration of Game: 45".

3 ADDITIONAL BLAND ROOMS — DAVID ROWE

MINING ROOM (Dwarf) — DAVID ROWE
B/g mining features (but MUST be out of reach!); Possible track from behind camera with truck on it going behind rock in b/g (real truck & track); — PROPS
Dungeoneer must blast his way out eg disintegrating wall+flickering light. (NB Mining for gold) — ROBERT HARRIS

TROLL ROOM — DAVID ROWE
Matt room - entry Cam R side wall or f/g; Cliff face Cam R with ledge at a raised level for Dungeoneer to walk along; Exit by Cam R b/g door. No wall Cam L - huge void to give sense of size; TROLL bends down into room from Cam L; blanket light room. (Avoid greens as TROLL's face may be blue)

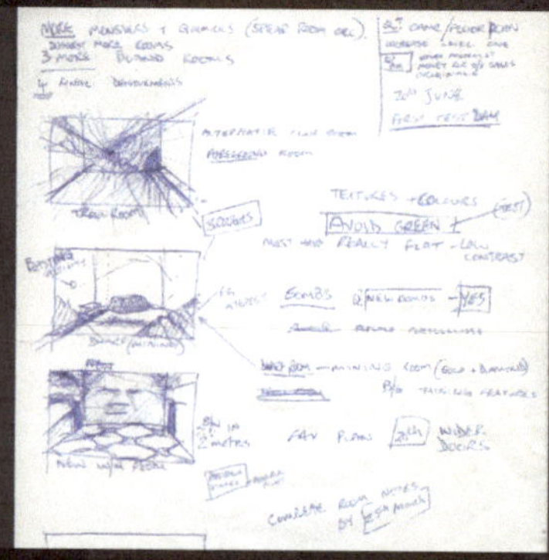

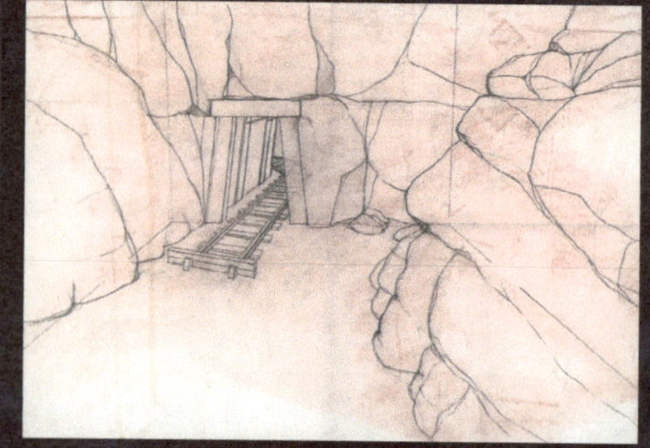

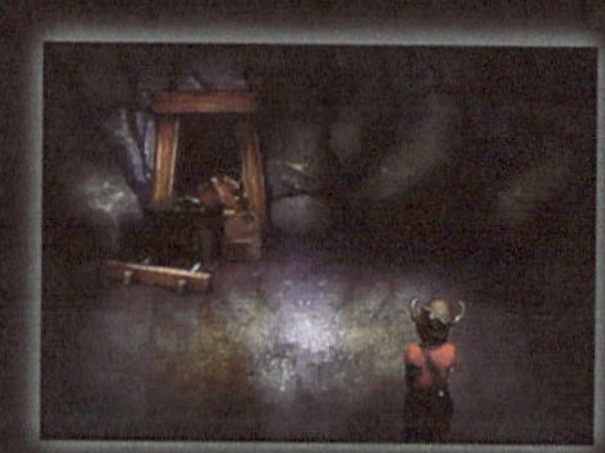

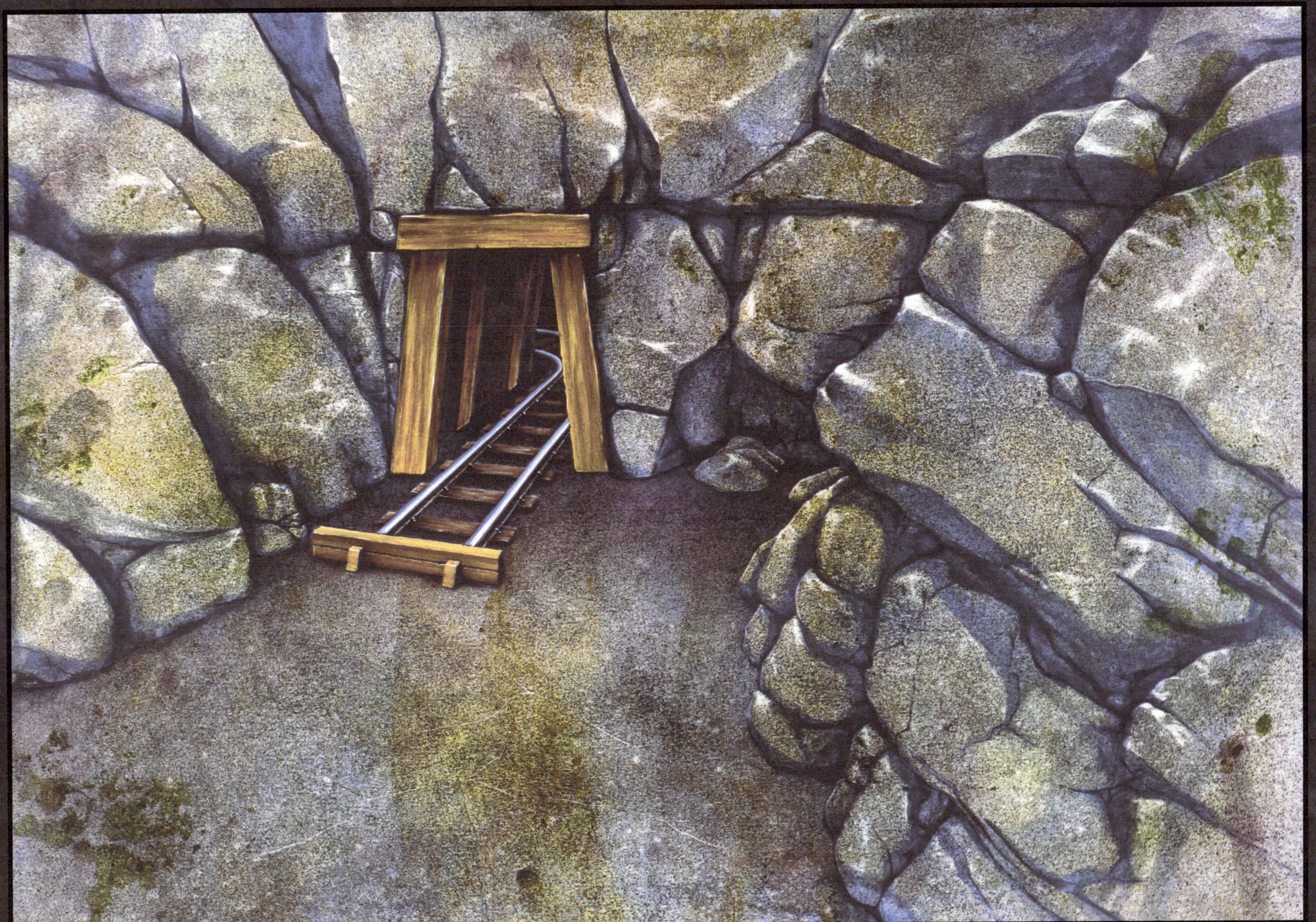

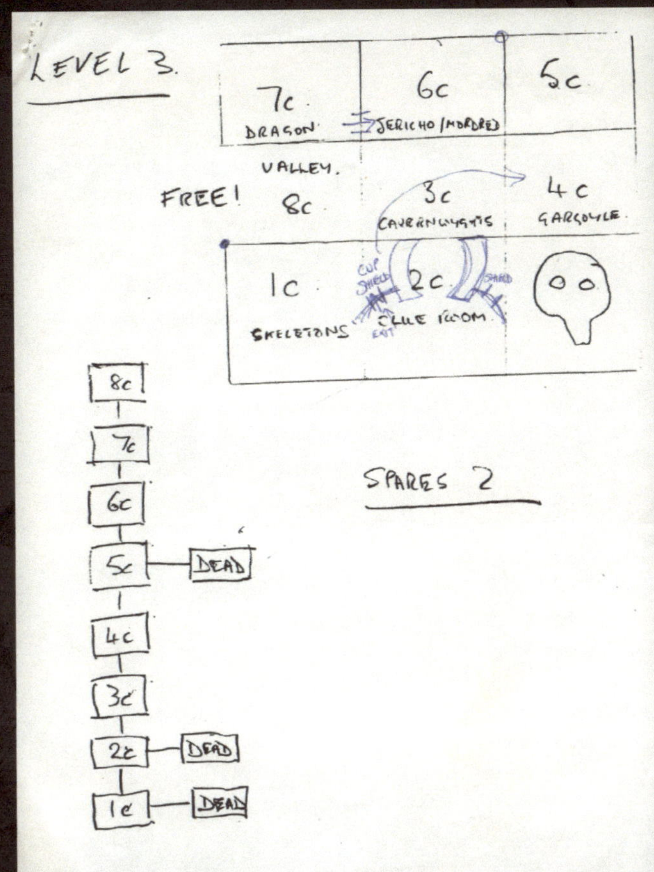

-2-

KNIGHTMARE SERIES 2 H128453-128465

Level 3

3/1c   Skeleton Rm
3/2c   3rd Level Clue Rm
3/3c   Cavernwights Rm
3/4c   Gargoyle Rm
3/5c   Medusa Rm
3/6c   Jericho/Mogdred Rm
3/7c   Crossing Room Three
3/8c   Valley Rm /Dismissal
3/9c   Chess Rm
3/10c Roulette Rm

Sprig of Energy
Travelling Glitz
Spellcasting

Skeleton Room 3.1c

The deeper and darker depths of the dungeon provided opportunities to invoke dank textures and giant tree roots.
The sequoia type roots in the foreground were replicated on the set with flat, blue painted matte boards which obscured the Dungeoneer if he strayed behind them.
The rough indicates that these foreground mattes were added later with a ball point pen to the sketch. This was probably after a phone discussion to talk over amendments. They served to make the room less 'boxy' in any event.

Right: *The colour rough for the Skeleton Room included suggestions for foreground sequoia roots to help give the room a more contained and less room-like feel.*

Below: *The key lines were traced through for the final artwork. Matte panels had to be created to mask the Dungeoneer should he stray behind tree roots.*

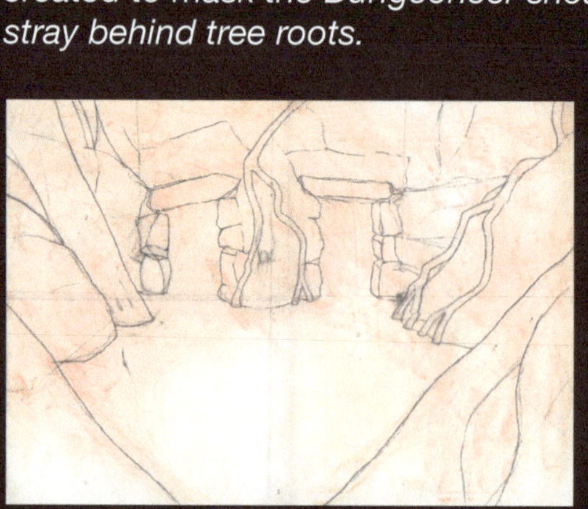

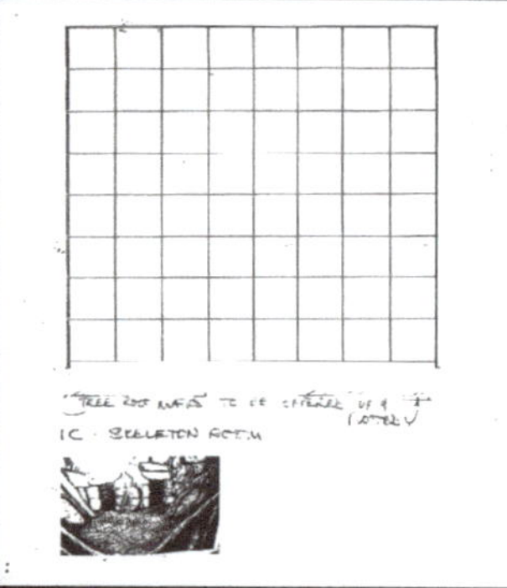

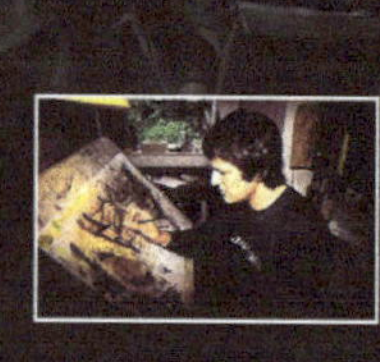

Working on the painting circa 1986.

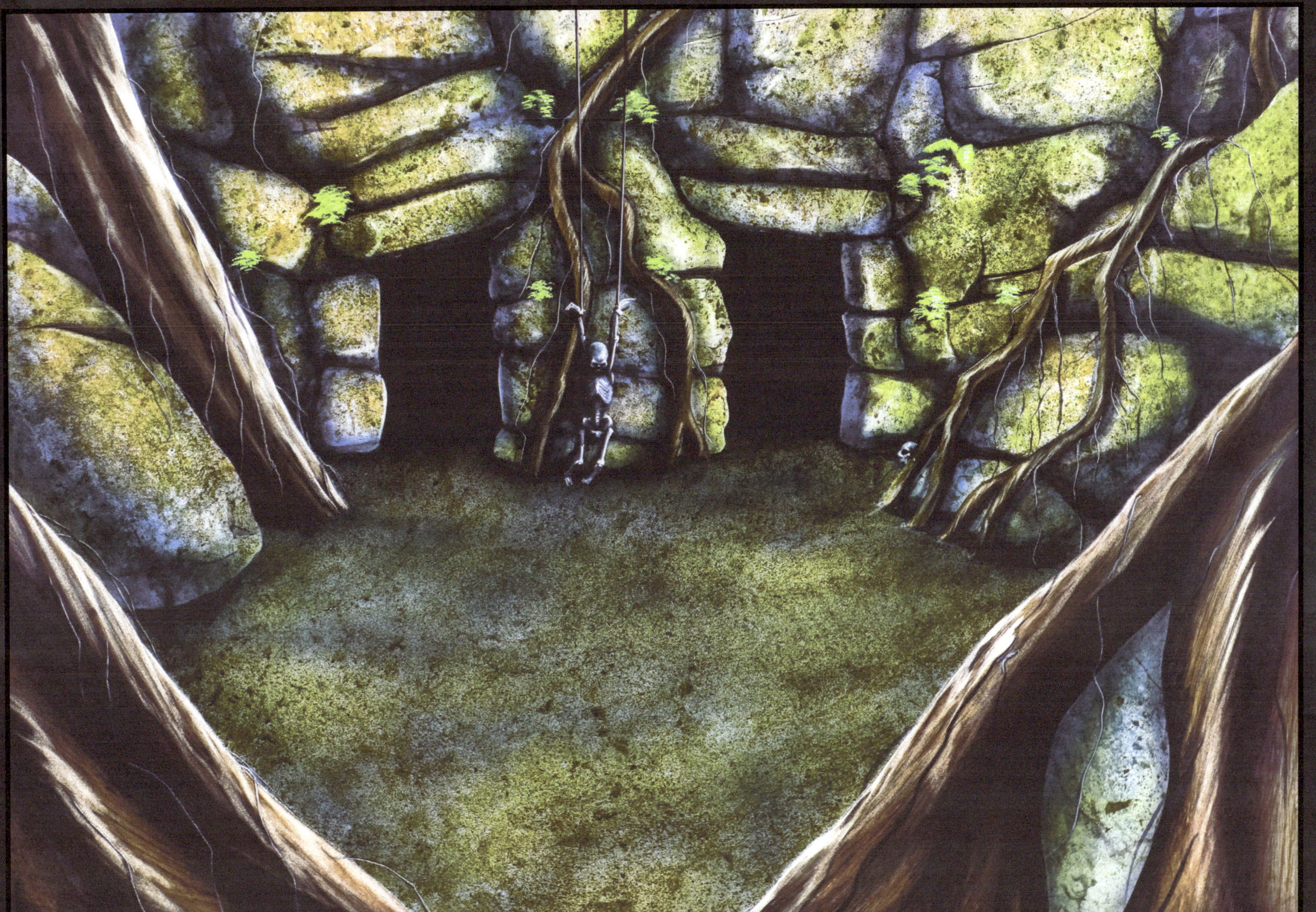

3rd. Level Clue Room 3.2c

The quick visual representation of the final artwork came into its own again with the Third Level Clue Room. A number of pitfalls were spotted and resolved over the phone. The curved stairs were impractical on many levels and would have taken many hours of teamwork which, in the end, would have been wasted.

The shields were within reach of a Dungeoneer descending the stairs and so were placed safely on the back wall.

The side doors were changed to arched and a quick ball point note whilst on the phone placed them on the back wall.

The changes gave more scope for coming up with variants of the room.

Below: *The original faxed brief; the floor plan for props; A relit broadcast composite.*

Far right: *The plain lit originals allowed for the architecture to be reworked and re-imagined in new scenarios. This version is the Stained Glass Room.*

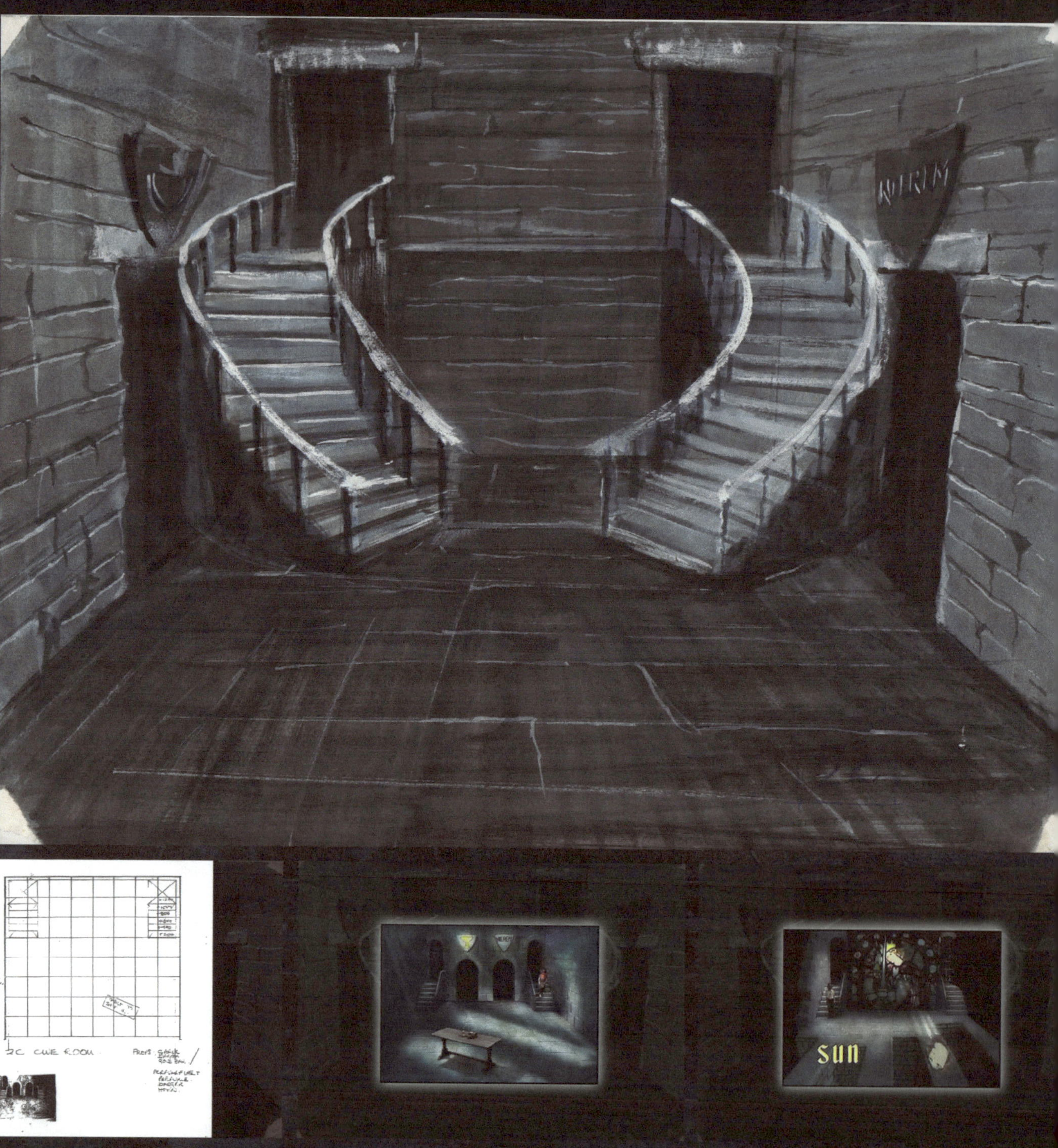

CHAMBER 1, LEVEL 3

A VERY NASTY DANGEROUS LOOKING ROOM but with no special features. Adevnturer falls to position forground. Lots of skeletons scattered about here. No other clues. Use Wraiths if necessary. 2 exits.

CHAMBER 2, LEVEL 3 (LEVEL 3 CLUE ROOM).

MULTI-LEVEL. Bring ADVENT DOWN STAIRWAY and into position behind Altar/table again, only reverse directions from last time (Merlins room). ROOM has two apparent exits with shields above. One shield is decorated with a CUP (thin steamed grail-type). The other is embossed with the word NILREM. Clue present on altar/table: perfume flask (old Fashioned with large lettering on it saying: "SMELL ME". Flask should contain real perfume.) Also horn (for blowing) and dagger. Food is also present. Correct option here is to leave dagger. NILREM DOOR CHOICE TRIGGERS WIPE-OUT.

CHAMBER 3. LEVEL 3 Cavernwyghts be here. Two exits. One is locked (door with large keyhole). Cavernwyghts block off access to escape door. Solution is to remove top from perfume and leave it on floor. This room should be full width for shadow effects and full-void depth.

CHAMBER 4. LEVEL 3. THE GARGOYLE ROOM! think this should be a full depth/width chamber, but the gargoyle must be huge and should dominate the entire facing

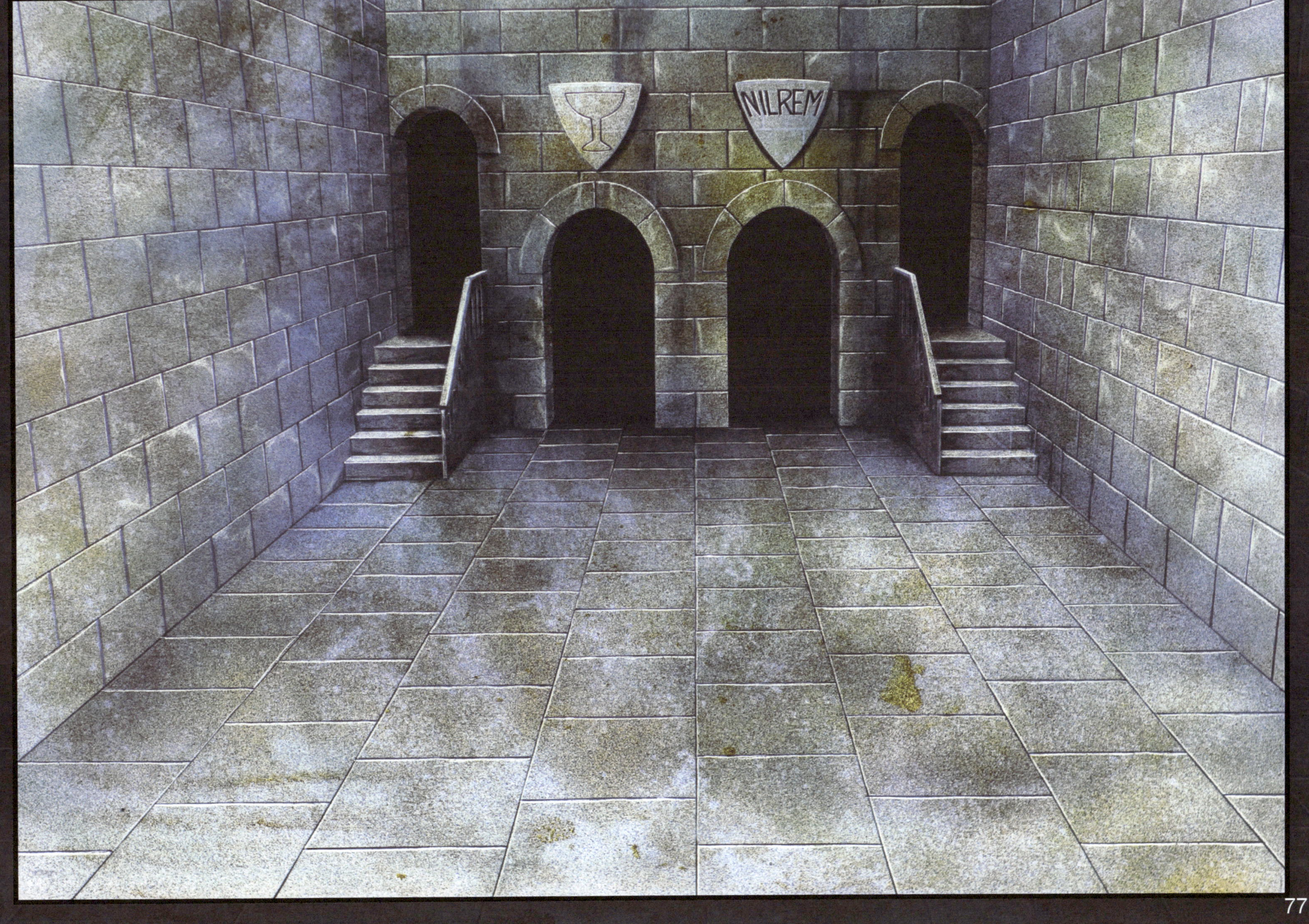

NILREM

Cavern wight Room 3.3c

Another from the deeper levels. The impression of deep caves that could be submerged at high tide was enhanced by the addition of flotsam and other potentially washed up objects.
The scene was finished off with wave marks in the sandy floor to add a sense of life going on there when nobody was present.

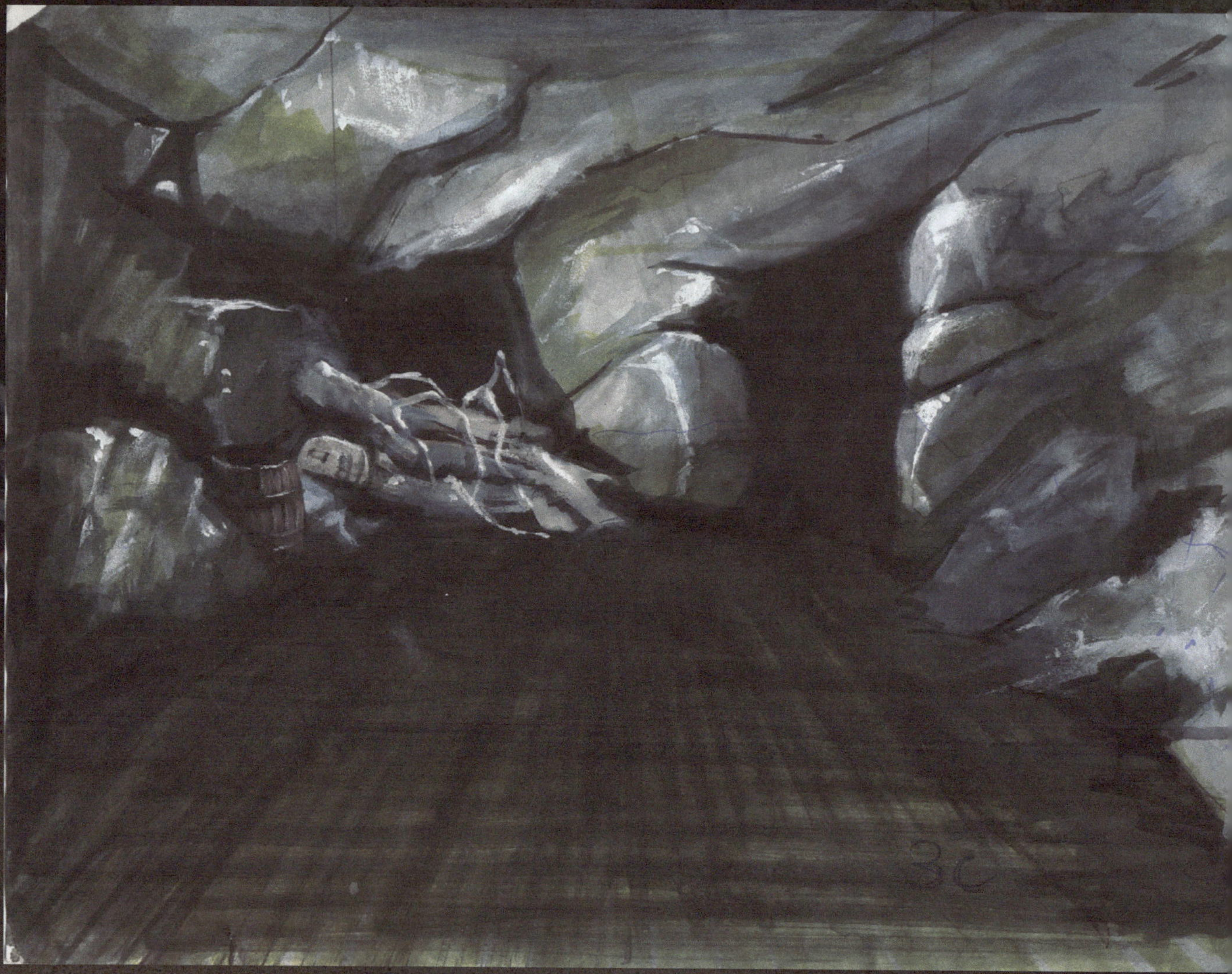

Right: *Colour roughs were made using a combination of marker pens and acrylic inks for washes before being detailed with ink and brush and white gouache highlights.*

Below: *The original faxed brief; The tracing sheet; Faxed floor plan for the props; The broadcast composite, complete with painted and physical props.*

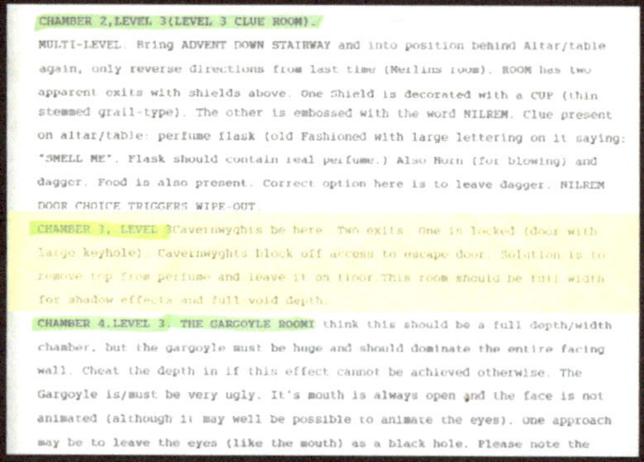

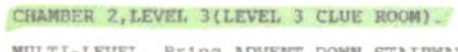

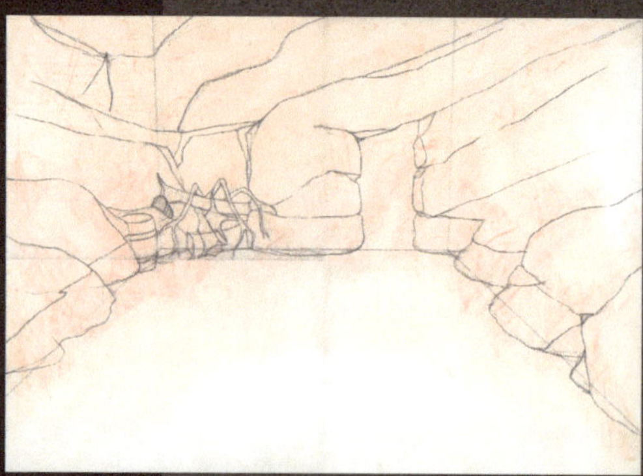

CHAMBER 2,LEVEL 3(LEVEL 3 CLUE ROOM).

MULTI-LEVEL. Bring ADVENT DOWN STAIRWAY and into position behind Altar/table again, only reverse directions from last time (Merlins room). ROOM has two apparent exits with shields above. One Shield is decorated with a CUP (thin stemmed grail-type). The other is embossed with the word NILREM. Clue present on altar/table: perfume flask (old Fashioned with large lettering on it saying: "SMELL ME". Flask should contain real perfume.) Also Horn (for blowing) and dagger. Food is also present. Correct option here is to leave dagger. NILREM DOOR CHOICE TRIGGERS WIPE-OUT.

CHAMBER 3, LEVEL 3Cavernwyghts be here. Two exits. One is locked (door with large keyhole). Cavernwyghts block off access to escape door. Solution is to remove top from perfume and leave it on floor.This room should be full width for shadow effects and full-void depth.

CHAMBER 4.LEVEL 3. THE GARGOYLE ROOMI think this should be a full depth/width chamber, but the gargoyle must be huge and should dominate the entire facing wall. Cheat the depth in if this effect cannot be achieved otherwise. The Gargoyle is/must be very ugly. It's mouth is always open and the face is not animated (although it may well be possible to animate the eyes). One approach may be to leave the eyes (like the mouth) as a black hole. Please note the

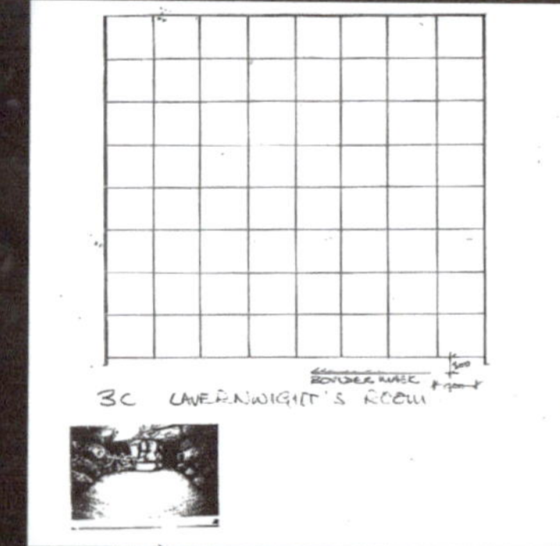

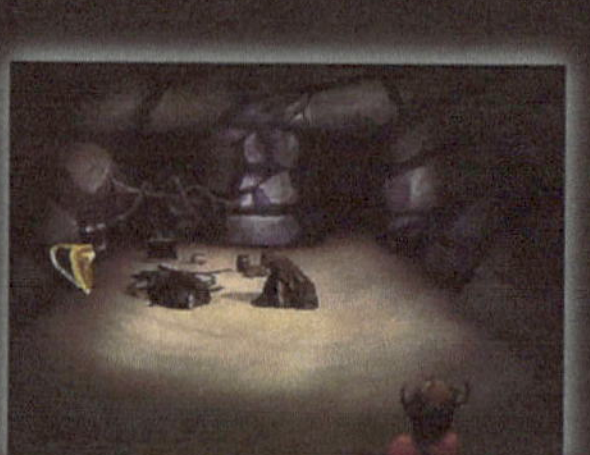

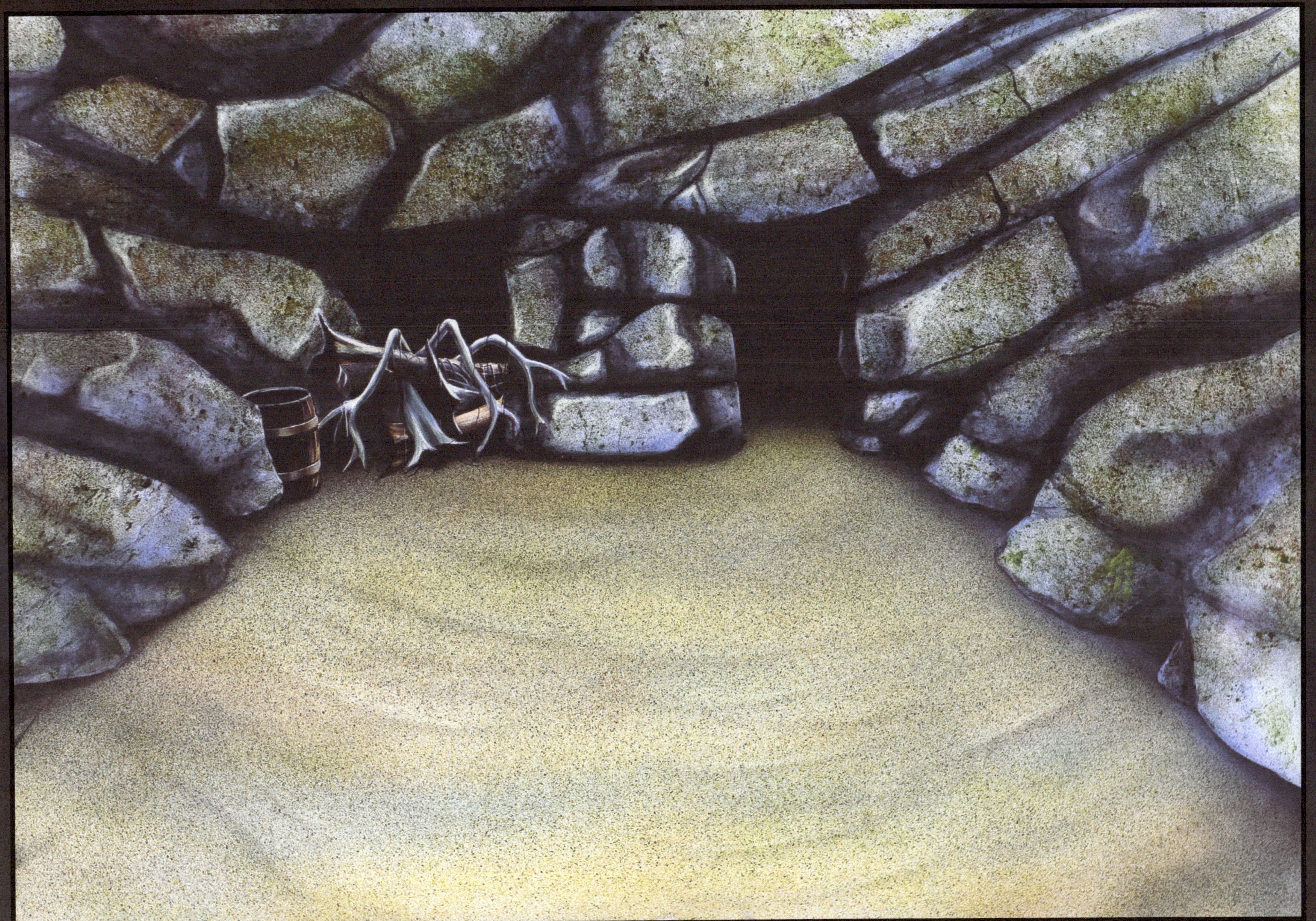

Gargoyle Room 3.4c

The rough and the grid drawing show the almost central position of the gargoyle's head. The drawing also shows the repositioning required to help accommodate the door to the right on the back wall.

The head had to be distinct so that it could be picked out and re-coloured at the post production stage: blue for miserable and red for cheerful.

There was an additional technique applied to some of the paintings, that of using an old toothbrush, dipped in inks and then stroked with the thumb over the paint surface. This gave more randomly sized spots.

Top left: *The original faxed brief*

Top right: *Subdivisions on the grid enabled exact positioning of doors and detail. I aimed for a grim and anxious expression.*

Middle right: *The colour rough.*

Middle left: *The key lines, drawn onto tracing paper, included small adjustments including moving the head to the left so that it didn't obscure part of the door.*

Bottom left: *The Gargoyle's head was isolated and recoloured to show his mood swings. Blue was for gloomy.*

Bottom right: *The artwork was further modified later to make way for a real talking mouth.*

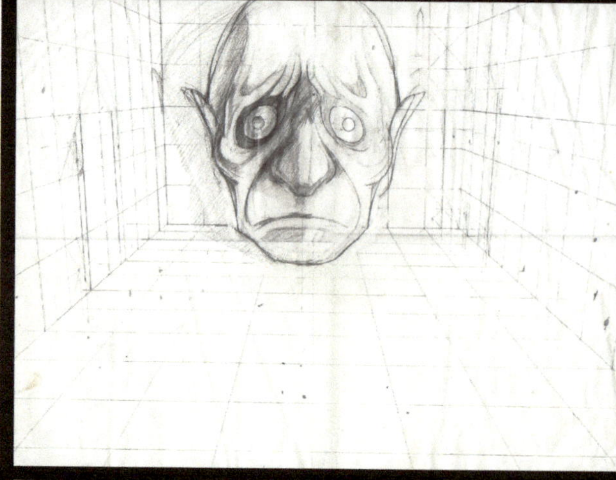

CHAMBER 3, LEVEL 3 Cavernwyghts be here. Two exits. One is locked (door with large keyhole). Cavernwyghts block off access to escape door. Solution is to remove top from perfume and leave it on floor. This room should be full width for shadow effects and full-void depth.

CHAMBER 4 LEVEL 3. THE GARGOYLE ROOM I think this should be a full depth/width chamber, but the gargoyle must be huge and should dominate the entire facing wall. Cheat the depth in if this effect cannot be achieved otherwise. The Gargoyle is/must be very ugly. It's mouth is always open and the face is not animated (although it may well be possible to animate the eyes). One approach may be to leave the eyes (like the mouth) as a black hole. Please note the Gargoyle is NOT a mask, but a drawn feature of the room. There should be provision on to the rear of the chamber (and to one side) for a door to be revealed. Please discuss how!

IMPORTANT NOTE: THIS room needs to change colour as mood of the Gargoyle changes. We can do this through mixer, but room probably best supplied in neutral shades so that we can best achieve this. Again, please consult.

CHAMBER 5. LEVEL 3. NO SPECIAL FEATURES. 2 OR 3 EXITS This chamber is an extra option and can be deleted if necc.

CHAMBER 6. LEVEL 3 A complex and composite scene. Really two rooms in one but as

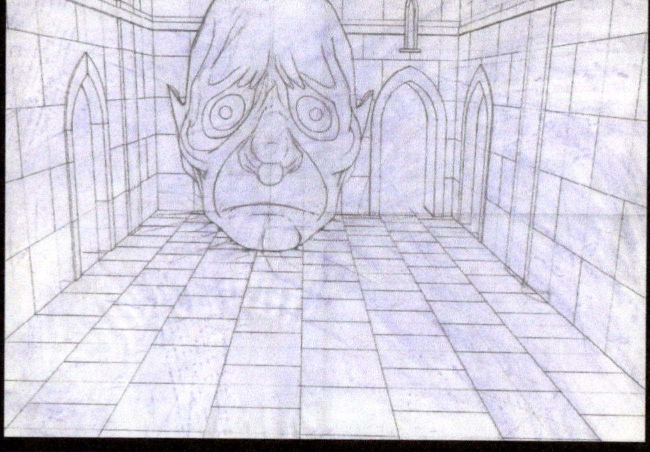

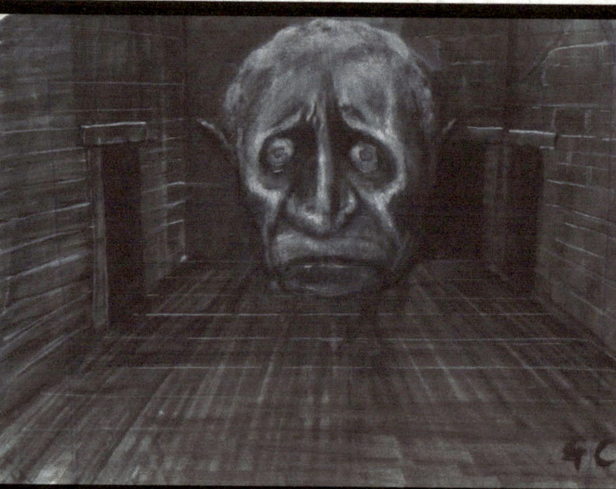

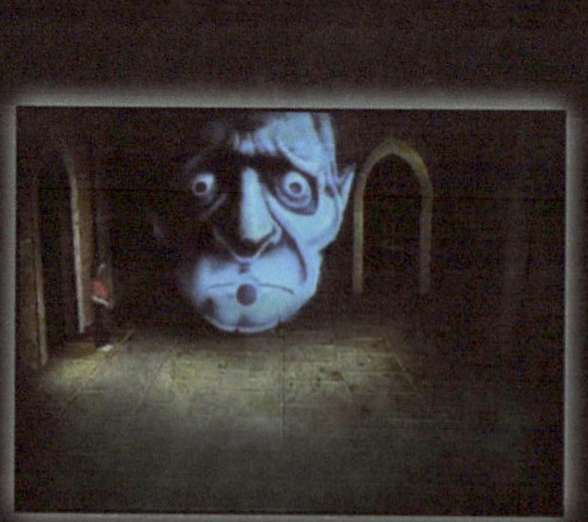

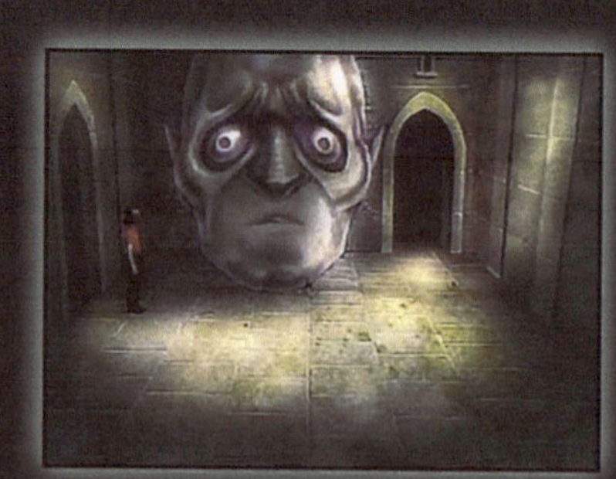

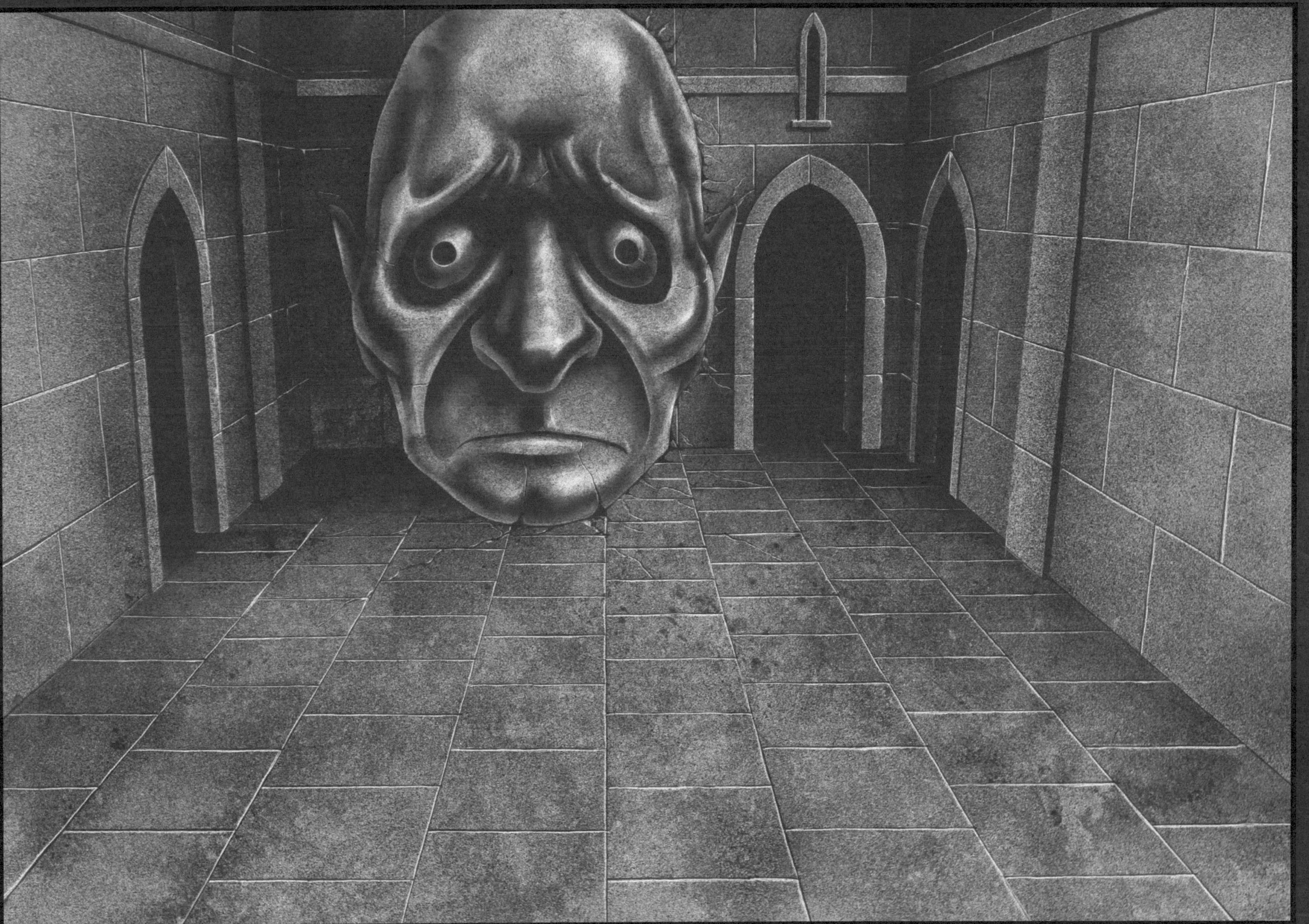

Jericho/Modred Room 3.6c

The wall had to be supplied as a separate kit that could be re-assembled to make a wall across the entire width of the set. The perspective for each brick was carefully matched to its position in the wall and then laid out and numbered on a separate sheet. The wall could then be shown to collapse, block by block to reveal the altar and the chamber beyond.

From Top Left: *faxed brief; colour rough with Biro noted corrections; trace sheet; floor plan fax; Wall kit with labelled and numbered sections; a Broadcast composite screen; The Jericho room complete with the full wall.*

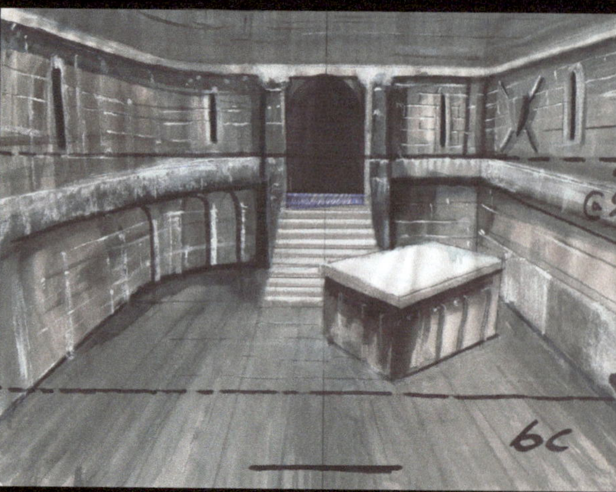

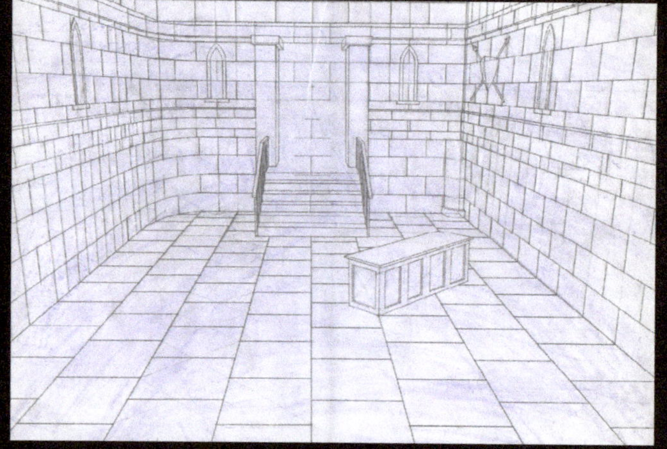

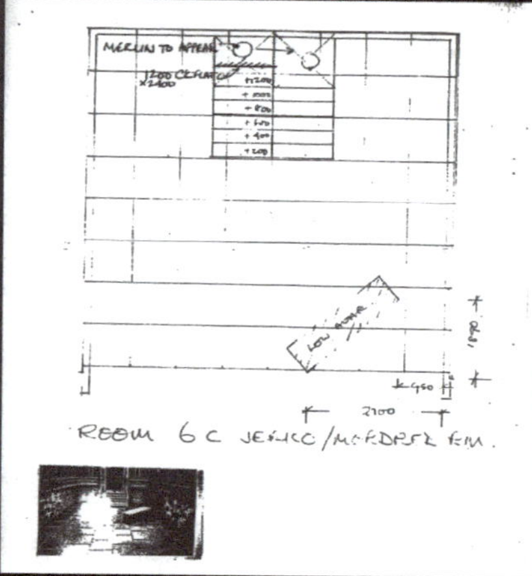

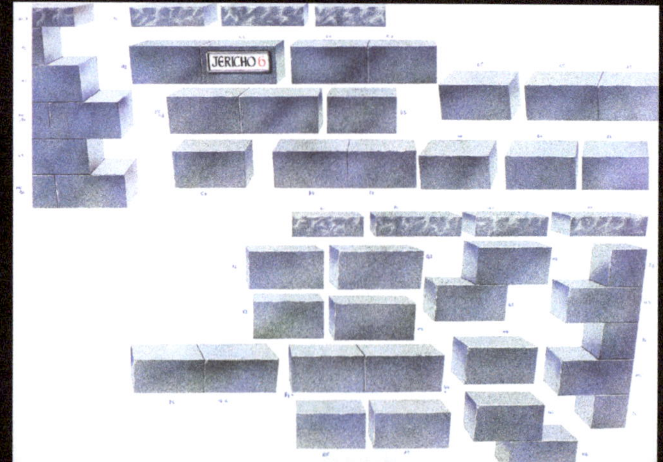

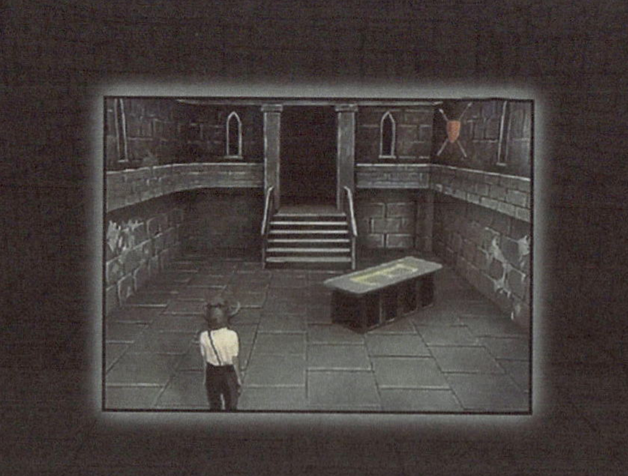

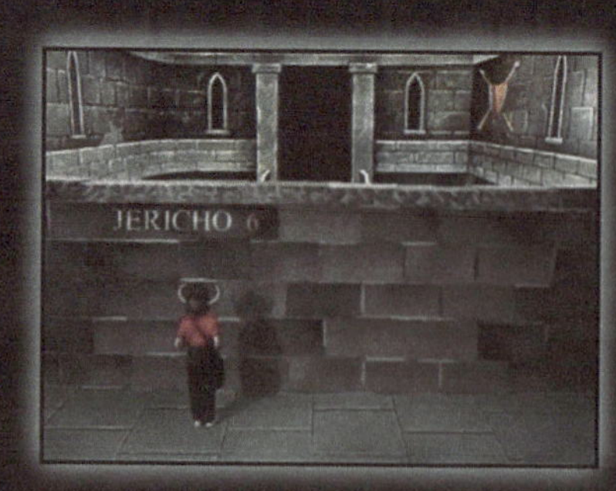

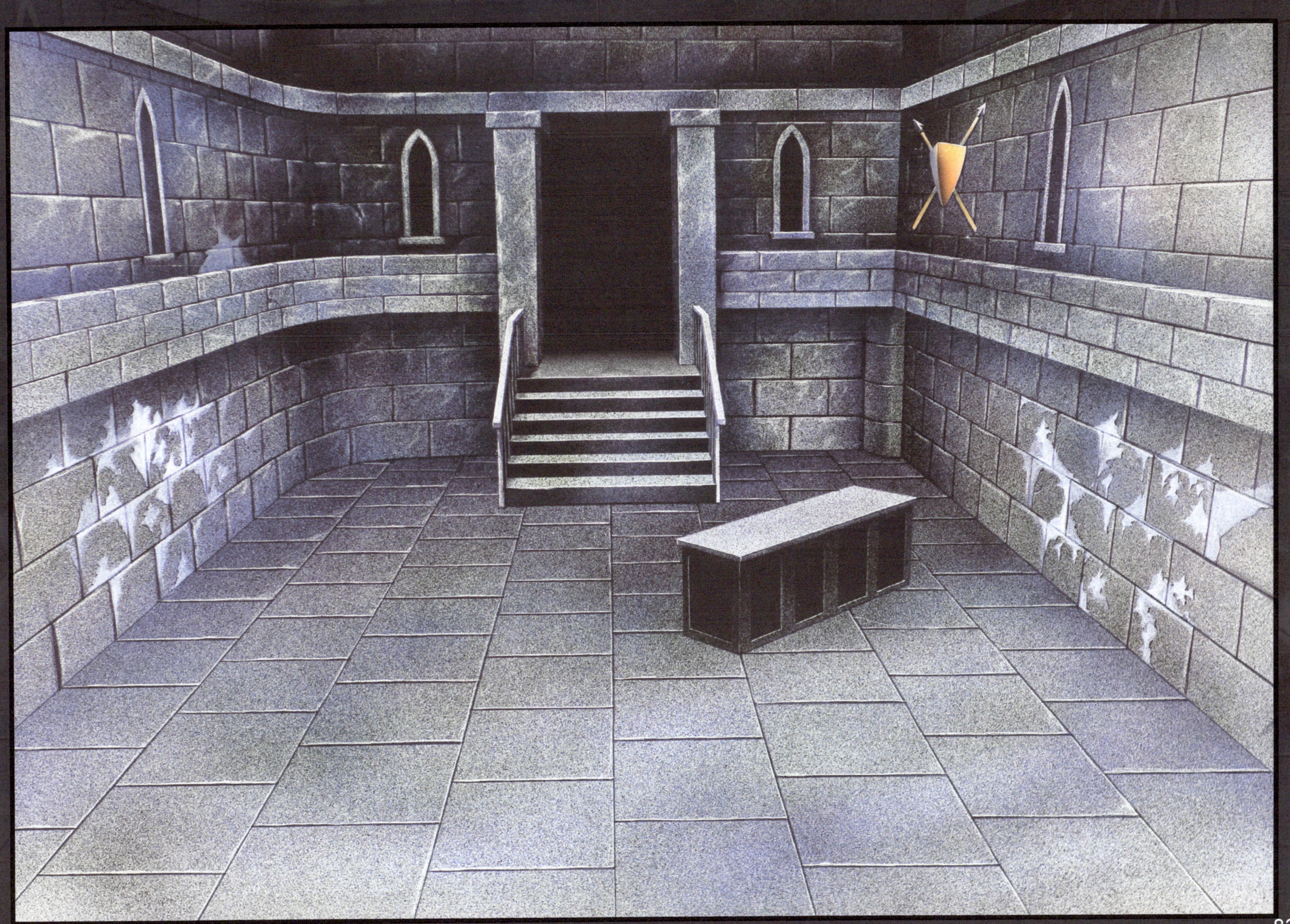

Crossing Room 3
3.7c

There were a number of roughs for this room before we agreed the final artwork. Eventually the process worked and because the rejected drawings were only rough sketches, time lost was kept to a minimum. I painted an eyelid on a separate sheet, using the same textures, which was used to animate the slow opening of the dragon's eye.

From Top Left: *first rough; second rough, which was still not right; a fax back and all becomes clear!; Heavily annotated, faxed final rough; room detail fax so that the set designer could fit the blue block walkway; the tracing sheet; the composite showing added flame and smoke effects.*

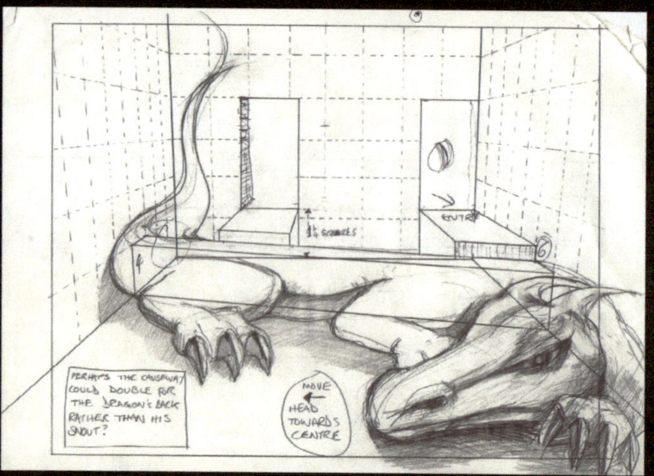

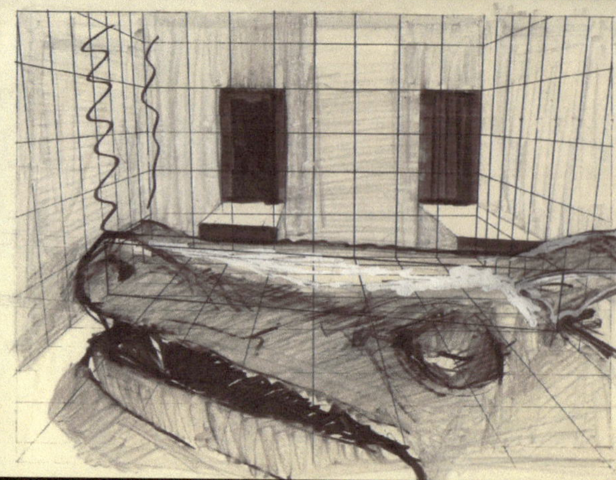

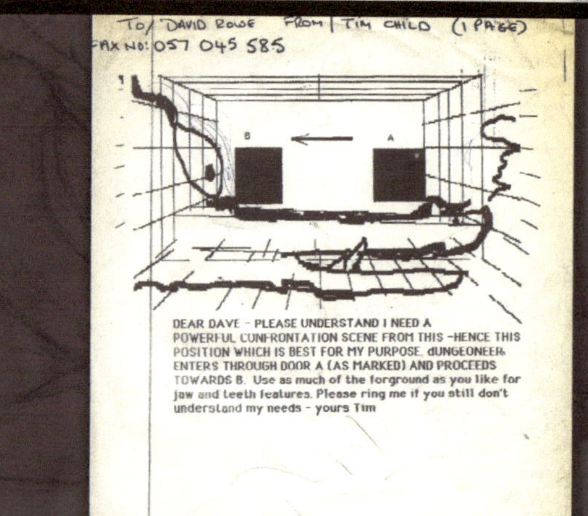

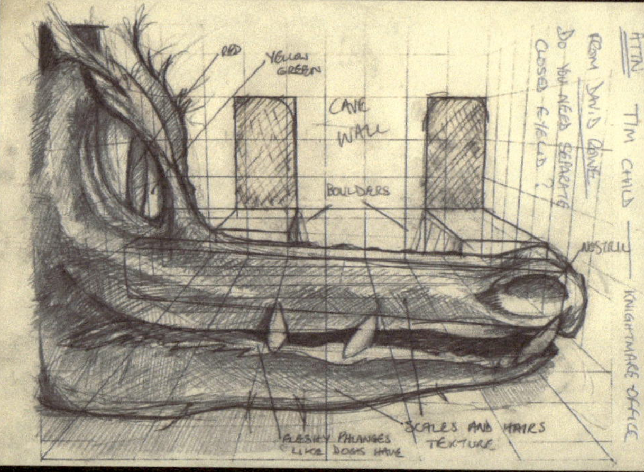

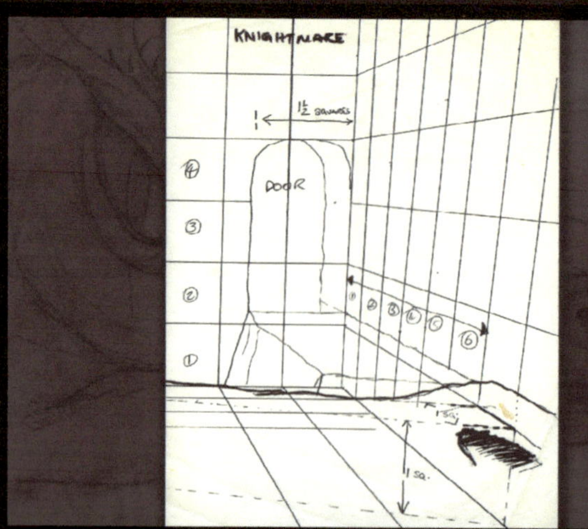

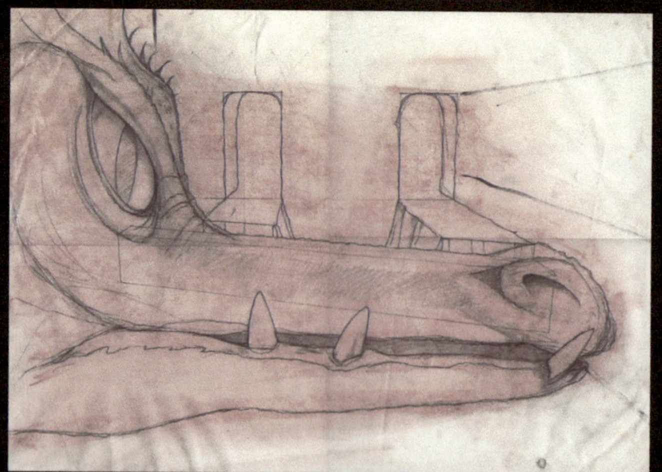

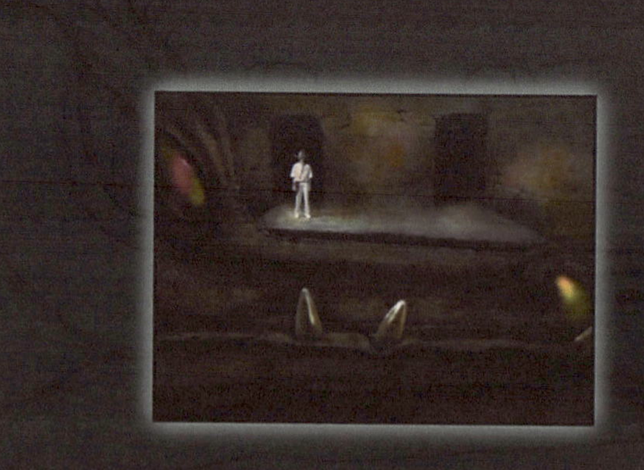

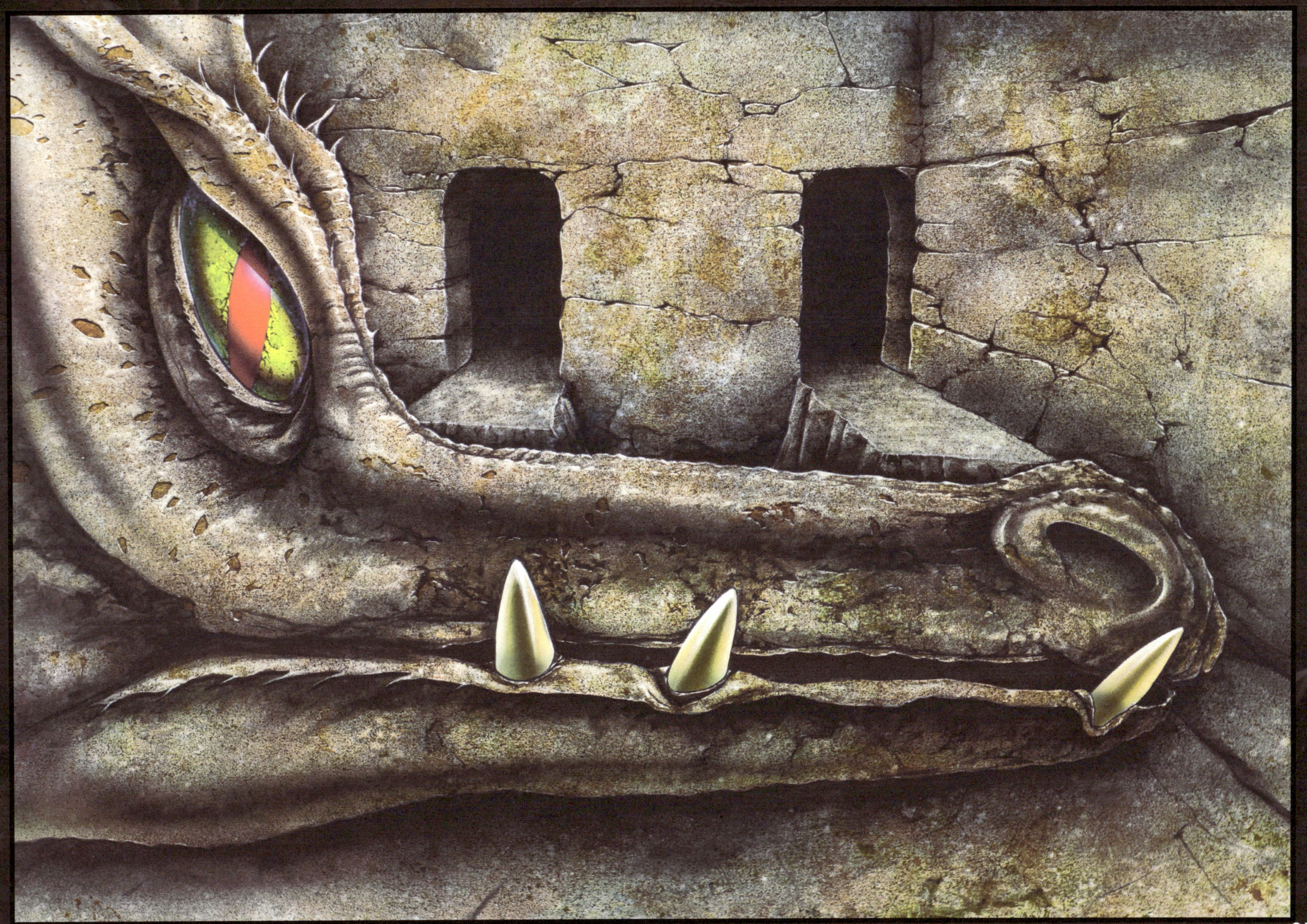

Valley Room/ Dismissal 3.8c

The Valley Room provided a reassuring exit scene for the watching audience. It showed that the team was safe and well and able to return to their own world.

Right: *The sketched drawing for the dismissal room shows pecked lines that indicate the geometry of the studio.*

Below: *The original faxed brief; Key line tracing; The faxed studio floor plan. The rock acted as a table and was included as a blue prop; The Dismissal or Valley Room was used to show the winning (or losing) team walking off safely into the sunset.*

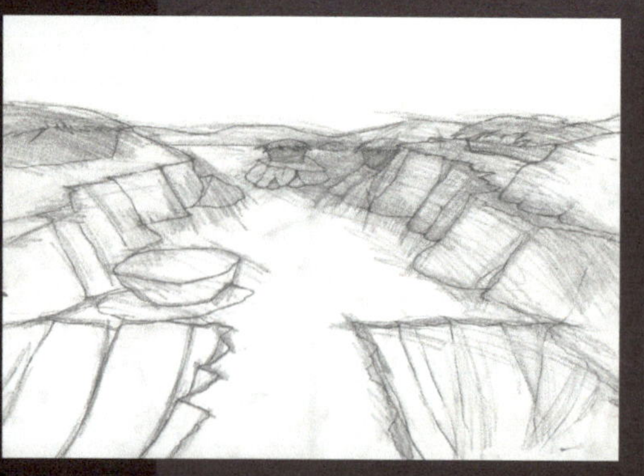

foreground as the Jericho wall allows, there should be provision for an altar/table. On this will be placed the same shattered medallion which was used earlier to invoke Merlin. Note the entry point of adventurer must be such that he will not mask this.

CHAMBER 7.LEVEL 3.THE THRESHOLD.

The last chamber. Here the dragon will appear. A good opportunity for an apparent multi-level chamber here as the Dragon (or lizard)will be ck'd in, and there's no need to put in ck staging to match. Thus three-quarters of the room can be taken up with a huge raised slab upon which the dragon stands/lies. The top of this could be about chin high to the adventurer. to the left handside is a footpath or gully leading to a portal exit to the rear.

CHAMBER 8. THE VALLEY.

THIS is the exterior scene, representing a pleasing fantasy world with a pathway winding away to the rear/. Only the floor need follow geometry. There should be provision for a large flat stone (central and slightly forground) upon which the silver spurs may be found. This scene is also used (but with nothing on the stone) whenever an adventurer fails and is "killed off".

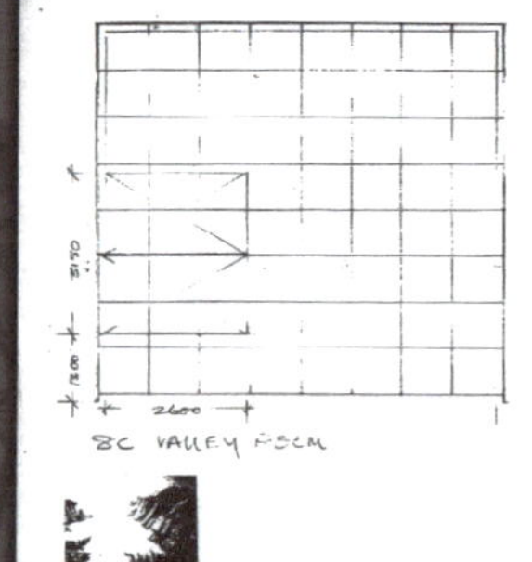

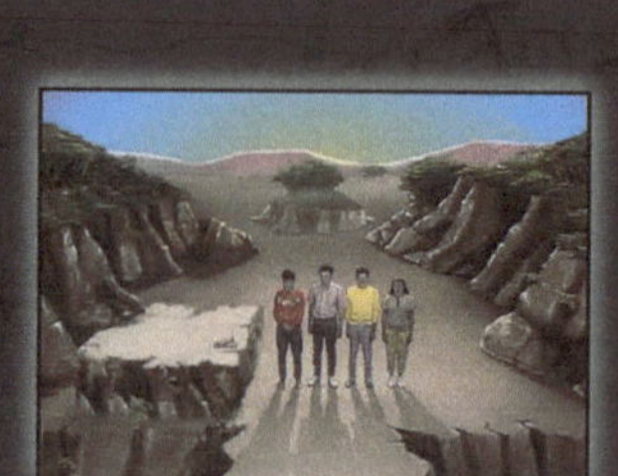

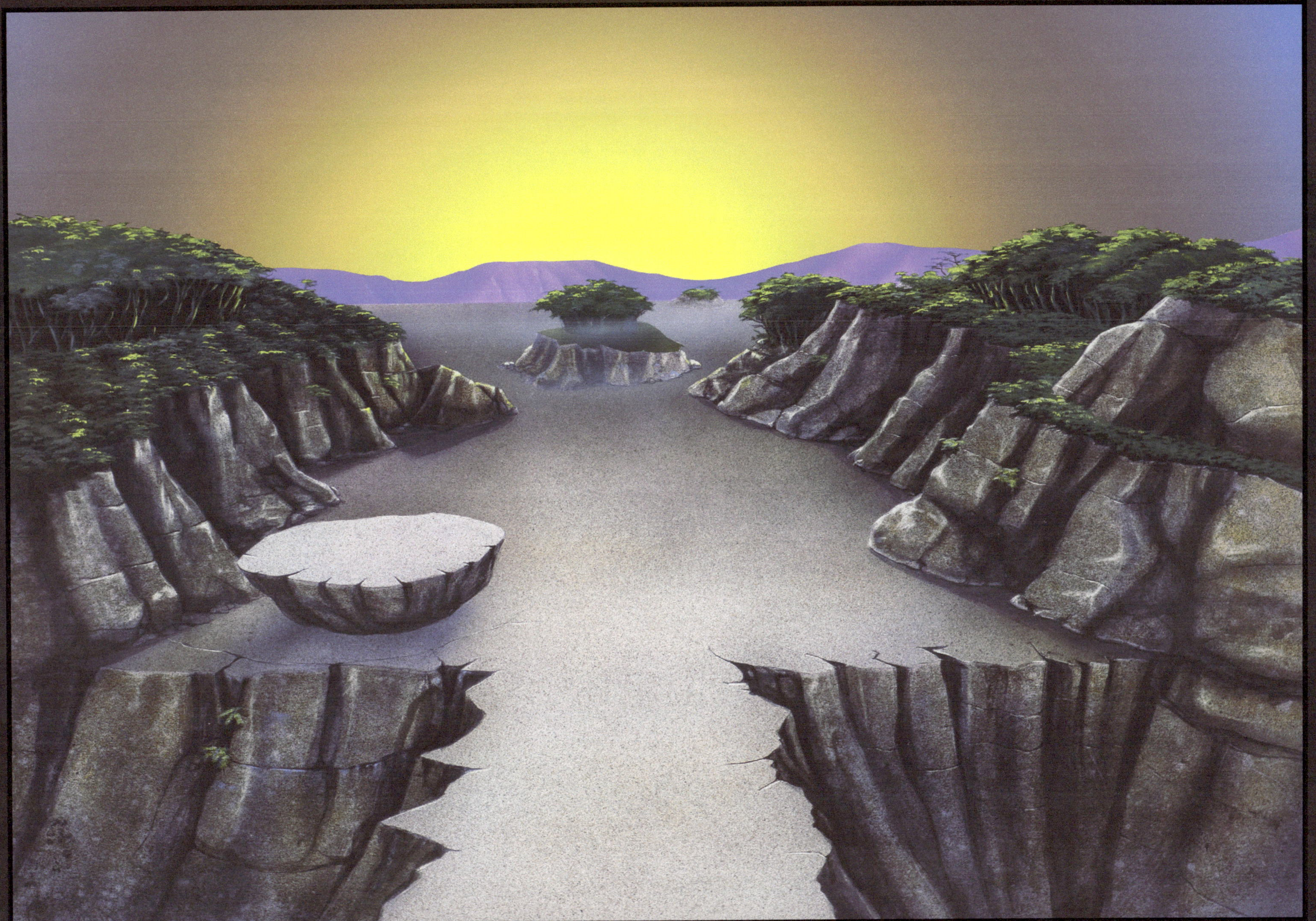

New Valley Room 3.8c

Tim explained in a fax that a darker, more brooding landscape favours the rolling of credits over the top. The brief was for a replacement to the original Valley/Dismissal Room.

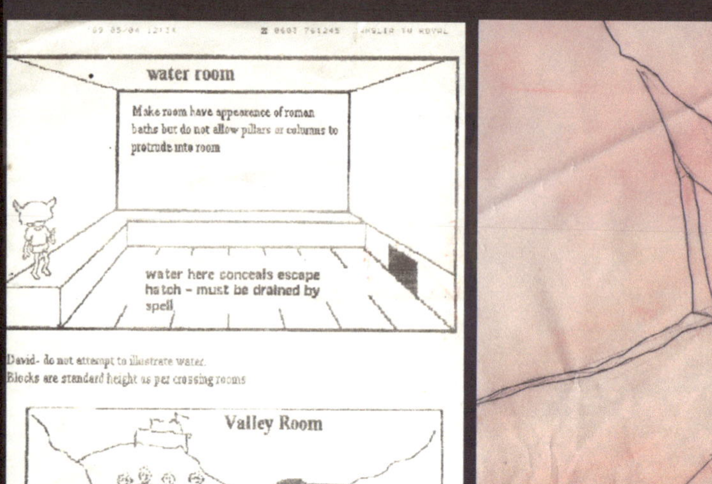

Top left: *The faxed brief which included an outline for the Baths Room.*

Top right: *The tracing for the new Dismissal Room had the studio floor lined in for reference.*

Bottom left: *Sketched rough for the new Dismissal Room. The final artwork was used as a background for The Dragon's Lair, one of the series of Knightmare adventure novels by Dave Morris.*

Bottom right: *The new valley room final set.*

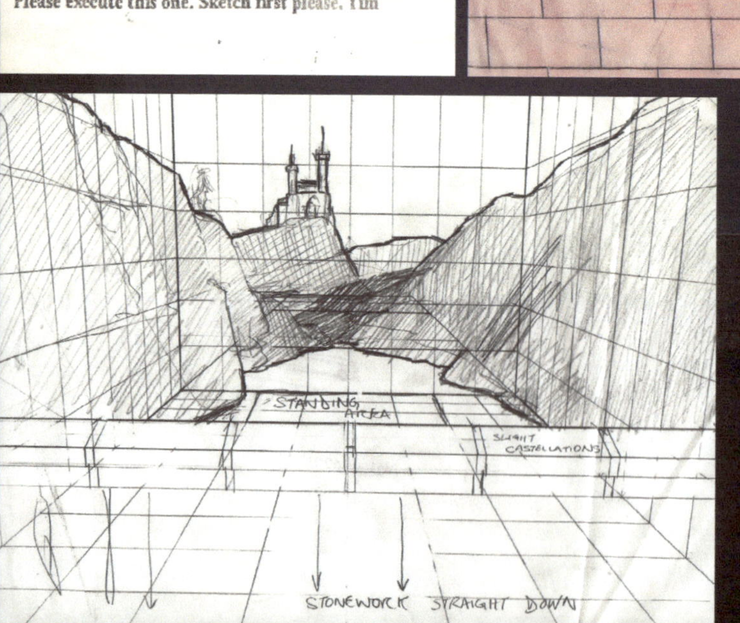

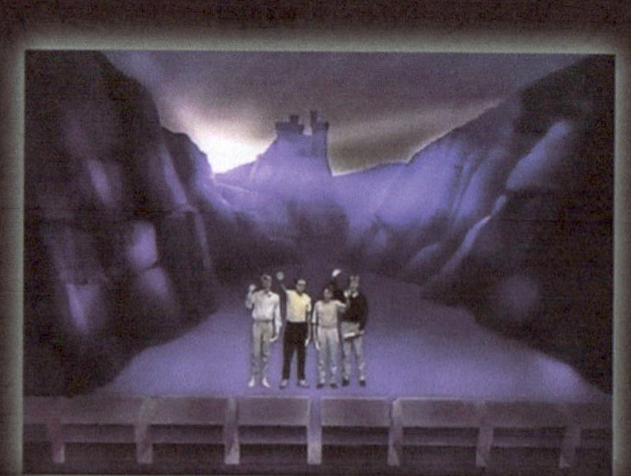

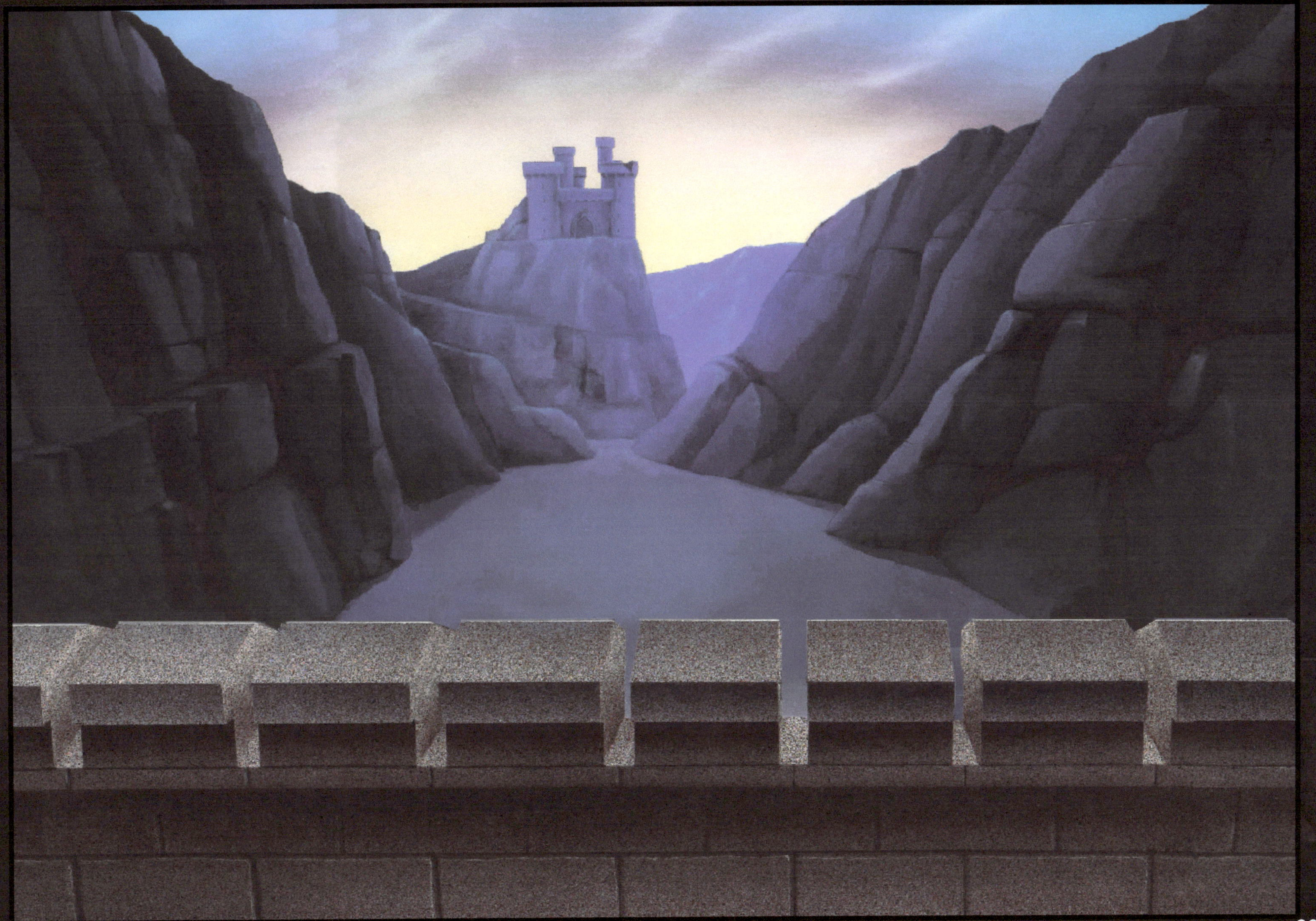

Chess Room 3.9c

I favoured a black and white marble texture for the chess board and the dry stone walls were inspired by the garden walls of my new home after my move to Mid Wales.

Right: *This tracing shows a lot of detail for the rubble walls from which, helpfully, my cottage walls are made.*

Below: *Original Meeting notes describing room details for my reference.*

My faxed rough indicating the various elements. The chess board grid might have been obvious, but then this was Knightmare and it was best to be sure.

The final broadcast composite.

A variation on the final set for the Chess Room.

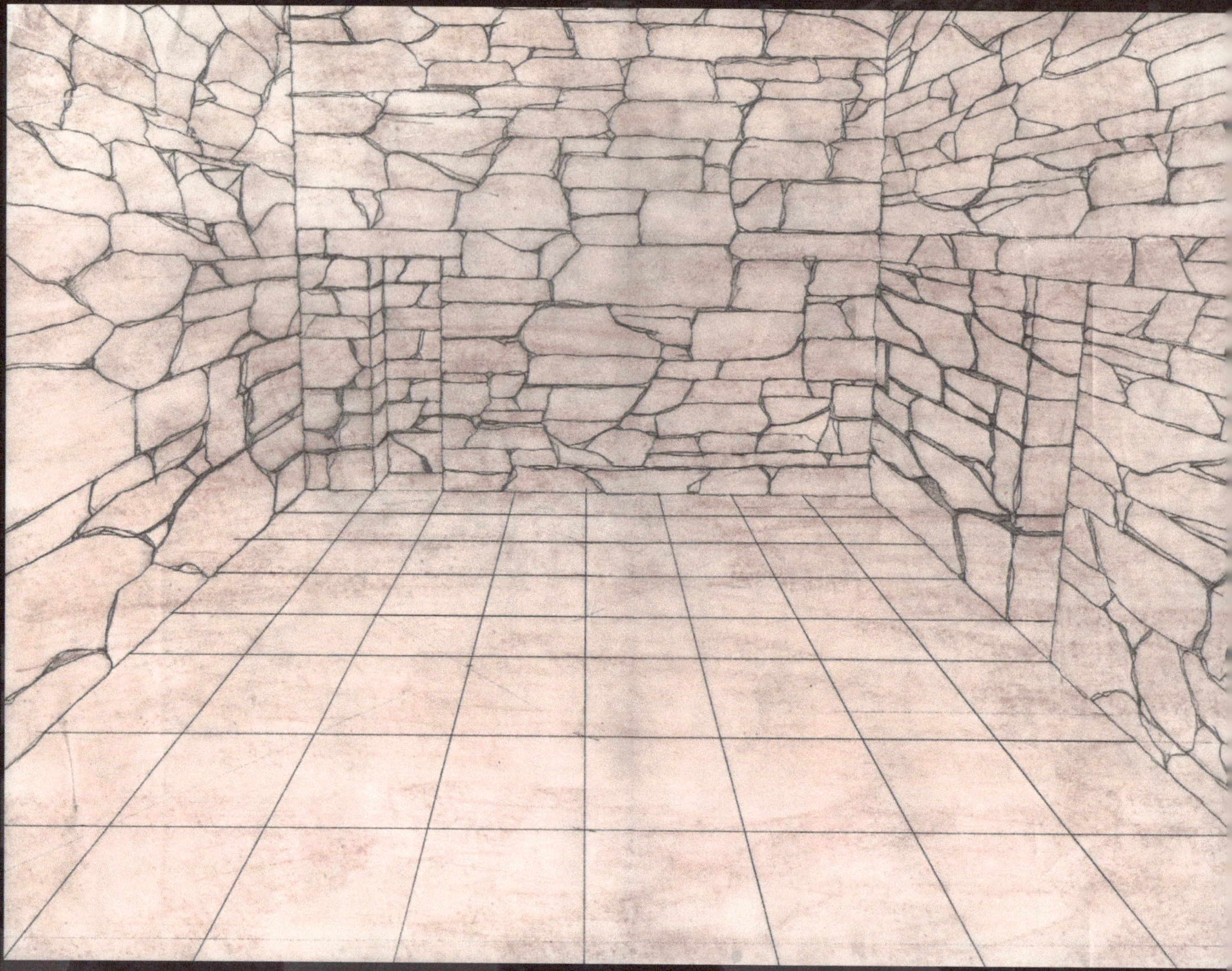

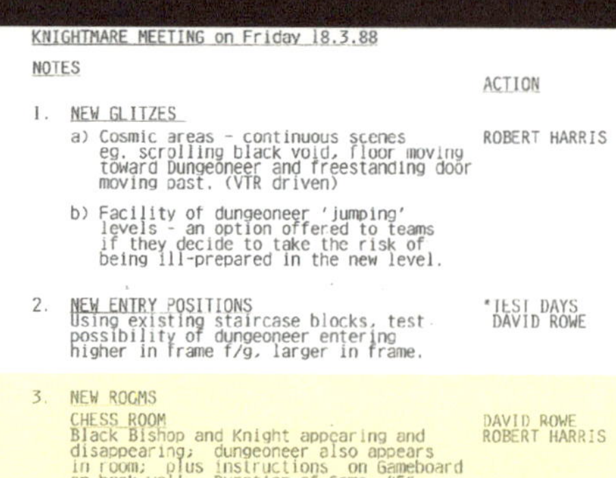

KNIGHTMARE MEETING on Friday 18.3.88

NOTES	ACTION
1. NEW GLITZES	
a) Cosmic areas – continuous scenes eg. scrolling black void, floor moving toward Dungeoneer and freestanding door moving past. (VTR driven)	ROBERT HARRIS
b) Facility of dungeoneer 'jumping' levels – an option offered to teams if they decide to take the risk of being ill-prepared in the new level.	
2. NEW ENTRY POSITIONS Using existing staircase blocks, test possibility of dungeoneer entering higher in frame f/g, larger in frame.	*TEST DAYS DAVID ROWE
3. NEW ROOMS CHESS ROOM Black Bishop and Knight appearing and disappearing; dungeoneer also appears in room; plus instructions on Gameboard on back wall. Duration of Game: 45".	DAVID ROWE ROBERT HARRIS

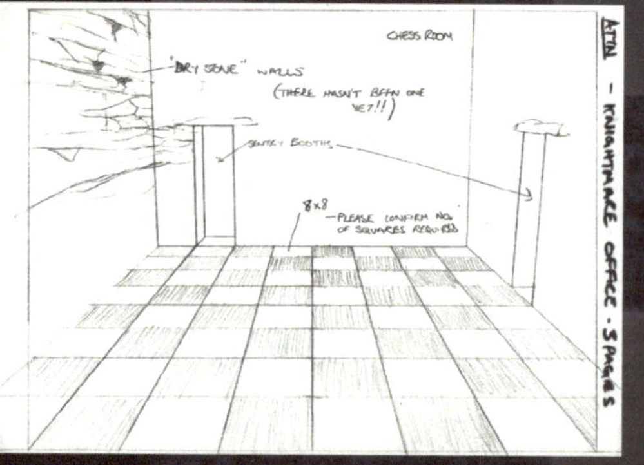

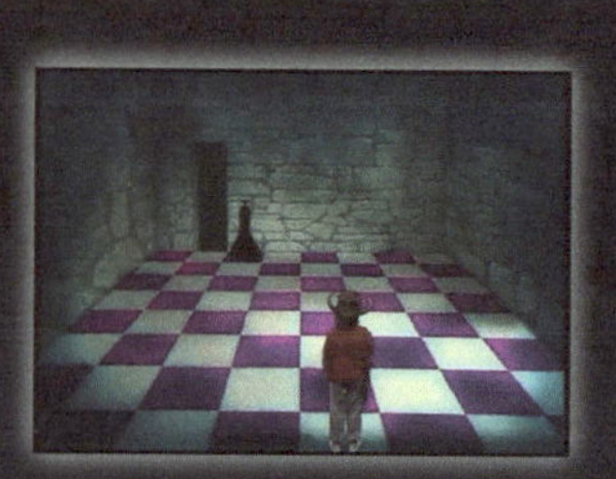

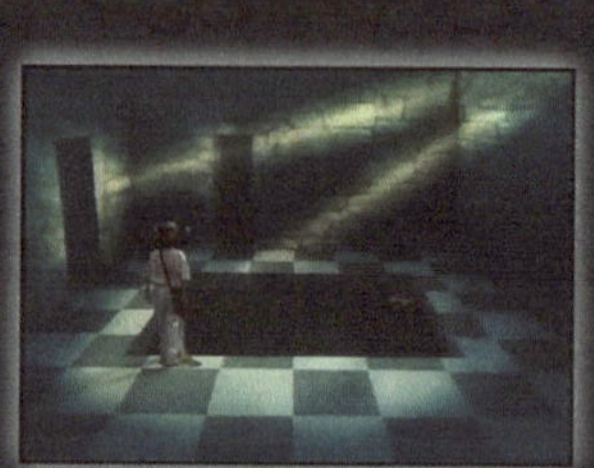

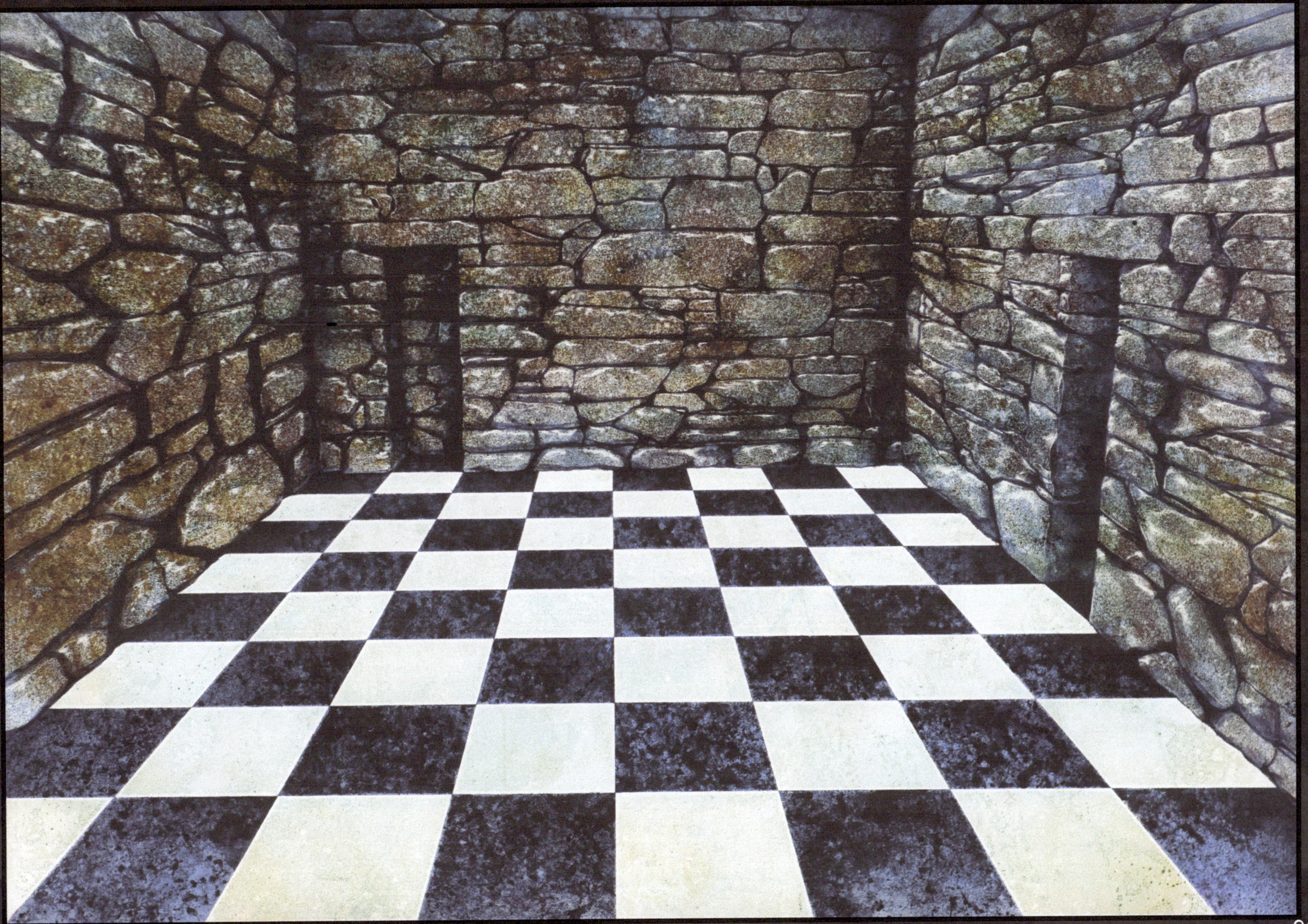

Right: *The initial drawing with notes and paint brush try outs. The drawing was handy when the painting was in progress.*

Far Right: *The ad featured prominently in computer game magazines and carried the cover image. I was attempting something otherworldly by depicting Treguard having twigs growing out of him and hair morphing into spiders.*

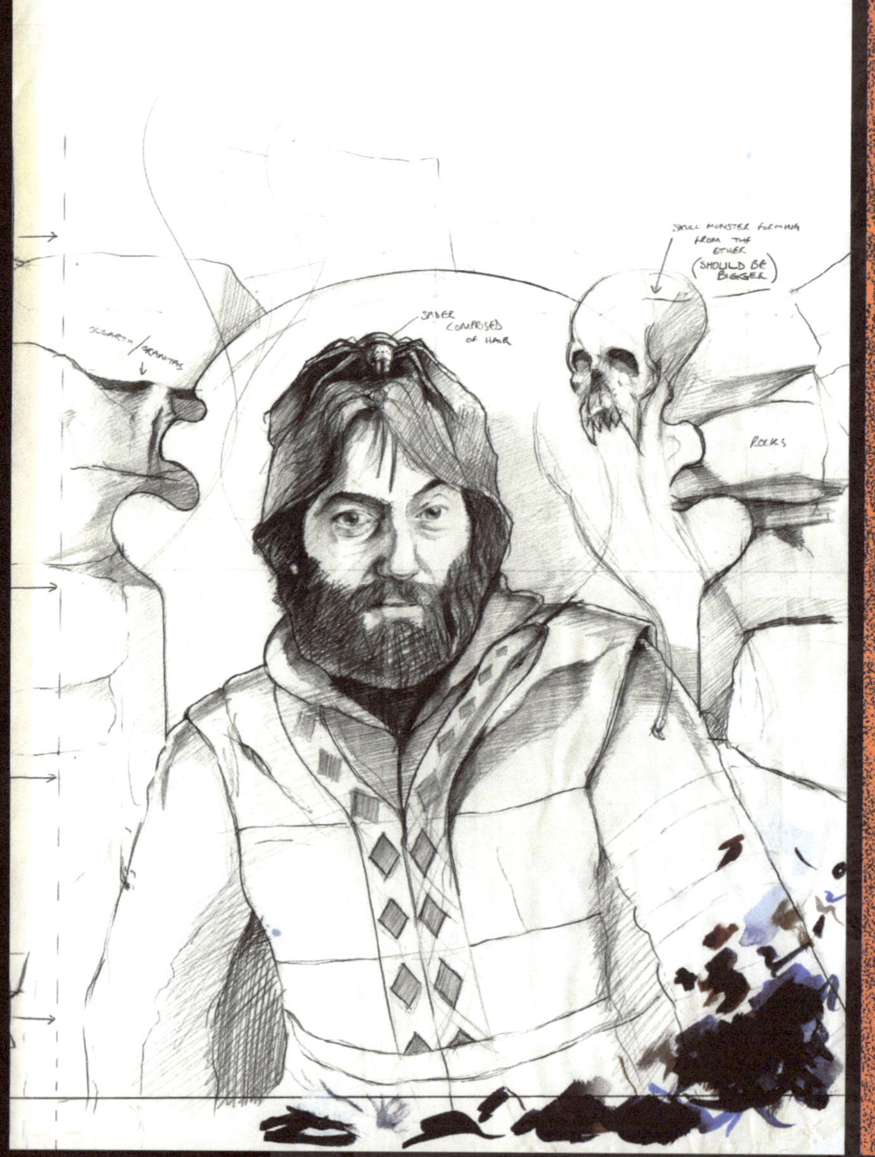

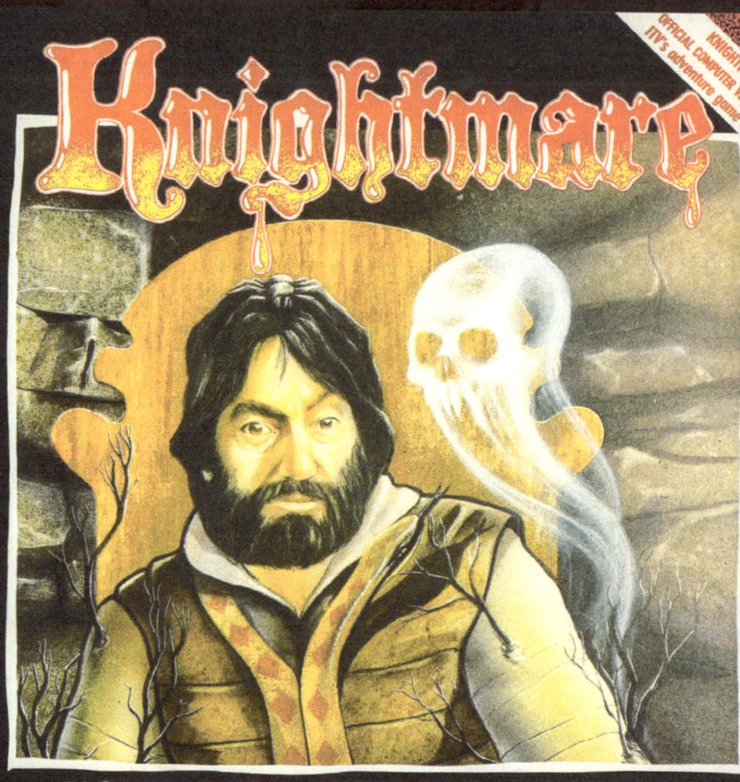

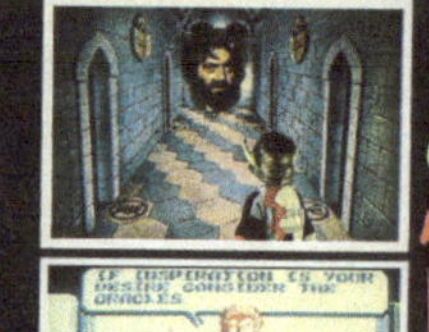

Knightmare the computer game uniquely combines the best elements of traditional adventuring with some hot arcade action and provides puzzles and riddles of a varying nature not found before in computer games.

Mail Order: Activision (UK) Ltd, Units 3 & 4 Lloyds Close, Finedon Road Industrial Estate, Wellingborough, Northampton NN8 4SR. Tel: (0933) 76768

Commodore 64/128 Cassette (£9.99) and Disk (£12.99)
ZX Spectrum 48k/128k/+ (£9.99) Amstrad CPC
Cassette (£9.99) and Disk (£14.99) Atari ST (£14.99).

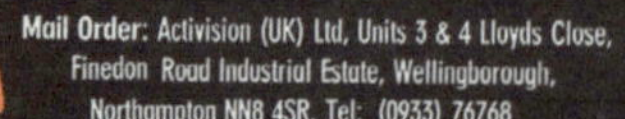

ACTIVISION.

Copyright 1987 Anglia Television. Game copyright 1987

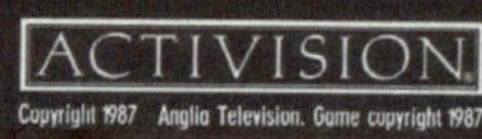

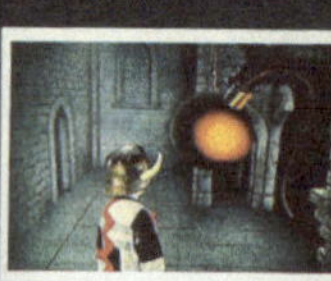

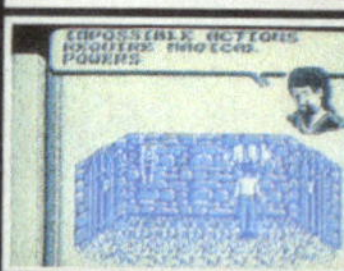

The Dungeon - Additional Rooms

There were additional rooms required that were to fit into the existing three levels for the third series of Knightmare. They are included in the this chapter so that the development chronology is apparent.
All the rooms that were created at this time are included here, whether they made it into the show or were left on the cutting room floor.

8 May 1990

To: David Rowe

Dear Dave,
Please find enclosed diagrams/grids/etc for what we will call the transporter room.
Sizes and depths are critical, so please follow plan.

All action in this room will take place in the rear of a void almost against the back wall.
Aspect is grid 3 (central VP).
Walls have been brought in slightly to give an arch-vaulted feel.
3 panel transporter pads are present at points D/E, where seen on floor, and also on C B and A. Final transporter pad is at final destination target (Point F).

These pads are six feet across and made up of three panels; each 2ft x 2ft. Floor C is 6 ft 6ins above floor E.
Ditto A above C.
Floor F is suspended from above (like hanging basket.)
H is a black void.
G is stone forground.
I is another black void or impassable drop.

Can you
a: (sketch and show)
b: illustrate.

Yours ever,

TIM

Water Room

The painting took into account the one metre high blocks that formed the chromakey props. The walkway continued down the left side of the room and across the back.

The baths were filled with water and the Dungeoneer and team had to cast a spell to drain the water out of the sluice on the right wall. Once drained, the Dungeoneer could cross the floor and exit the room.

This room presented a more single option puzzle for the adventure and was therefore quite inefficient in production terms.

Further uses were created which involved adding a new exit to the back wall right hand panel and placing a shark in the water.

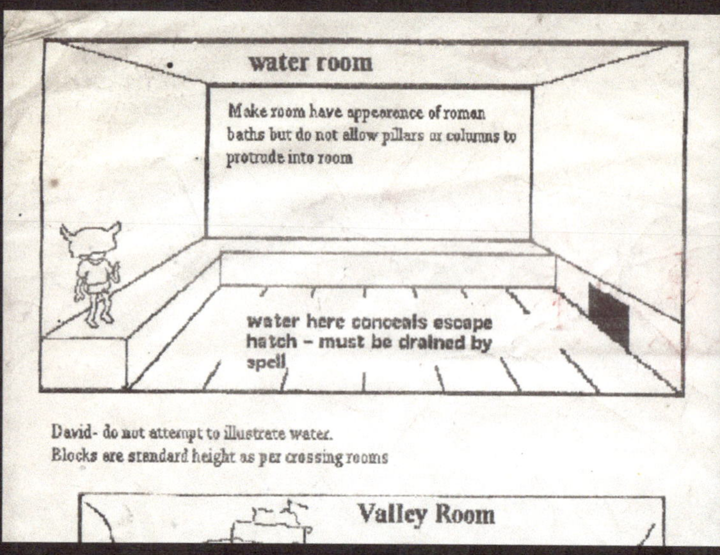

The faxed brief for the Baths Room which was added later.

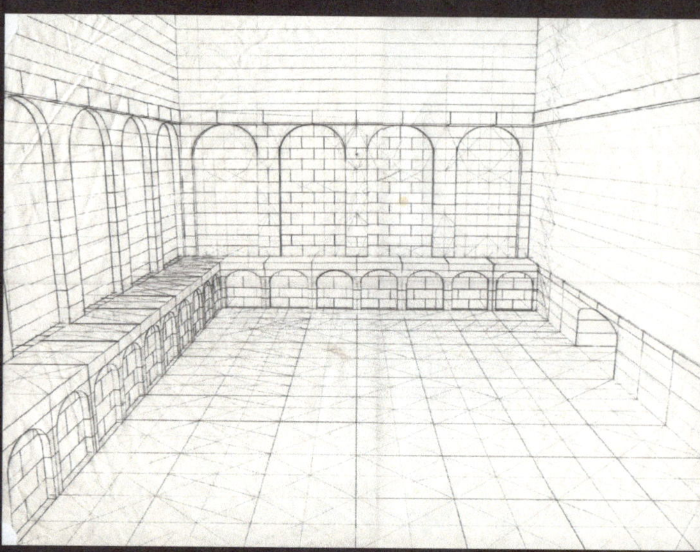

The drawing for the baths room was quite detailed to achieve the Roman Baths feel. Grid squares were bisected to add finer detail as can be seen here.

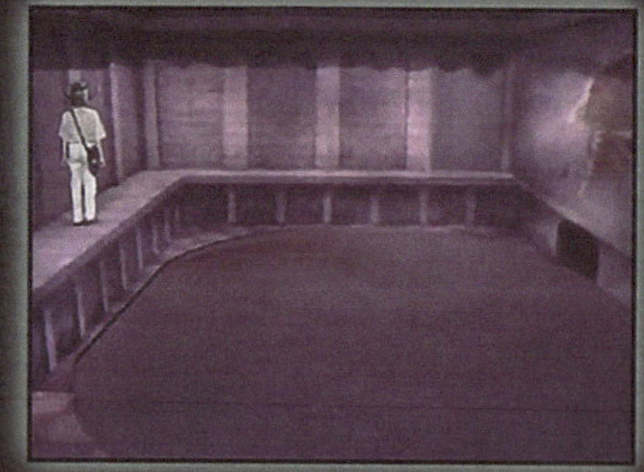

The water draining from the baths in the final composite.

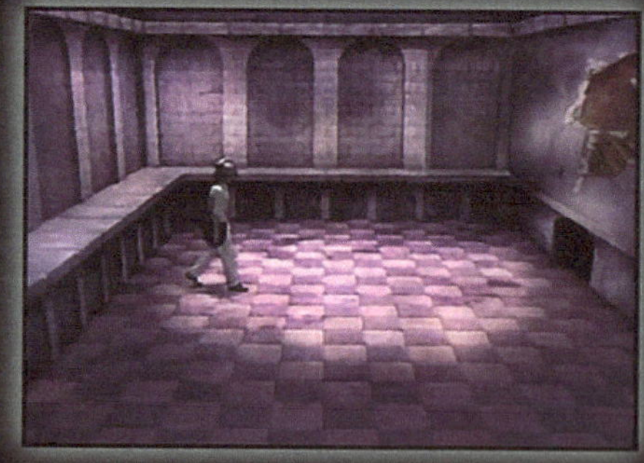

The drained baths allowed the Dungeoneer to progre[ss] from the room.

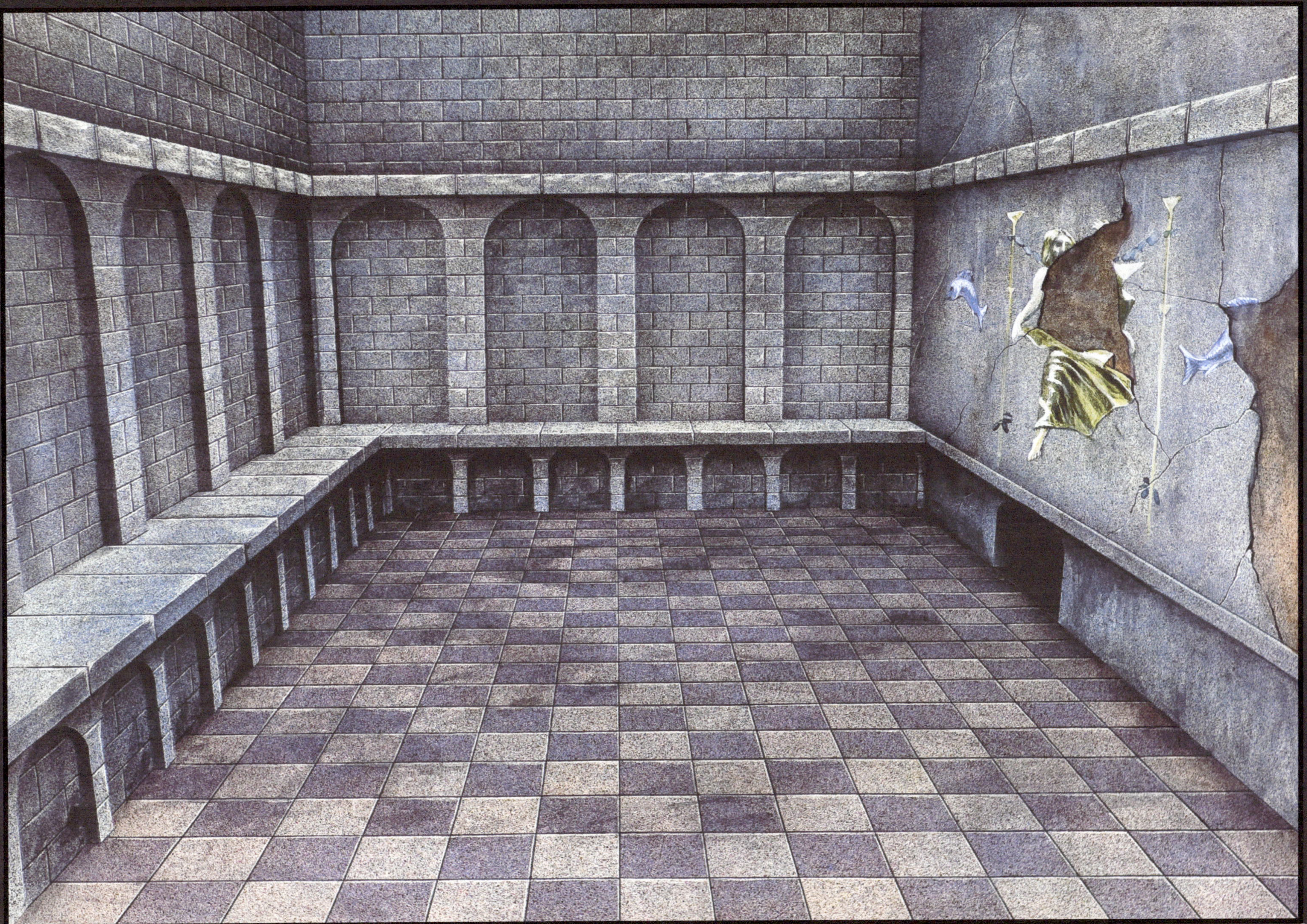

Egyptian Room

The Egyptian Room was a timing based conundrum. The team had to guide the Dungeoneer across the gap between laser bolts fired from the eyes of the cat statues. The exit door at the back of the room was added with the computer at a later stage as the puzzle evolved from that originally envisaged.
I hope that the hieroglyphics don't actually say anything!

Right: *Further detail was added at the tracing stage to avoid having to draw it an excessive amount of times. Red pastel was added to the back of the tracing paper. The colour depended upon the predominant hue of the painting.*

Below: *The rough sketch. It established the style, but the laser firing cat's eyes had to come from a higher trajectory; The next faxed rough incorporated the adjustments; The final composite complete with laser bolts shooting from the cat's eyes; The final set and a successfully timed escape.*

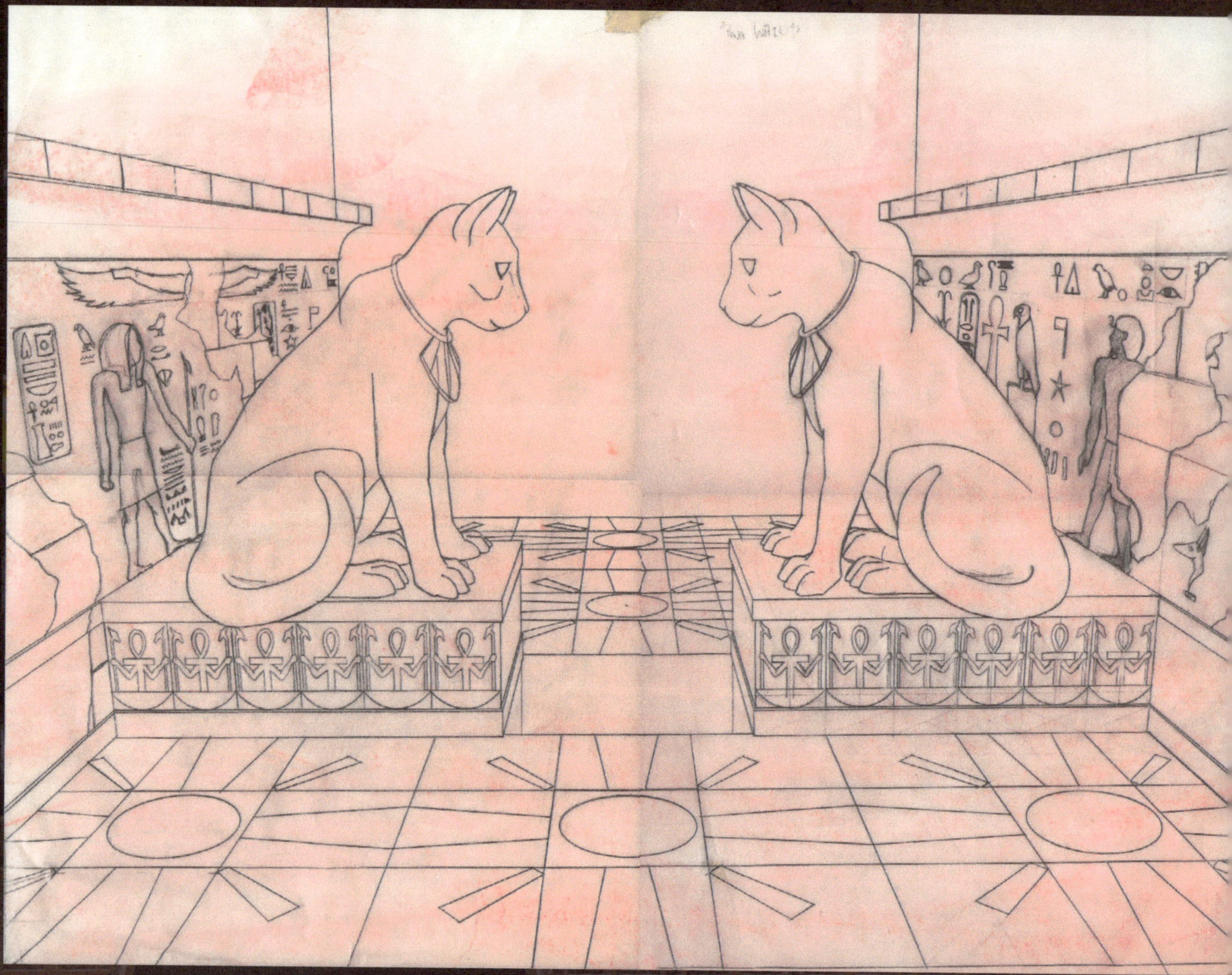

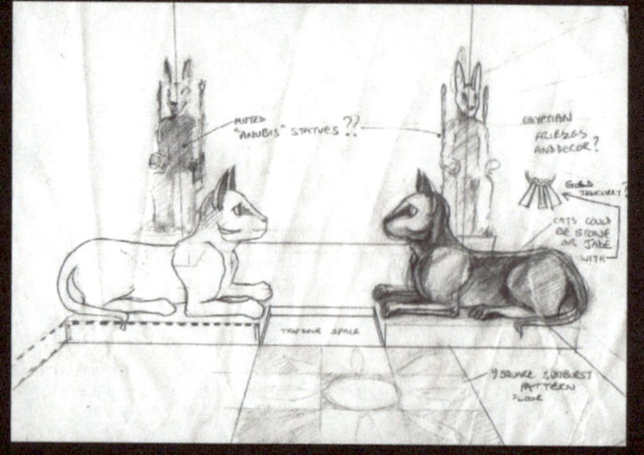

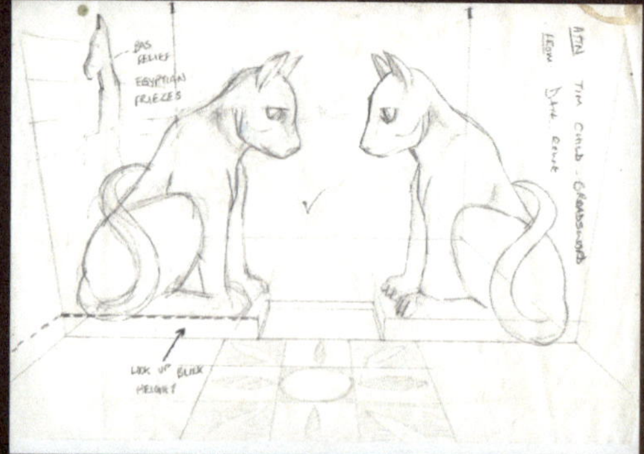

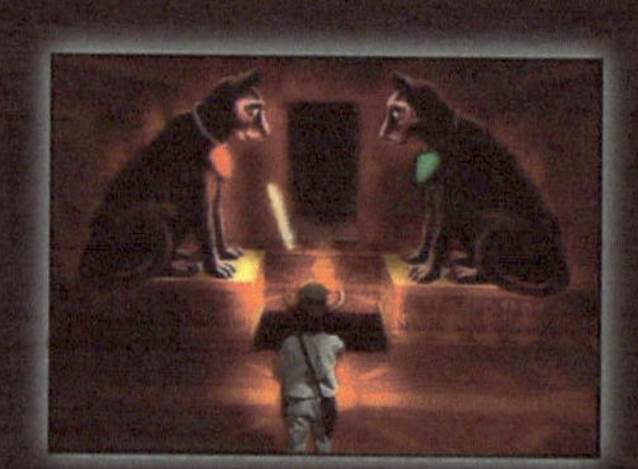

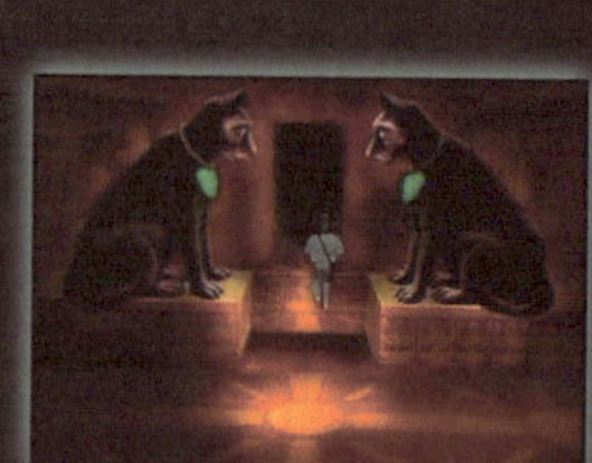

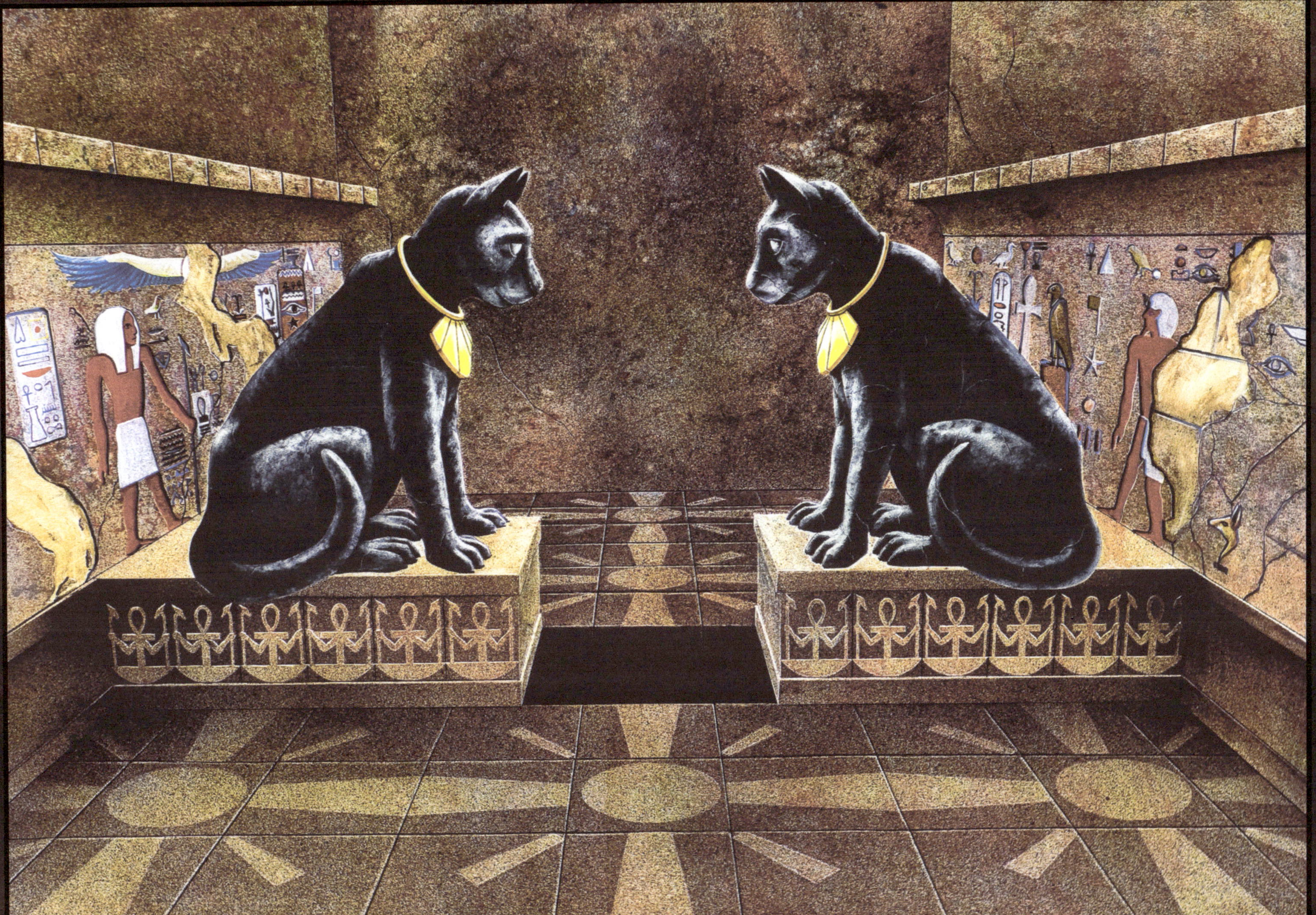

Causeway Room

The Causeway Room brief allowed a fair amount of freedom to interpret the scene. Space for the causeway had to be left as it was to be added later with computer graphics.
 The drawing was faxed to Tim Child using the half-tone capability which gave a good impression of pencil tone.
A portion of the finished artwork was cut into the background of the Transporter Room.

Right: *The annotated rough was faxed to Tim and the finished artwork was commenced once the go ahead was given.*

Below: *The faxed brief would have been supplemented with a phone conversation to make sure that there were no misunderstandings; Key line trace from the drawing; The computer was able to make the bridge collapse and fall as the Dungeoneer fled to safety.*

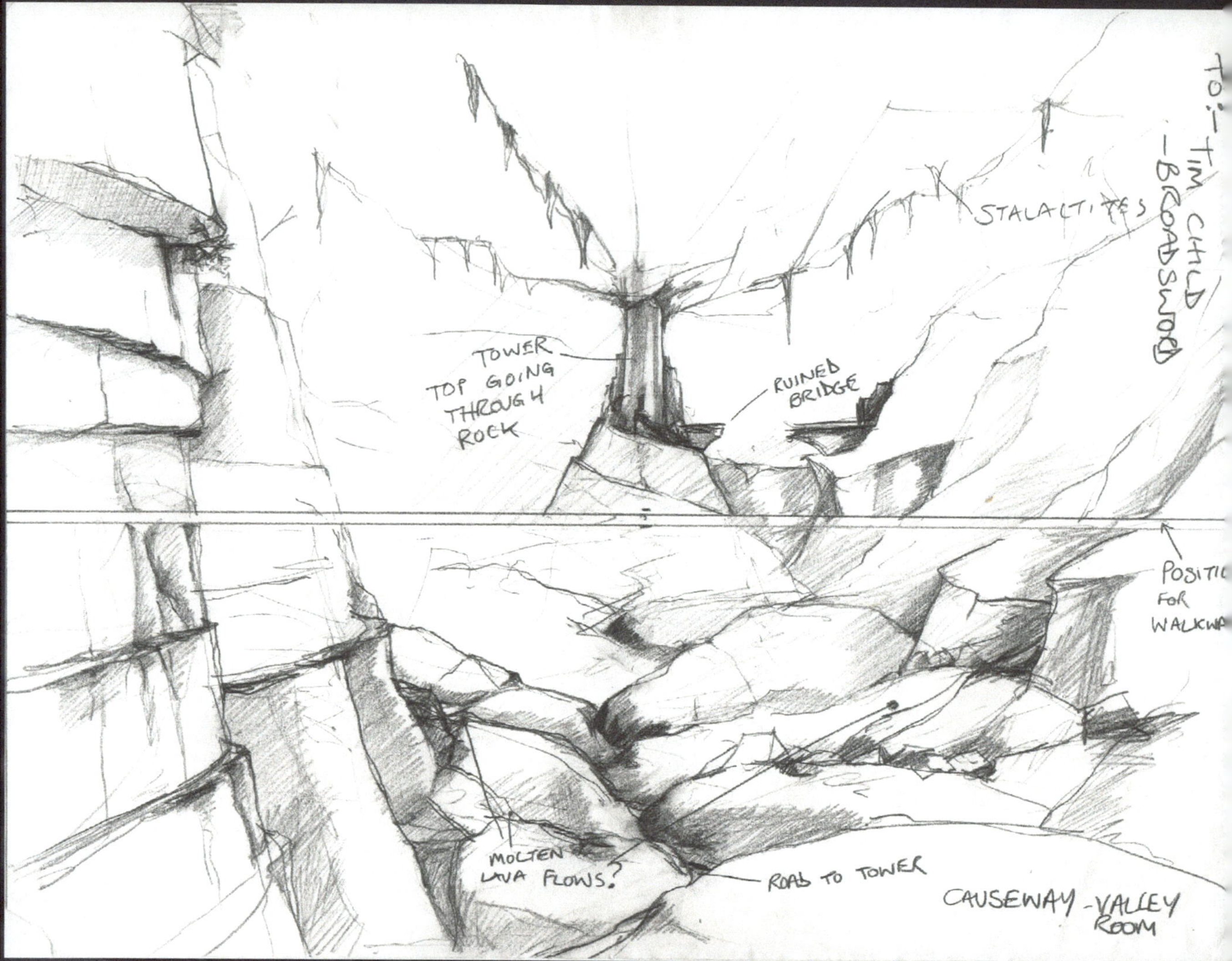

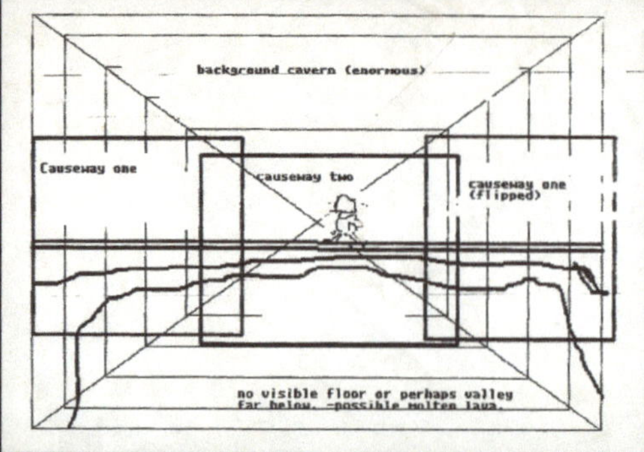

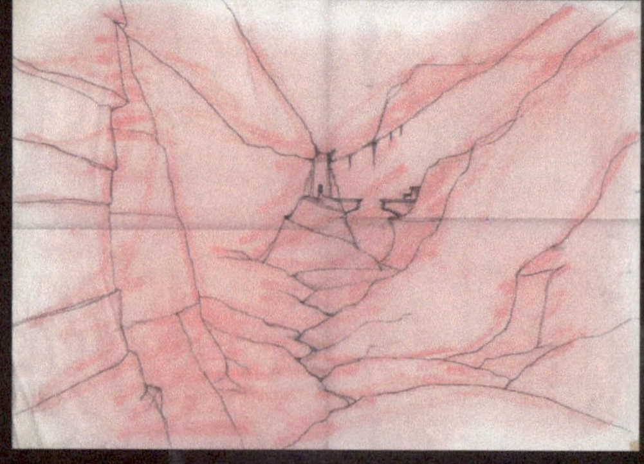

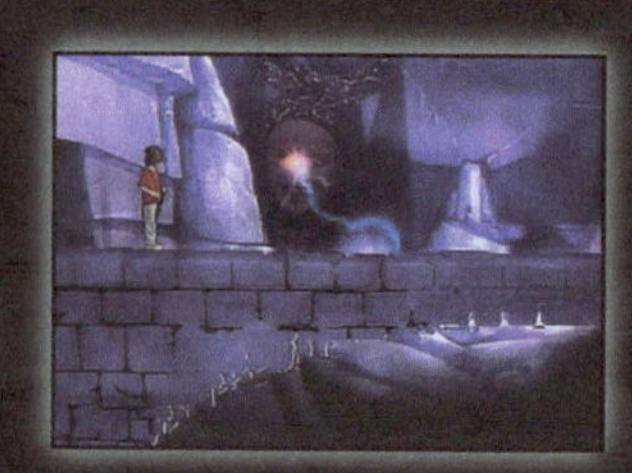

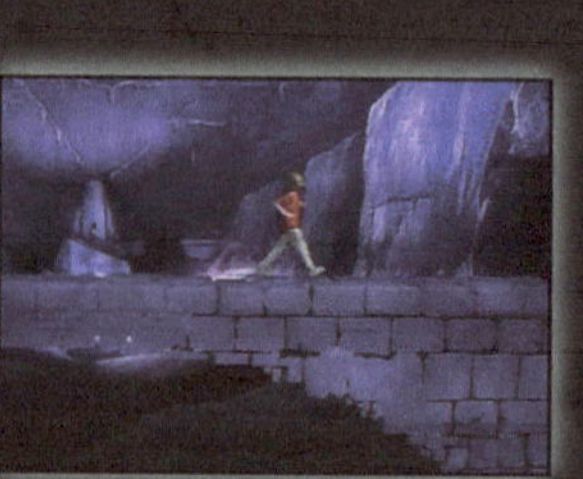

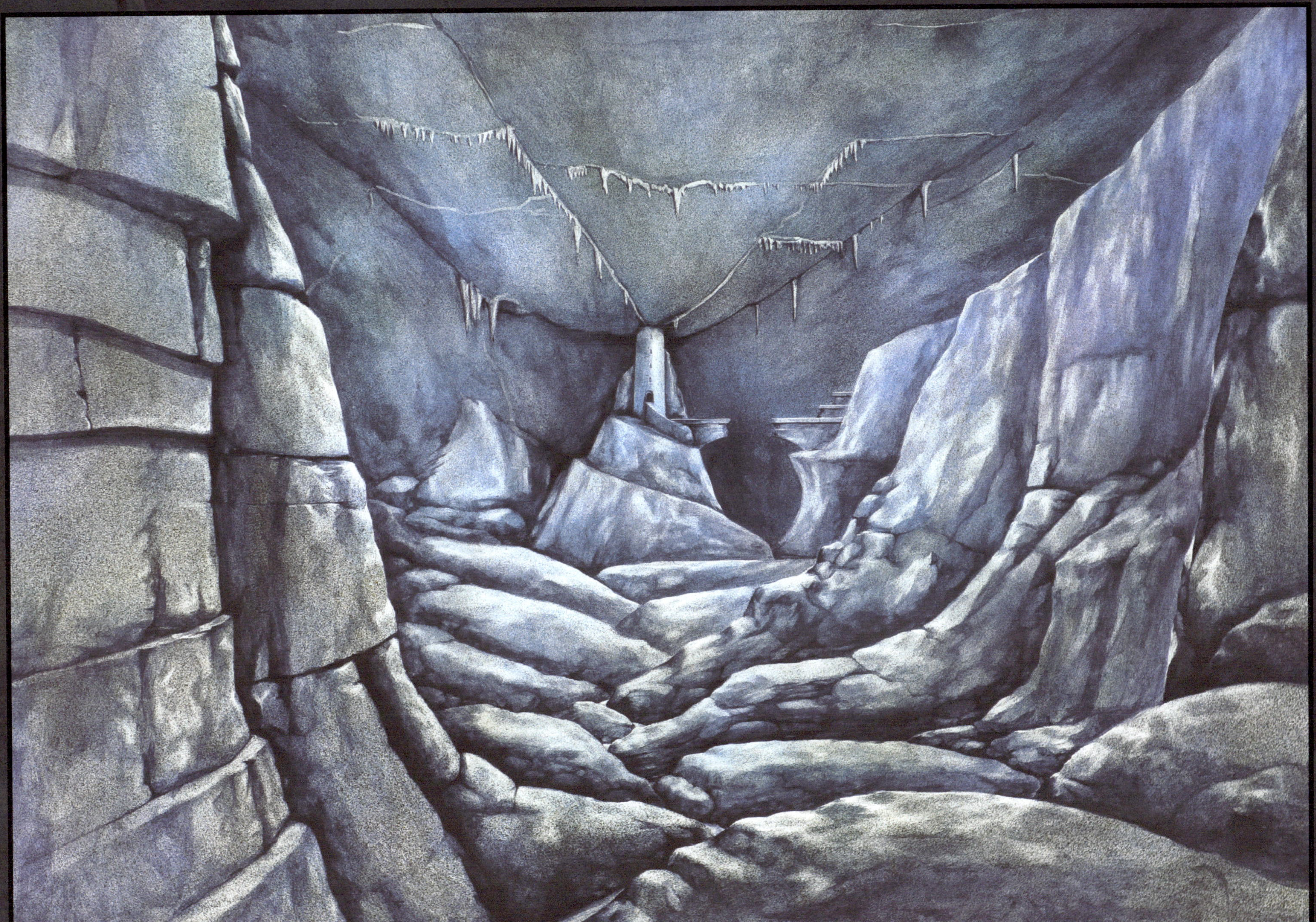

Turntable Room

The walls and floors of the chromakey studio were pencilled in to show positioning. The dimensions were also pencilled in to show the positioning of the turntable props. The image was drawn directly onto tracing paper which was then annotated, cut in two to fit through the fax machine and then sent to Tim for approval.

The turntable plinth was extended or bled into a point at the centre of the area which would be covered by the plinth. This allows leeway in the turntable's positioning which then would cover the top of the column. When used in the final broadcast composite, the painting was flipped horizontally to allow the Dungeoneer to enter left foreground.

Below: *The original faxed brief; The annotated tracing taped together after it had been cut in two prior to faxing; The final broadcast composite.*

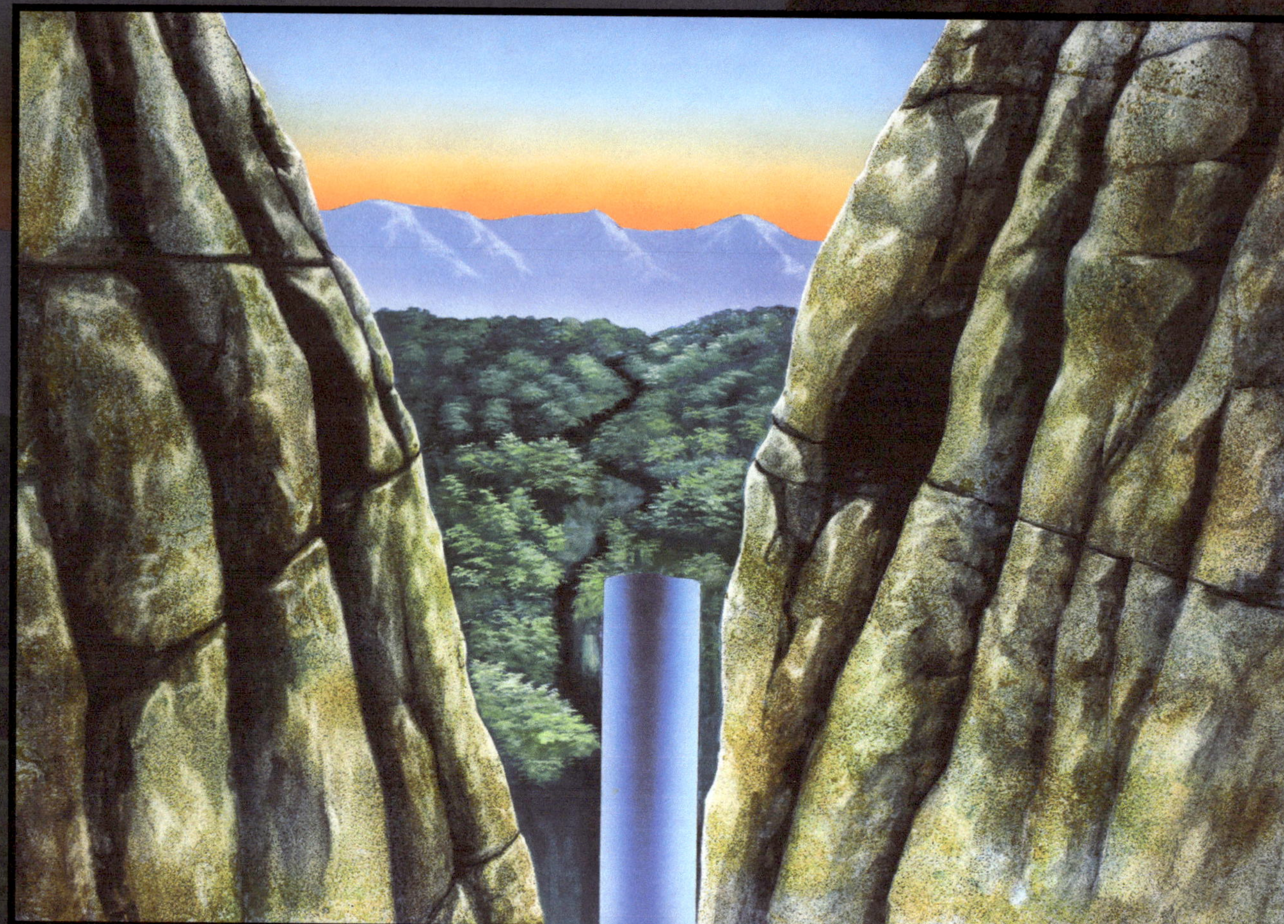

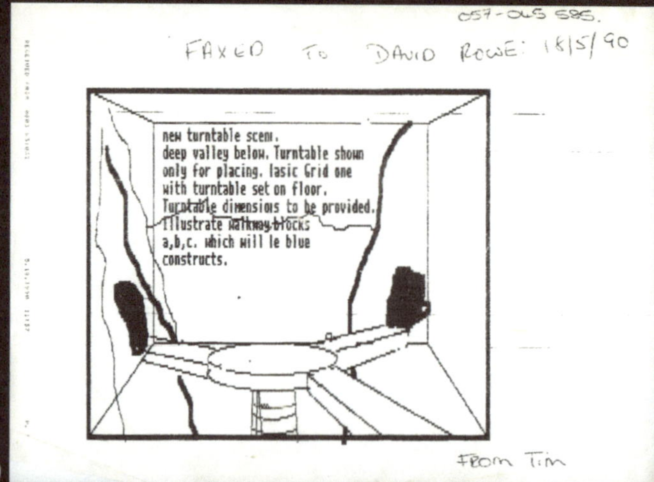

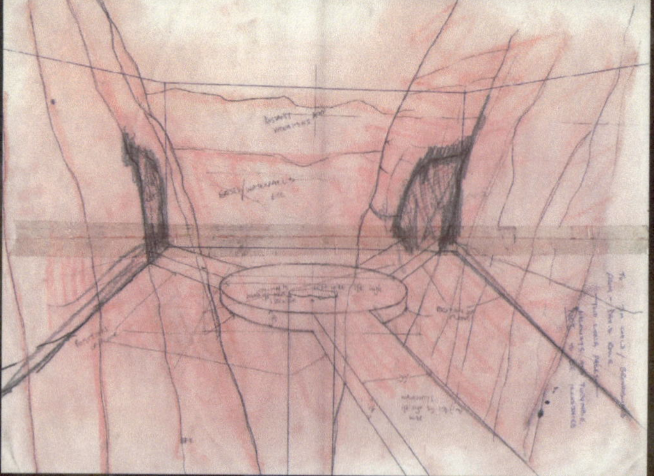

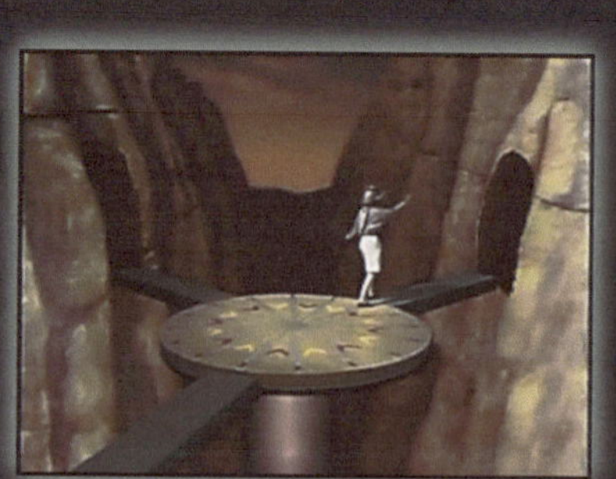

Bland Rooms

Bland Rooms were stock items that could be called into action when an idea for a room surfaced. They could lend themselves to a wide variety of scenarios unlike the more specifically designed rooms which often only suited a single story line.
There were a number of bland, flat lit rooms that allowed for a wide variety of options when it came to relighting and collage effects for specific rooms.

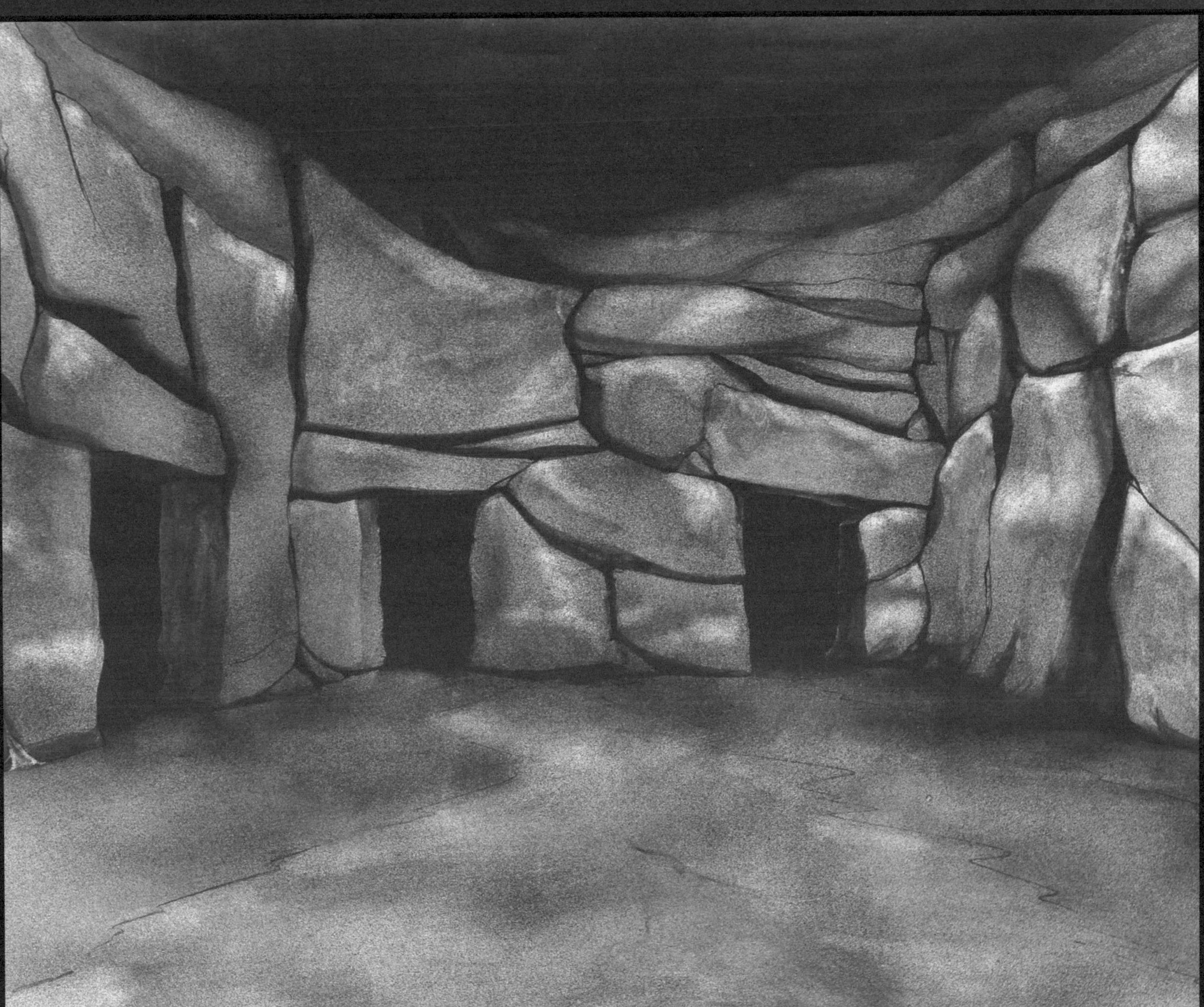

Death Valley

The brief for Death Valley required three views of the same room.
The Causeway Room and First Crossing Room with their split views paved the way. With the Death Valley Room, the ability to cut to different views was a big step forward that gave the impression of much larger spaces than the regular rooms that had been the norm until then.

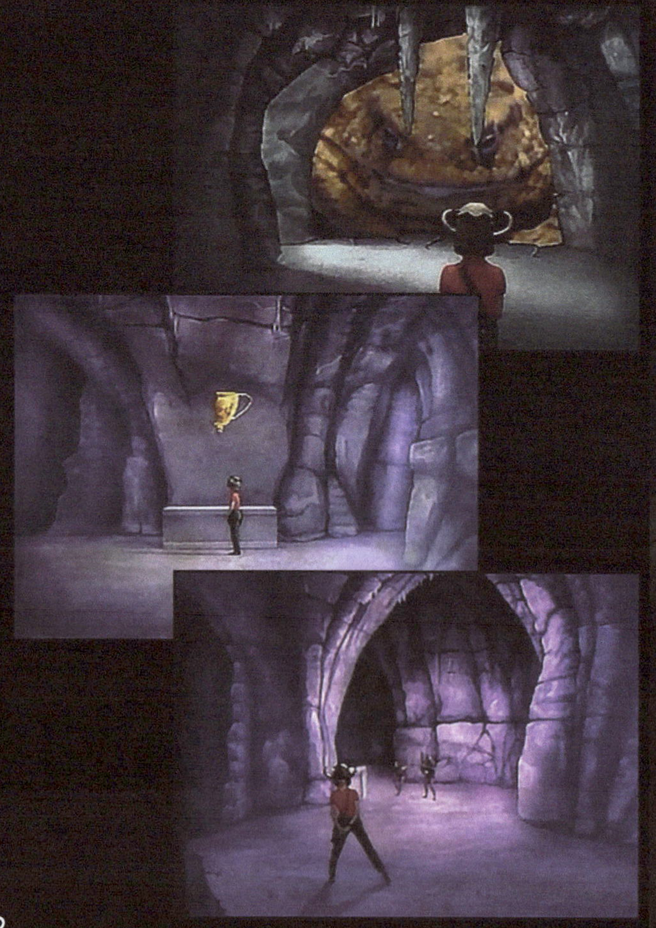

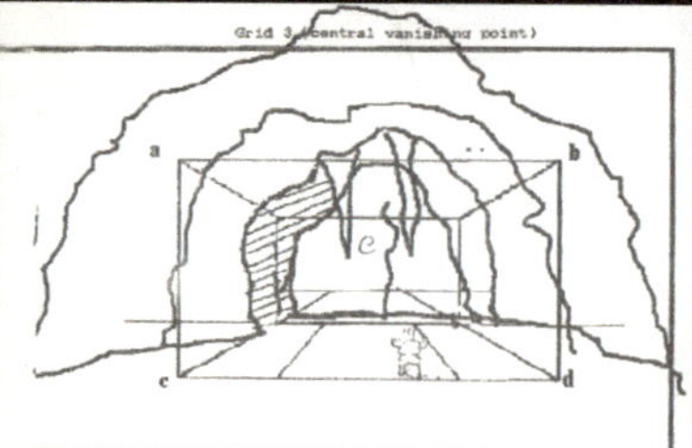

Death Valley 2 - scene 1.
Please note :we will take advantage of grid 3 to reveal the first part of a massive cavern, with enormous arch vault ceilings. Please notice that I have used the grid as a window here to help illustrate and that the actual framing for the scene is within a.b.c.d.
The cross-hatch area ///// indicates a turn to the left (round a corner into scene 2, with light pouring from that scene into this one.

note : Stalagtiles!
e = dead end.

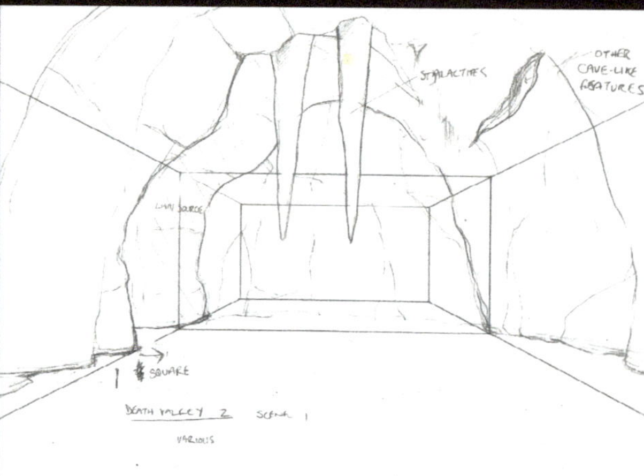

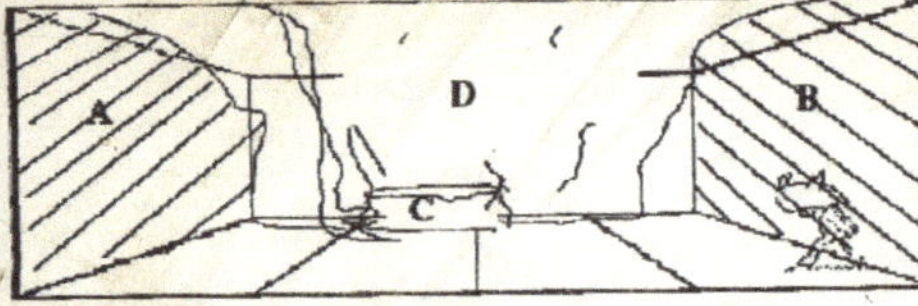

Death Valley 2-Sc 2

Death Valley 2 - scene 2 (Grid 3).
Key to contents:
a=entry to scene 3 with some charateristics of scene 3 contained therein.
b=Scene 1 - where we've just come from after turning the corner.
c=a stone alter (single standard block placed against rear wall.
d= huge rock plinth supporting ceiling, with central even textured area to allow manifestation or place wall monster.

OK?

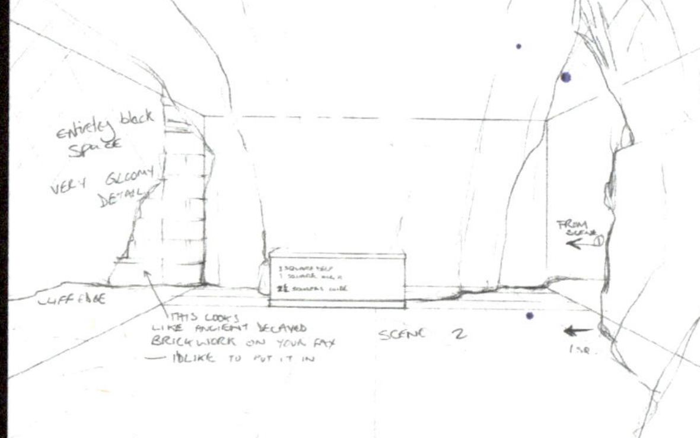

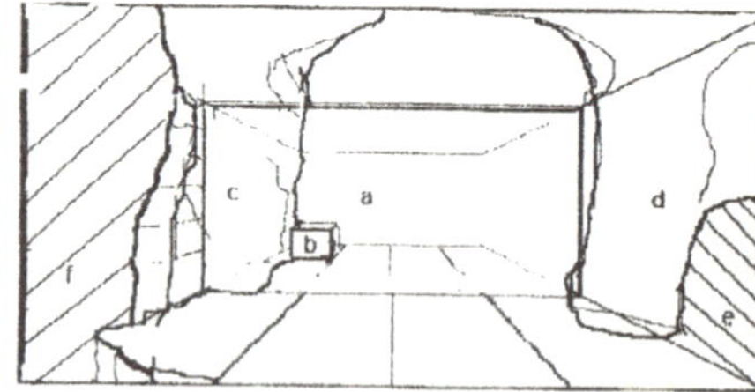

Death Valley2 scene 3.

Grid 3 (central vanishing point)

Key to features:
a=side view into Death Valley 2 Sc 2 with (b) altar.
c=supporting stone column (d in dvsc2). f = cliff edge with black hole. d = second supporting stone column. e = cave mouth. NB don't worry that this is cheated behind wall line – we will grab dungeoneer out early!

Call me with any queries – TC

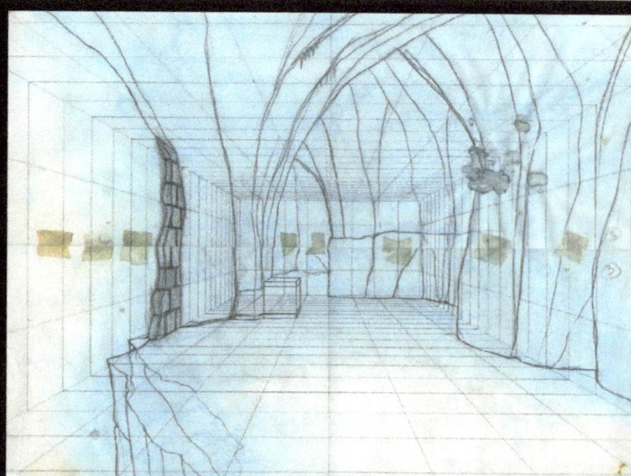

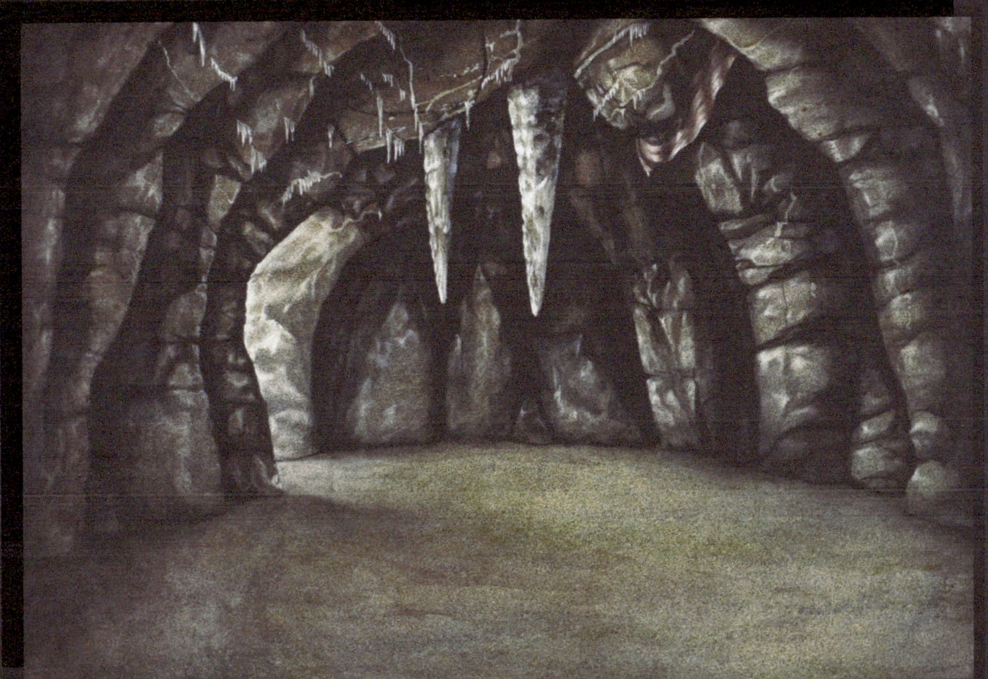

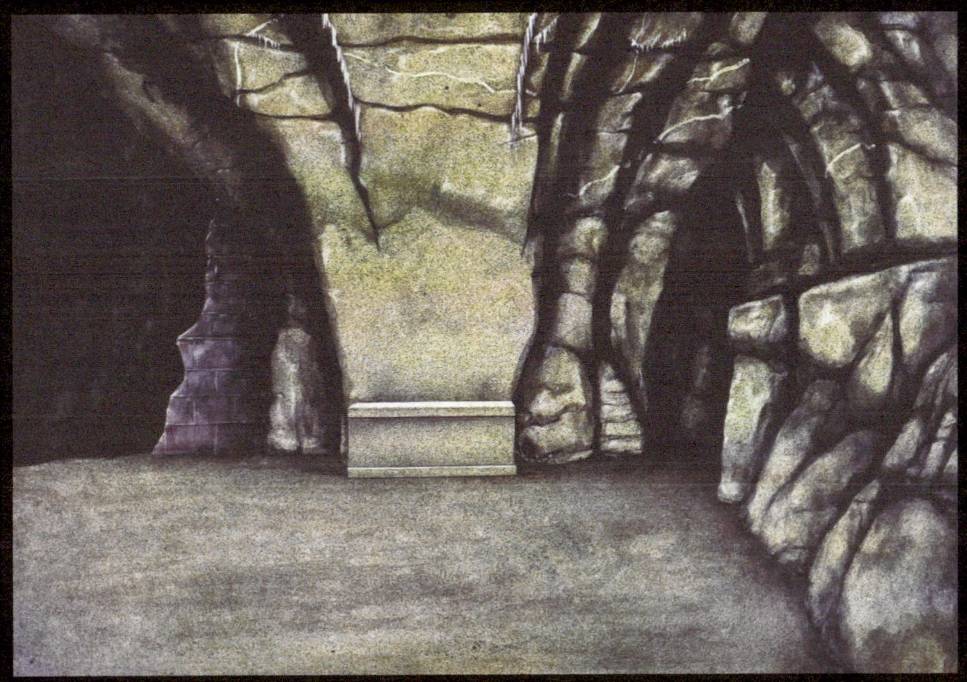

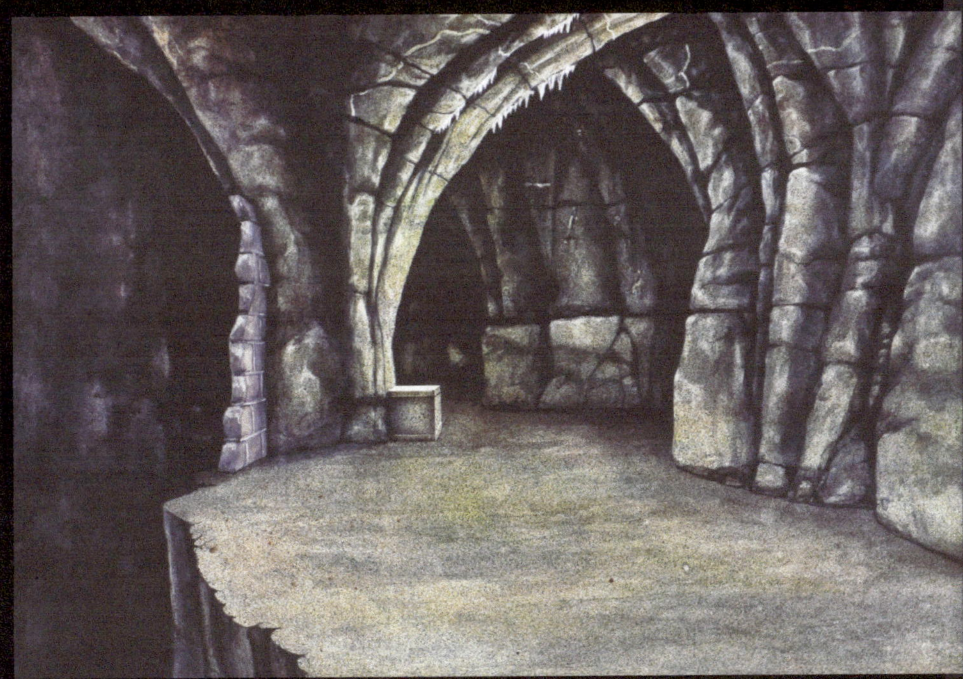

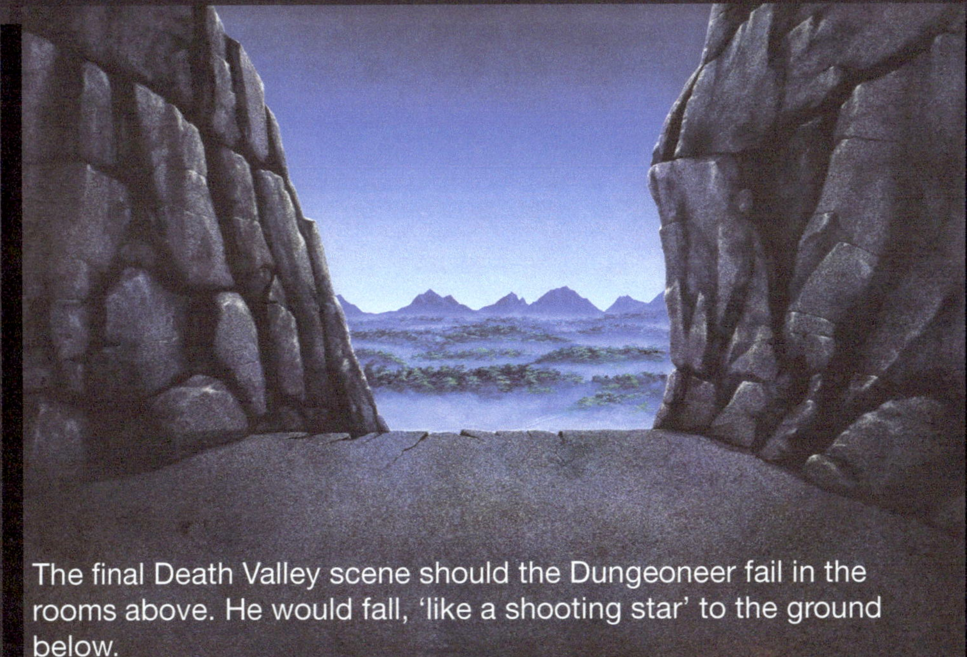

The final Death Valley scene should the Dungeoneer fail in the rooms above. He would fall, 'like a shooting star' to the ground below.

Mouse hole Room

Here is a painting that didn't make it through to the finished programme. I thought that the painting had been lost, but on closer examination, the pencil lines on the tracing had not been drawn over to transfer the image to illustration board.

This triggered a faint memory that the puzzle had been dropped from the show and therefore the room was not required and so the painting was not produced.

It is not difficult to imagine what conundrums and spells would have been invoked had this room seen the light of day.

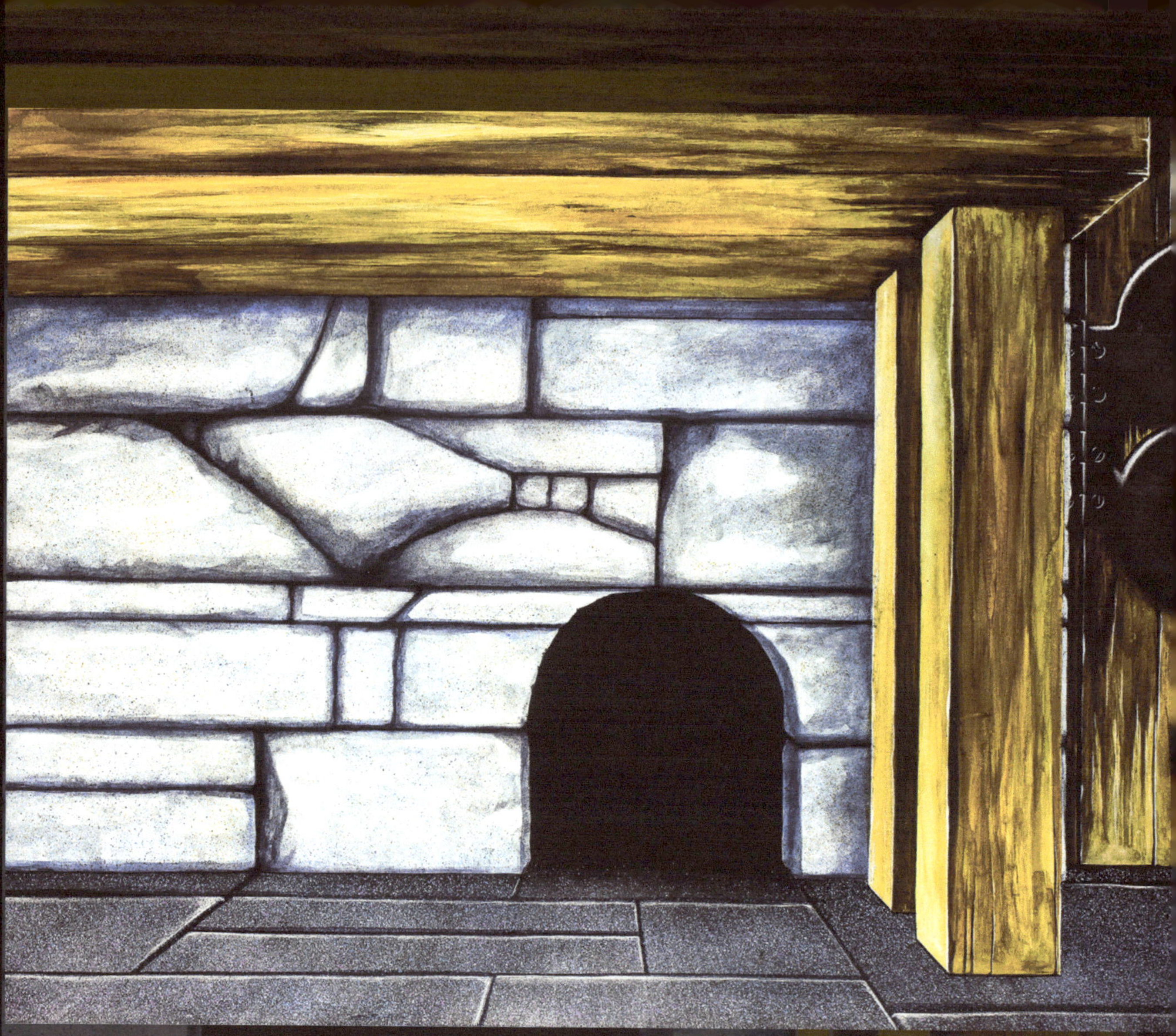

Right: *The finished artwork for the close-up.*

Below: *The rough sketch with key dimensions; The faxed brief from the Broadsword office; The rough sketch for the mouse hole close up; The key line tracing.*

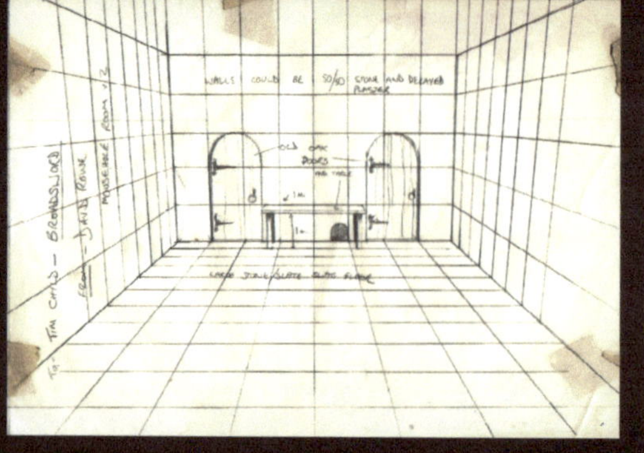

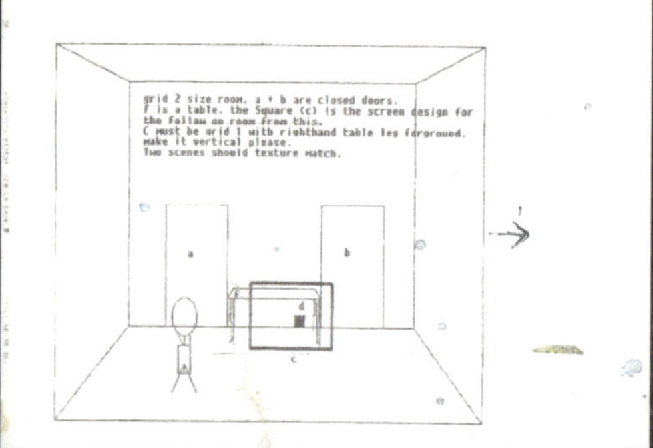

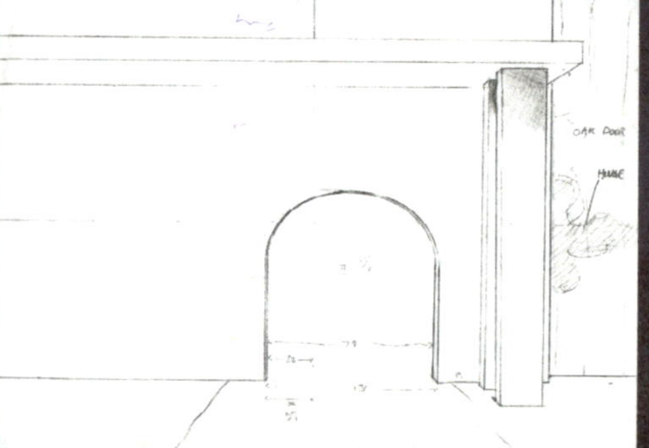

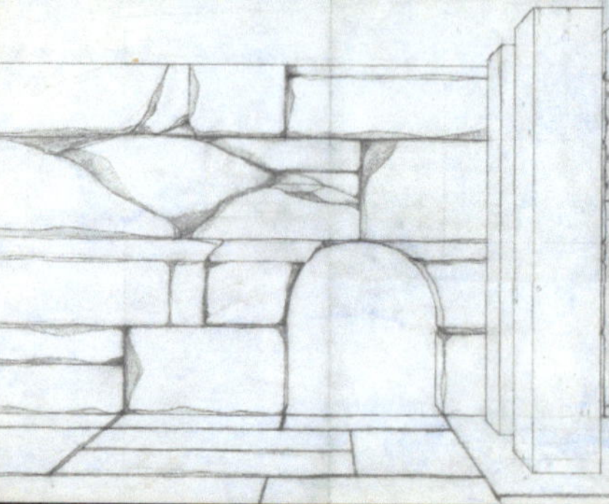

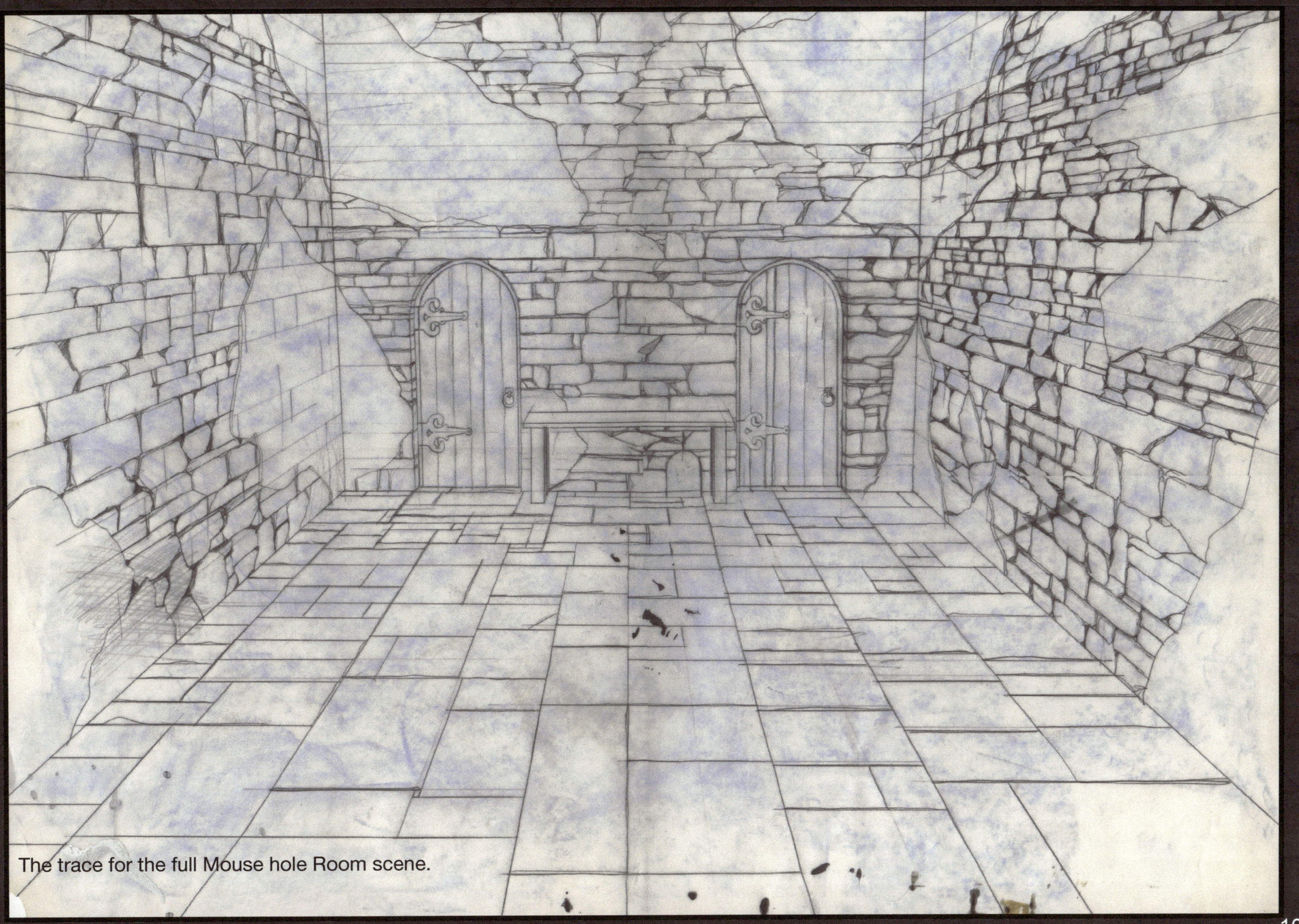

The trace for the full Mouse hole Room scene.

Transporter Room

The Transporter room was an ambitious undertaking which required precise placement of the various platforms.
It was important to demonstrate that I had understood the idea that I could execute the drawing to the exact dimensions indicated in the brief.
The rough sketch with the dimensions that were plotted on the grid was faxed for approval before the painting was commenced.
The arch-vaulted roof mentioned in the brief was added as was the crossing corridor and nave beyond although this was substituted in the final broadcast composite with a section of the Causeway Room painting.

Right: *The final tracing, ready for transfer to the illustration board.*

Below: *Original explanatory brief from Tim; Diagram with key; Fax from me to show my understanding of the requirements of the room; The broadcast composite in action.*

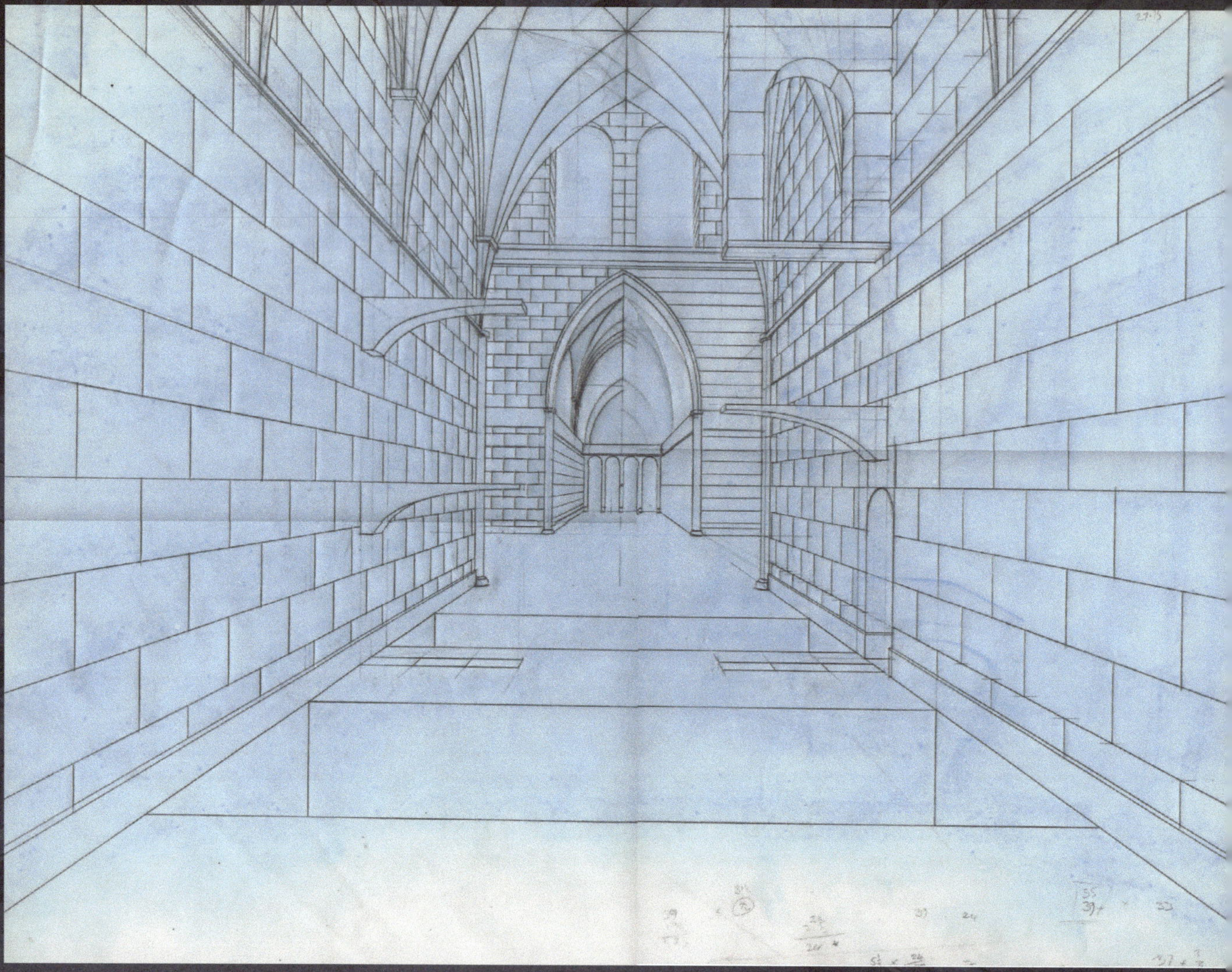

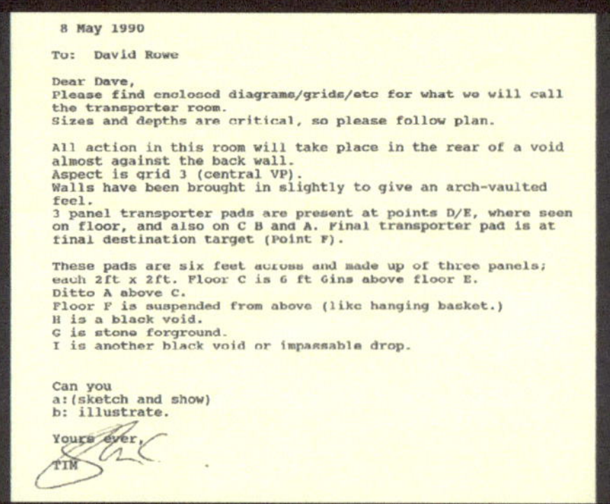

8 May 1990

To: David Rowe

Dear Dave,
Please find enclosed diagrams/grids/etc for what we will call the transporter room.
Sizes and depths are critical, so please follow plan.

All action in this room will take place in the rear of a void almost against the back wall.
Aspect is grid 3 (central VP).
Walls have been brought in slightly to give an arch-vaulted feel.
3 panel transporter pads are present at points D/E, where seen on floor, and also on C B and A. Final transporter pad is at final destination target (Point F).

These pads are six feet across and made up of three panels; each 2ft x 2ft. Floor C is 6 ft 6ins above floor E.
Ditto A above C.
Floor F is suspended from above (like hanging basket.)
H is a black void.
G is stone forground.
I is another black void or impassable drop.

Can you
a:(sketch and show)
b: illustrate.

Yours ever,
TIM

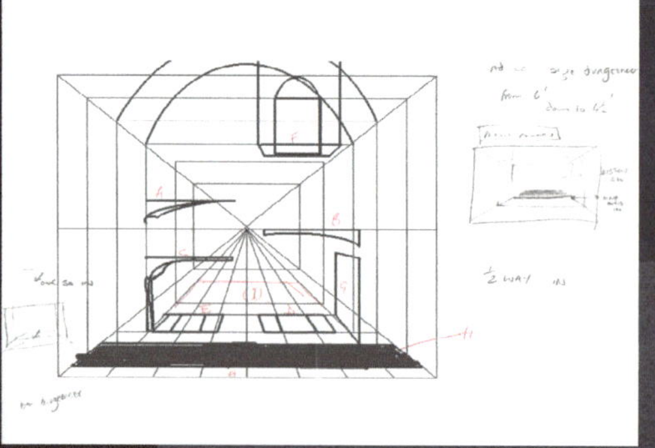

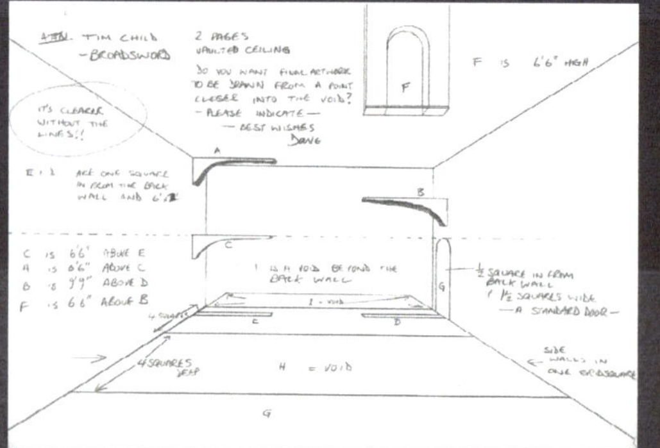

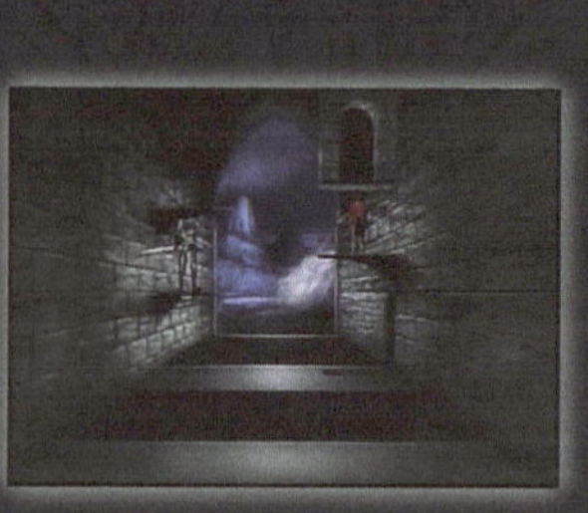

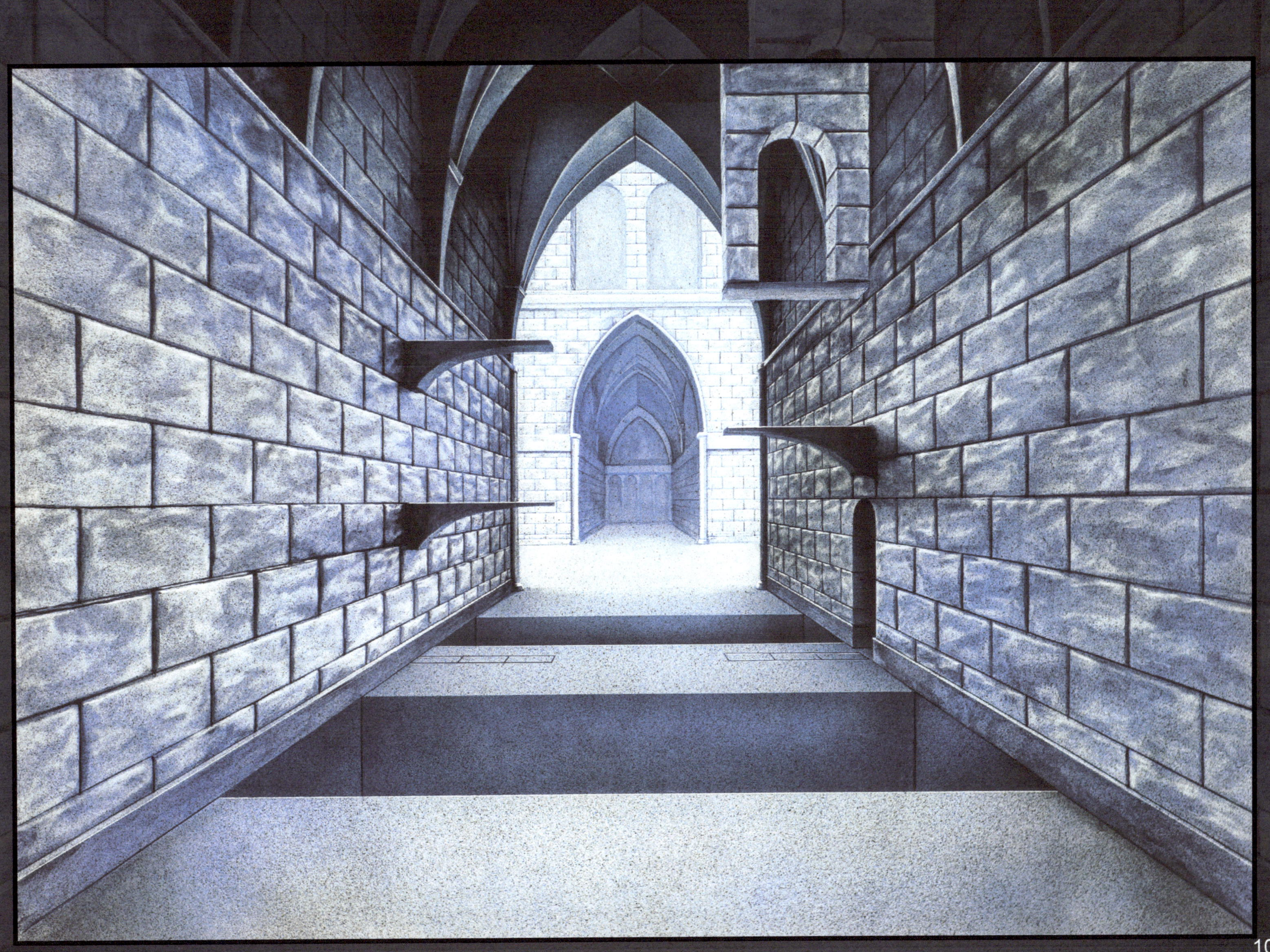

Twist Room

No brief for the Twist room survives. Perhaps the original idea for the room was different from the one that was broadcast which involved the room being rotated with a spell so that the Dungeoneer could use the doors. The ceiling in the original would not have made a good floor as the adventurer might have tripped over the central beam. In the broadcast composite, the floor was duplicated, flipped and placed over the original ceiling. This was a simple task as the room used the central vanishing point grid and so was symmetrical.

Right: *The finished artwork.*

Below: *The patched up tracing after it had been cut in two and faxed to Tim; A Dungeoneer confronts the twisted Twist room; The final composite, flipped.*

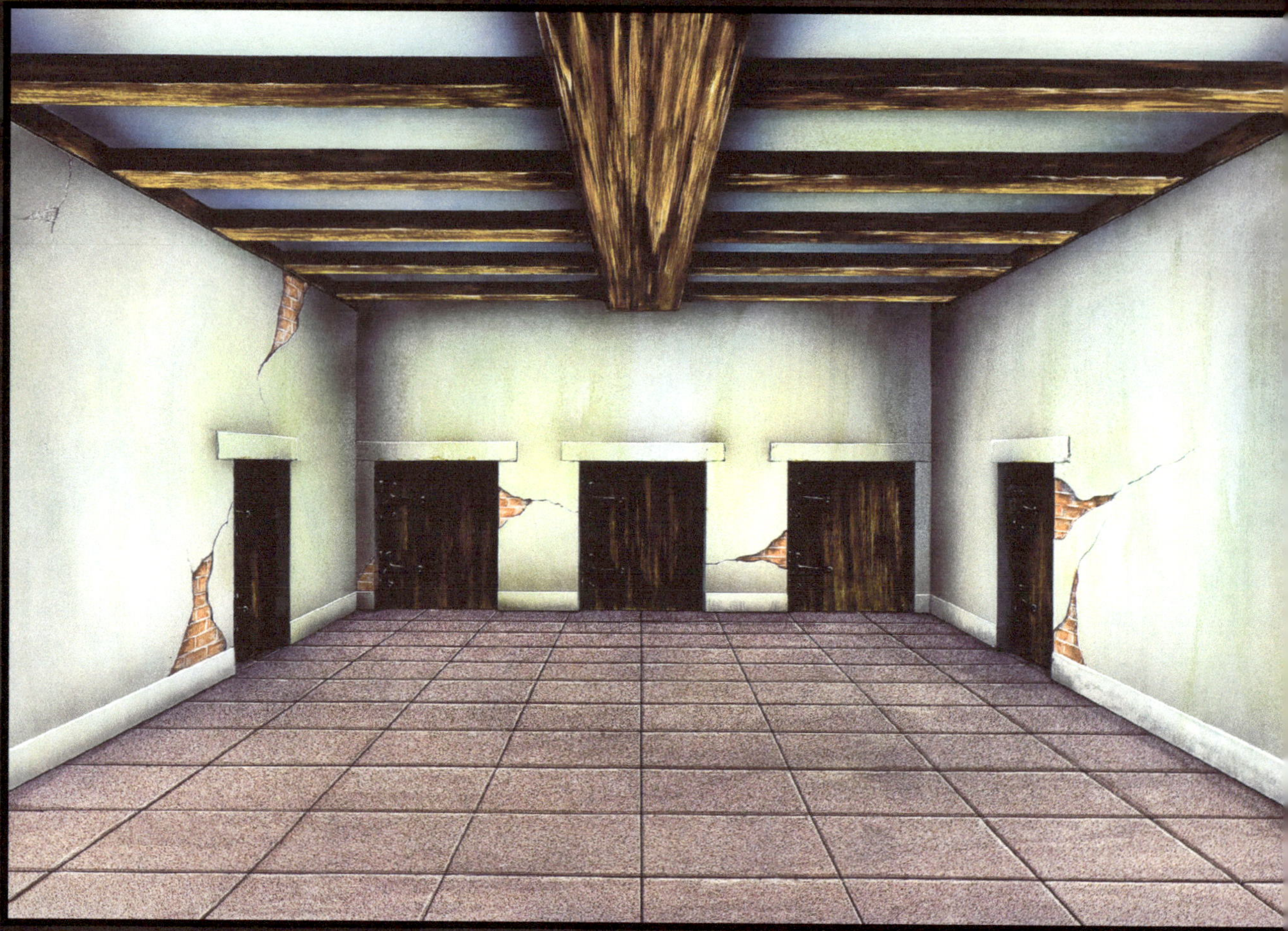

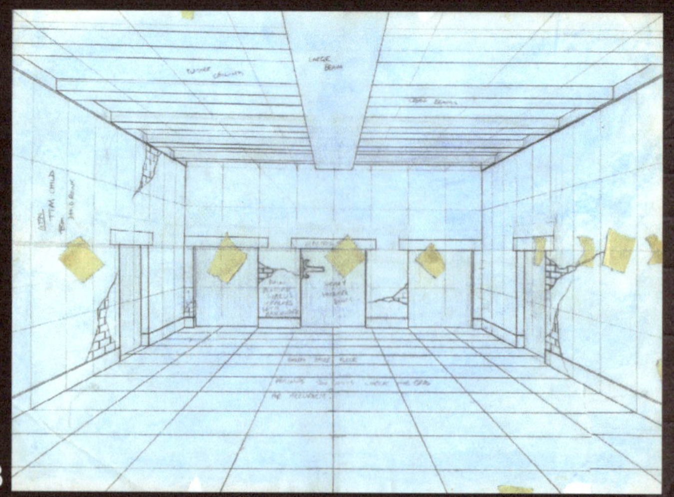

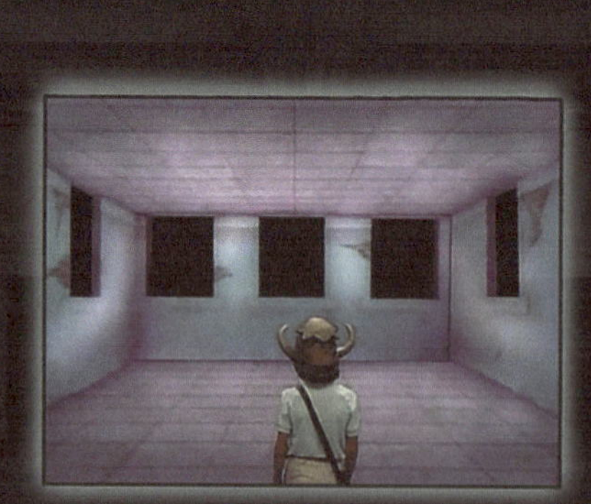

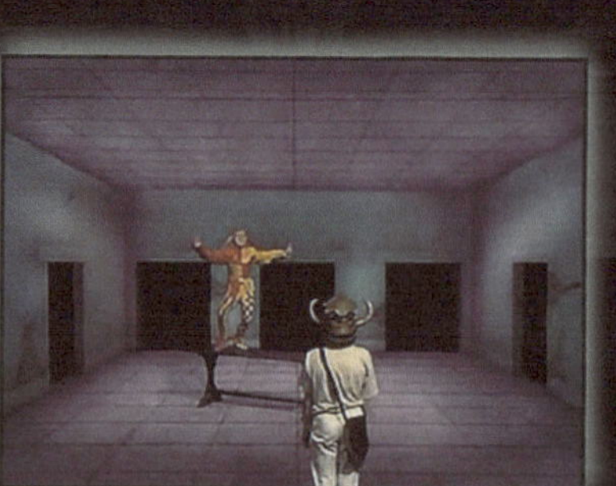

The Henge

The Henge was a composite comprised of two separate elements: the background and the monument stones. This meant that either could be used in different contexts bringing wide ranging scope for unfolding scenarios.

The notes on my drawing indicate that the leading edges should be straight. This was because the blue flat props that had to be made to mask the Dungeoneer's entry would have straight edges.

Right: *The composite scene as it was intended to be put together, ready for CG lighting to be added.*

Below: *The rough from Broadsword, annotated during a follow up phone call; A rough sketch for the Henge background, addressed and subsequently faxed; A further fax with more notes as the brief was tied down; The finished background painting.*

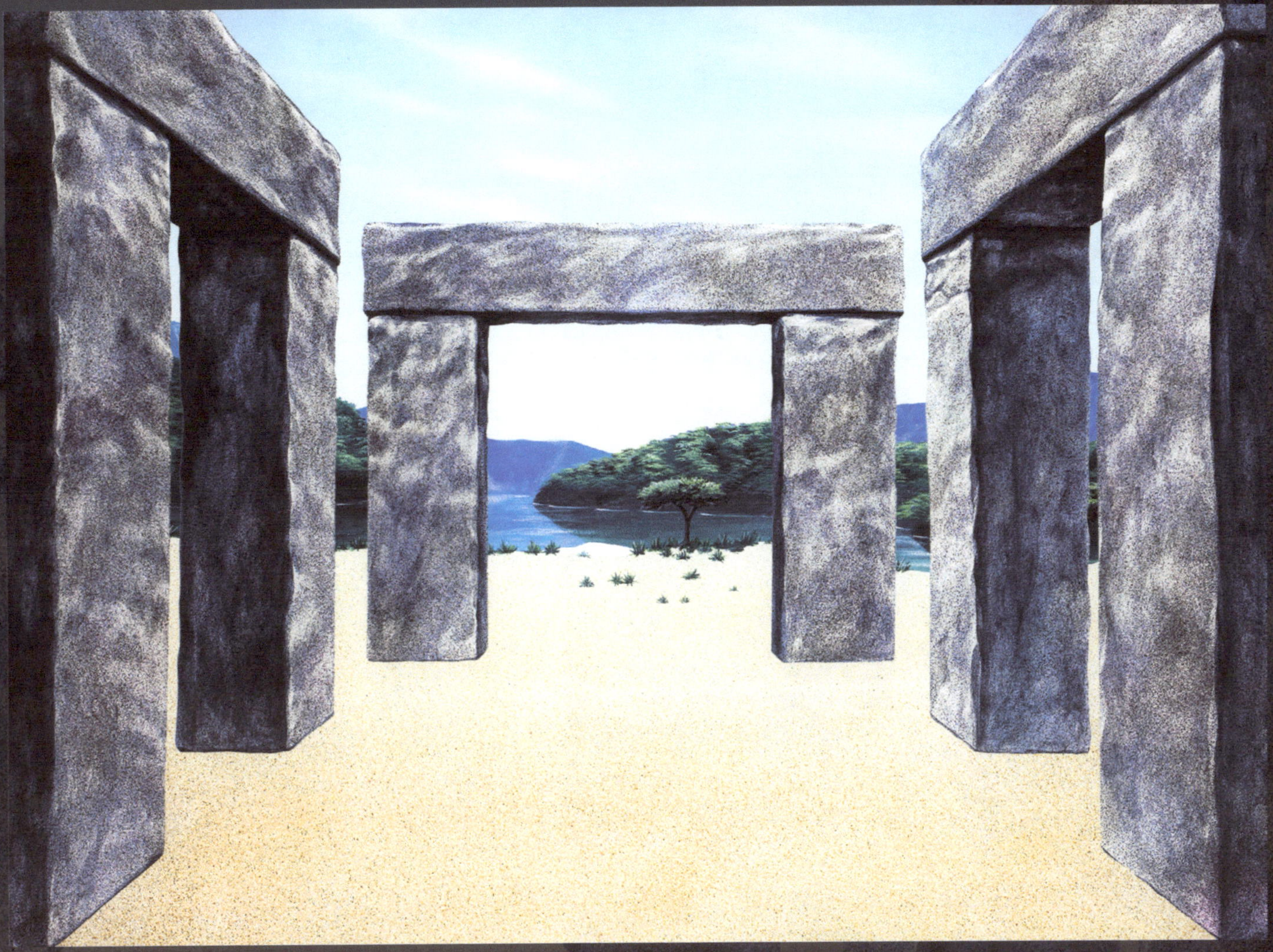

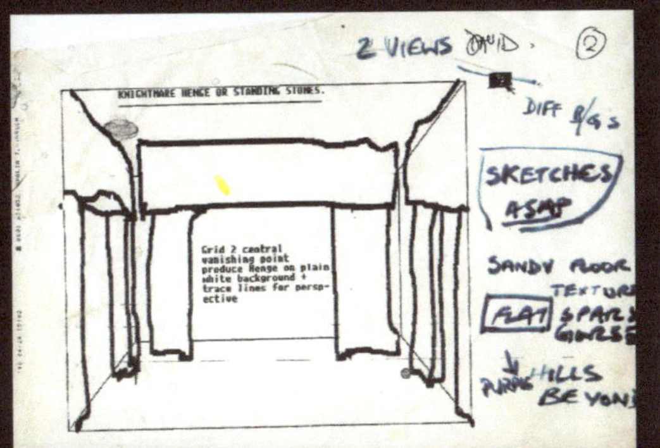

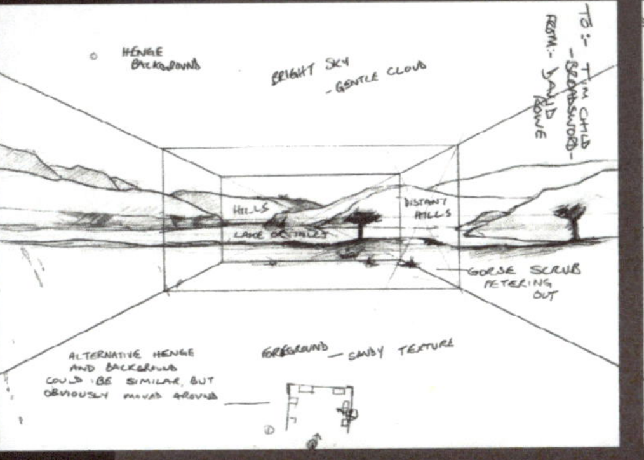

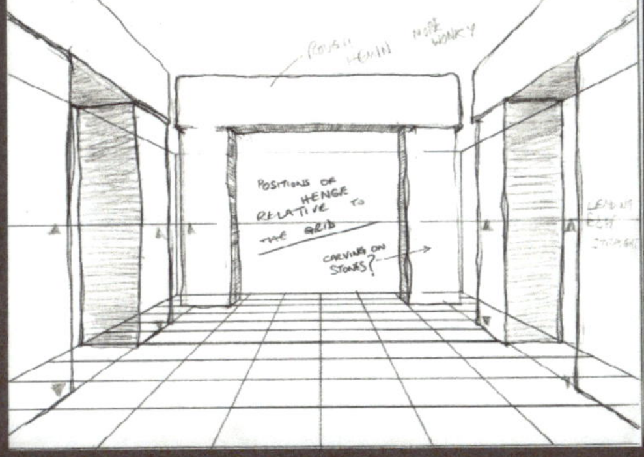

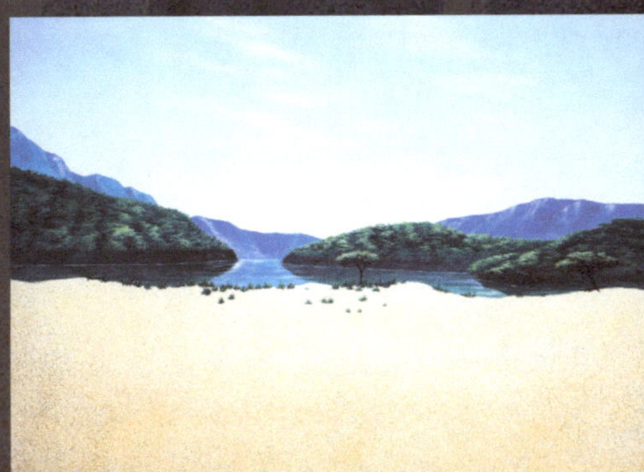

Vale of Banburn

The Vale of Banburn continued the plan to be able to have cut scenes within the same section of the dungeon.
This allowed for a more open plan feel to the scene and added variety to the type of location.

Top Left: *Sketchbook thumbnail doodles helped to begin to get a feel for the scene.*

Top Right: *The final composite for the first view.*

Middle Left: *Plan view of the Vale's three floors indicating viewing positions.*

Middle Right: *Looking back from view two.*

Bottom Left: *This rough included a 'note to self' to get a move on. The caricature is meant to be Tim.*

Bottom Right: *View three by the waterfall at the end of the Valley.*

Facing page, Bottom Right: *The drawing was copied with amendment notes added and posted back to me.*

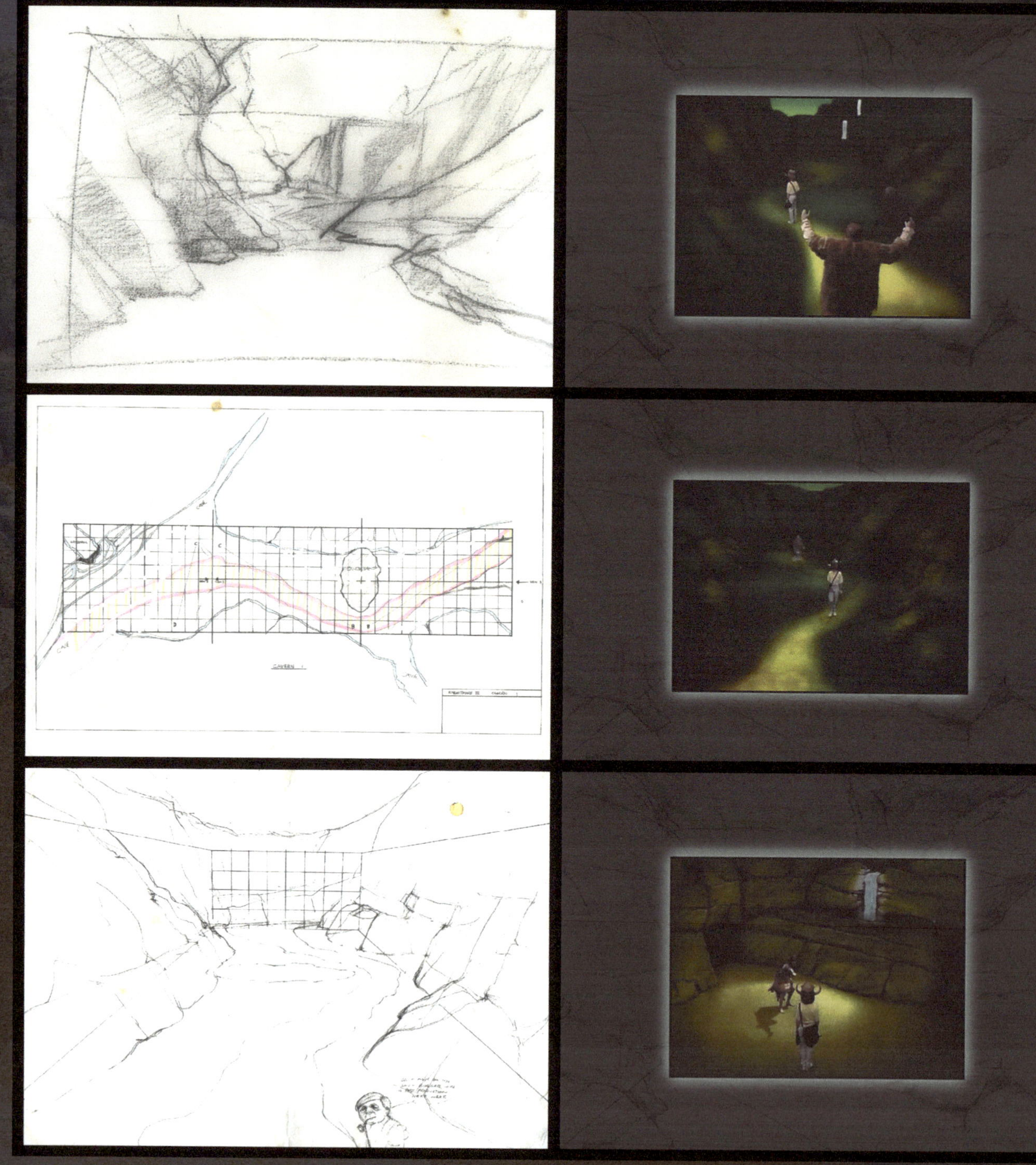

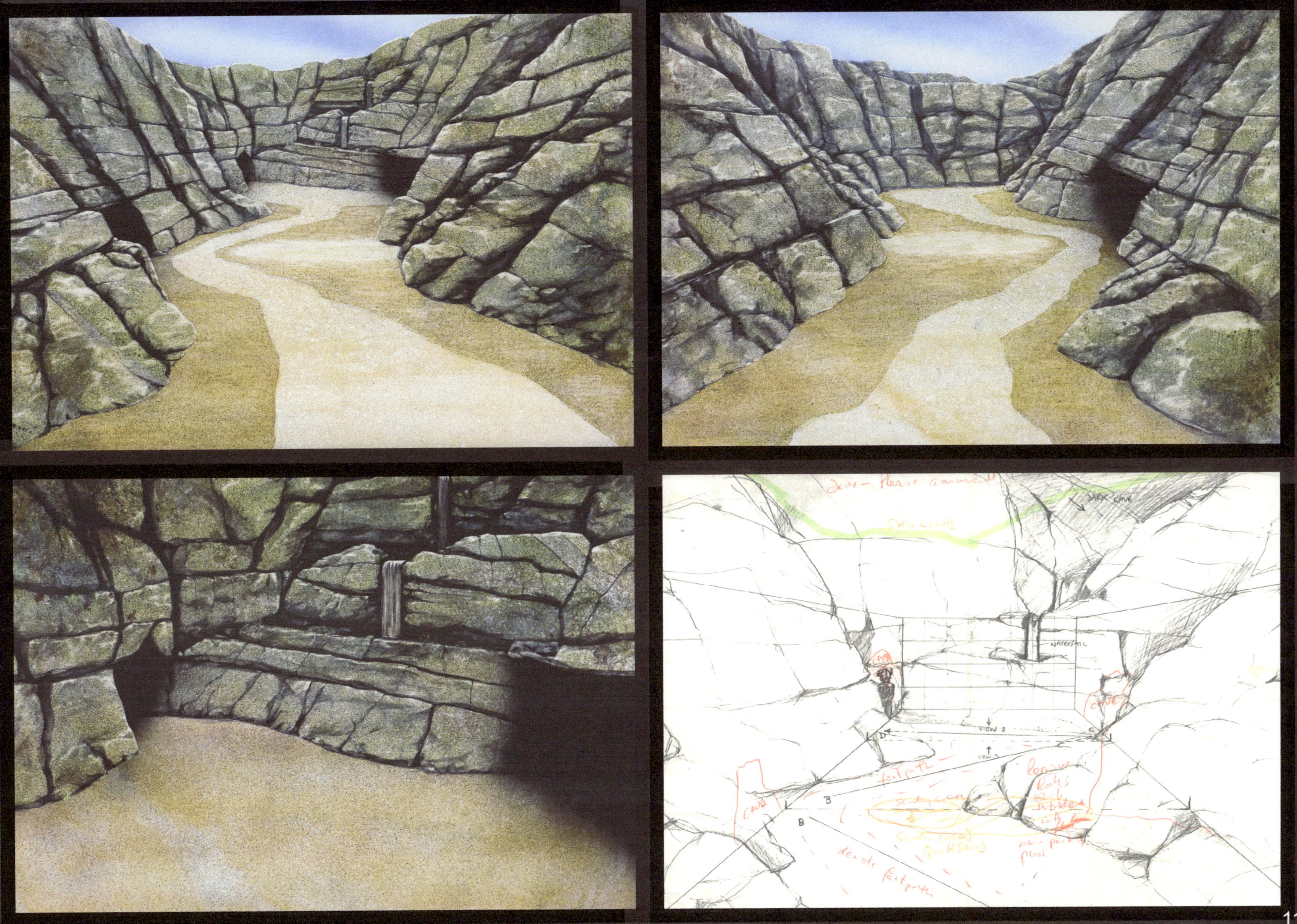

Lord Fear HQ

This was one of the last paintings that I did for Knightmare.

Exploring the concept stage presented the opportunity to try out a few ideas and get them over to Broadsword so that we could discuss them over the 'phone.

Once agreed, the drawing was made to show the key line features, cut and faxed to Tim at the Broadsword offices.

The mountain in the background has a flat top. It resembles a peak in the Brecon Beacons on the approach to Abergavenny from Monmouth. It always reminded me of a volcano and I was delighted to see that the CG team picked up on that for the broadcast composite.

Right: *The drawing utilised the second grid which had a lower horizon. Like many others, this was also cut into four and faxed to Tim with any additional notes.*

Below: *Early concept drawings; Concept close-up; Key line tracing; Broadcast composite.*

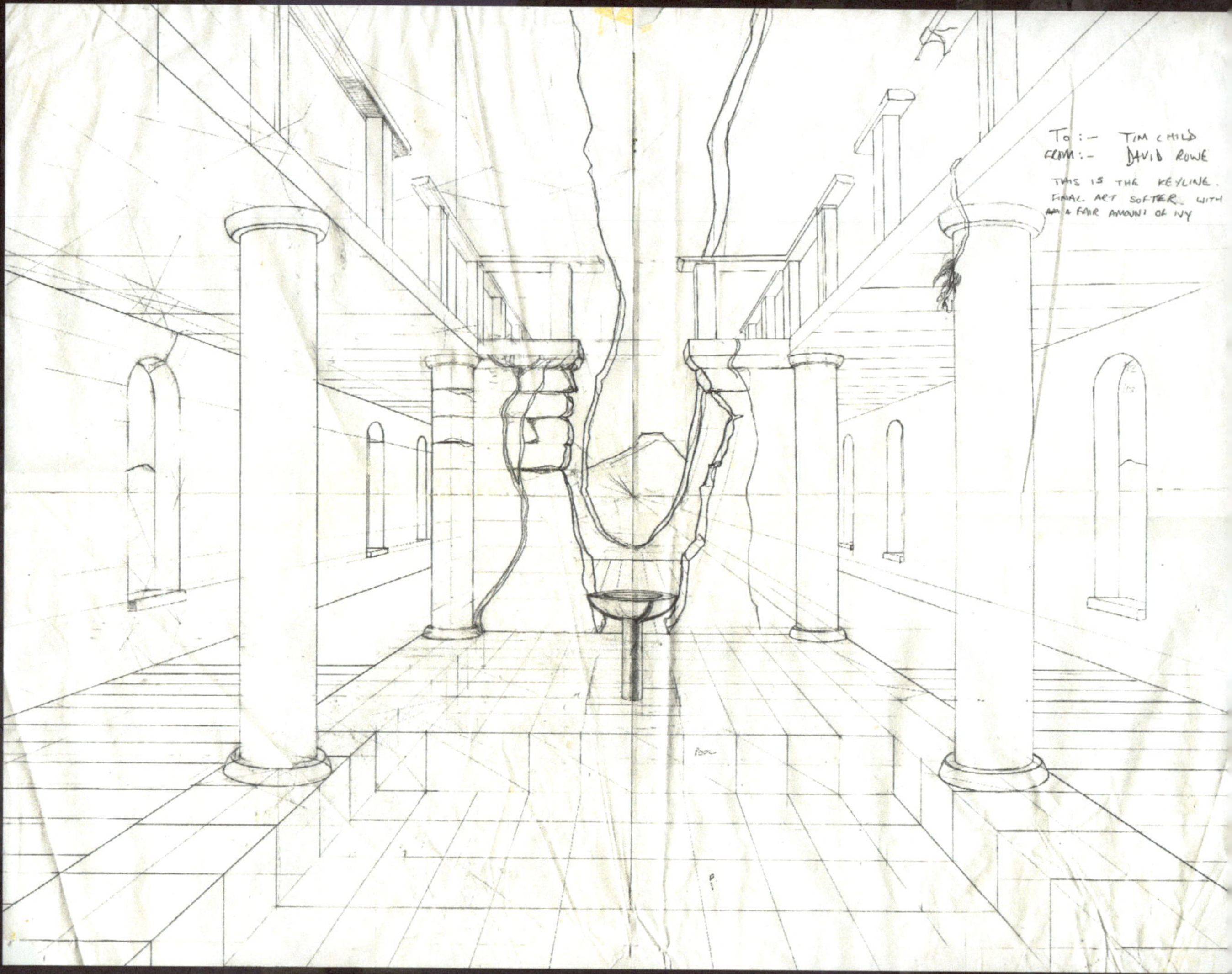

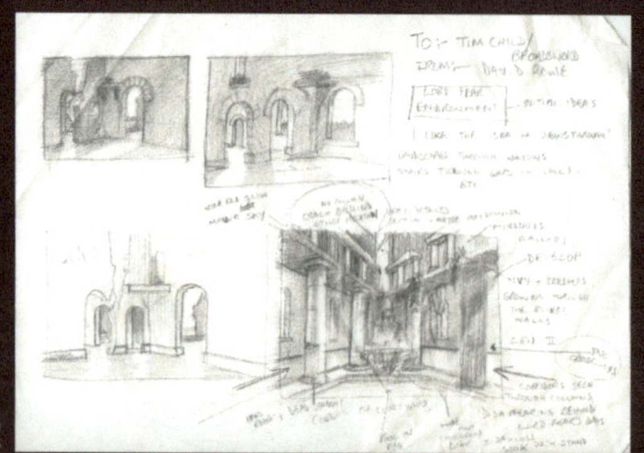

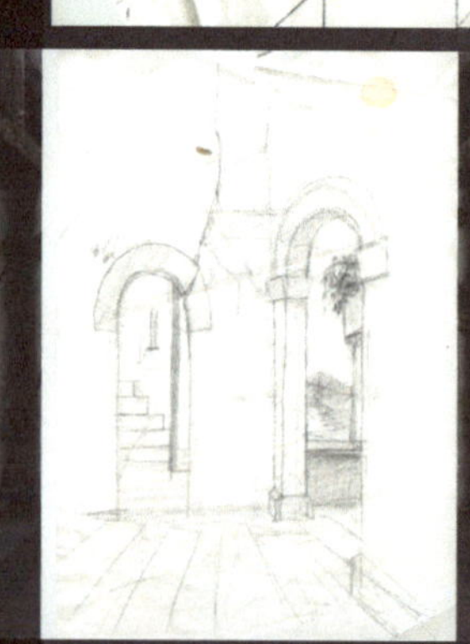

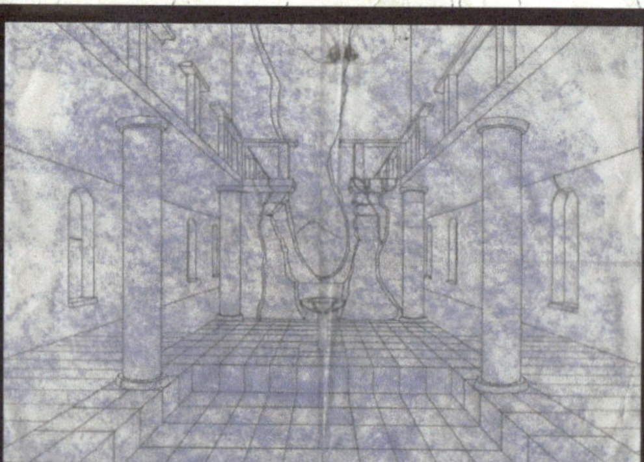

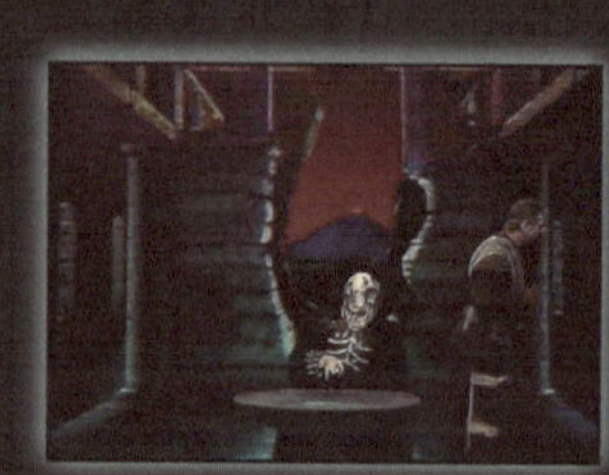

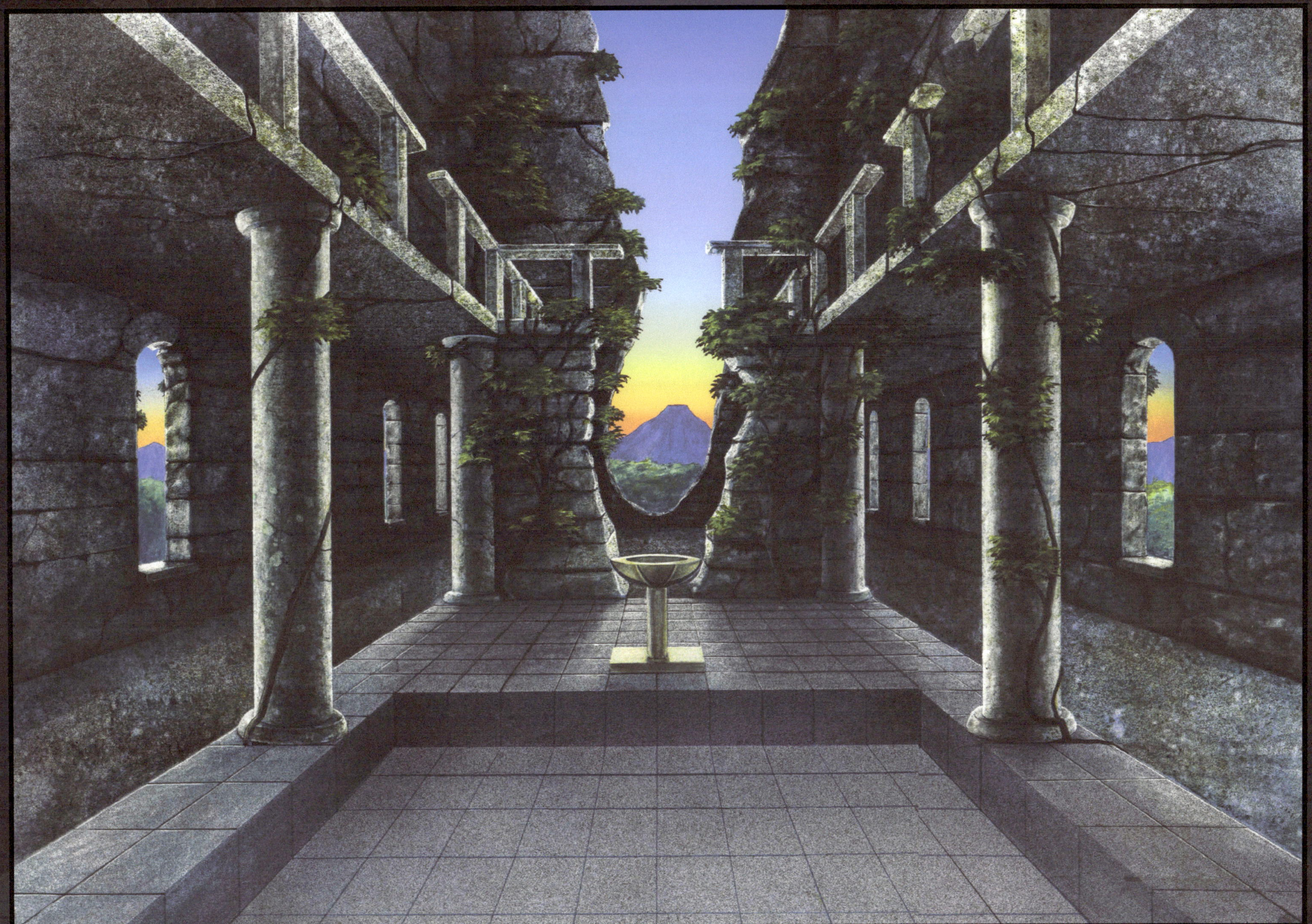

Geek Week

Google's Geek Week 2013 https://www.youtube.com/watch?v=74r-Eblqt9s remake of Knightmare saw the cast and development team get back together again.

Technology had moved on in leaps and bounds in the intervening years and the use of inks and airbrushes had become a distant memory for me. The original Lord Fear painting was scanned and imported into Photoshop, then reworked and relit. The close up images used 3D modelled columns which had granite-like textures applied adding bump-mapping and specularity before finally rendering with full radiosity lighting. The walls and windows were built up with Photoshop using sampled textures and manipulating them by hand.

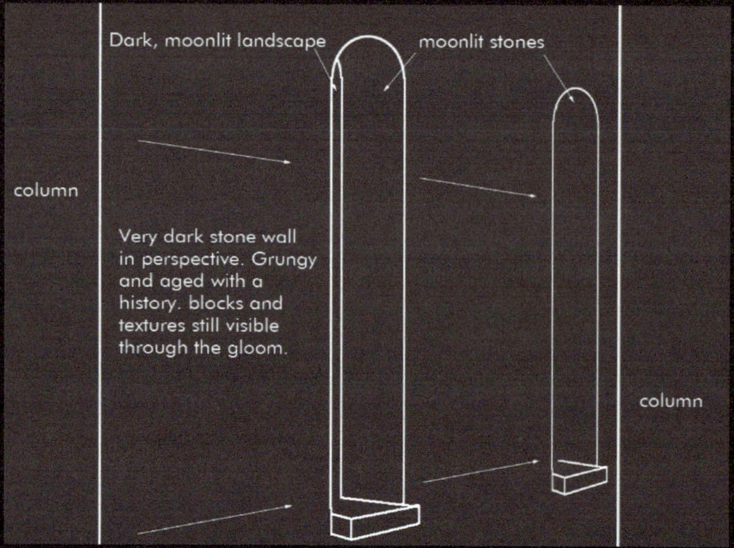

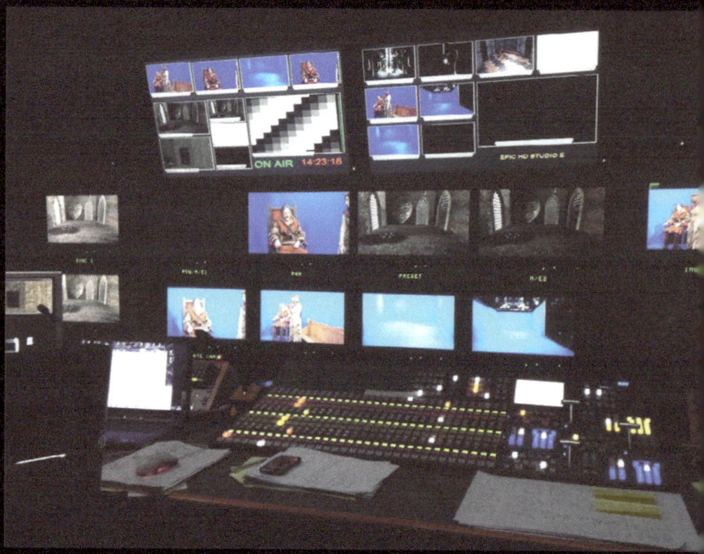

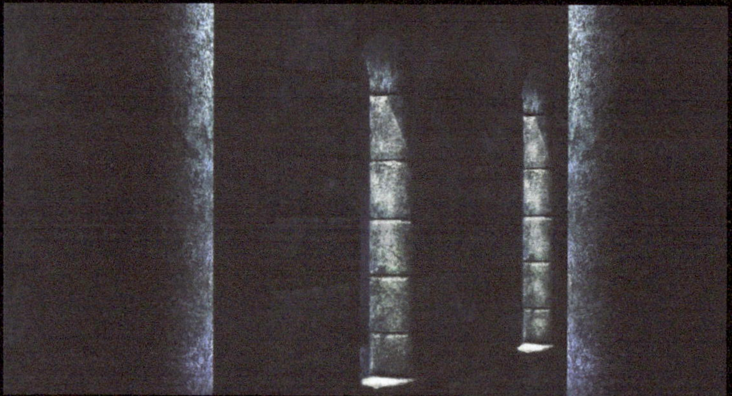

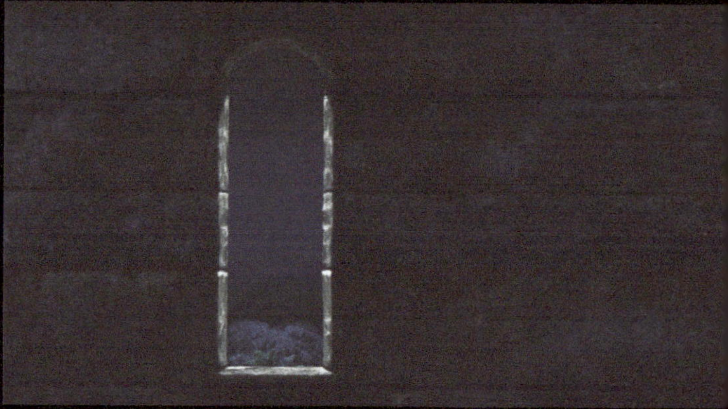

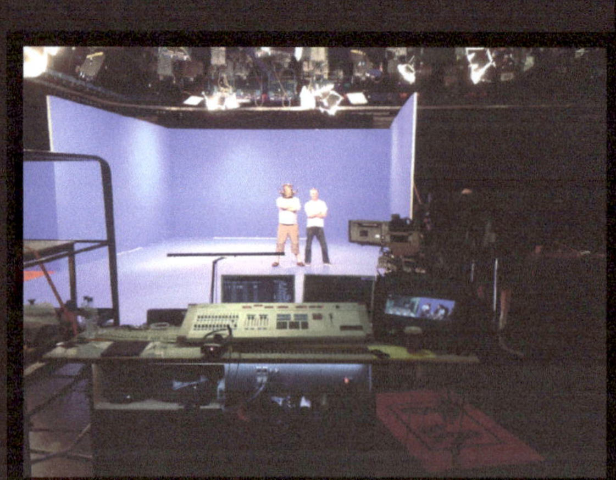

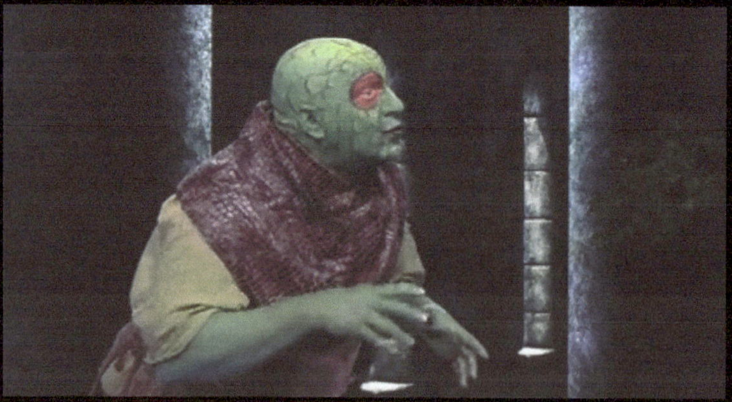

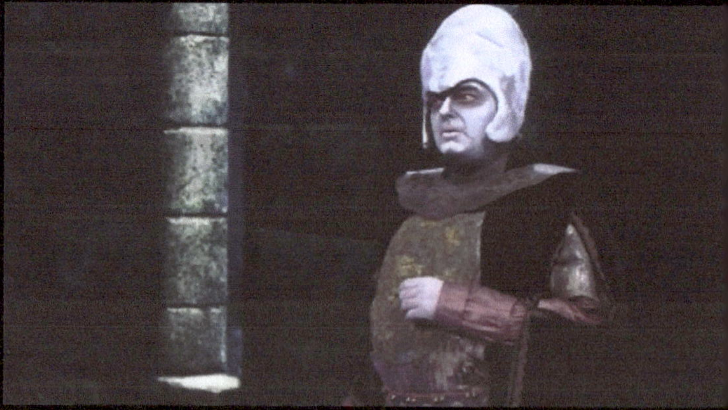

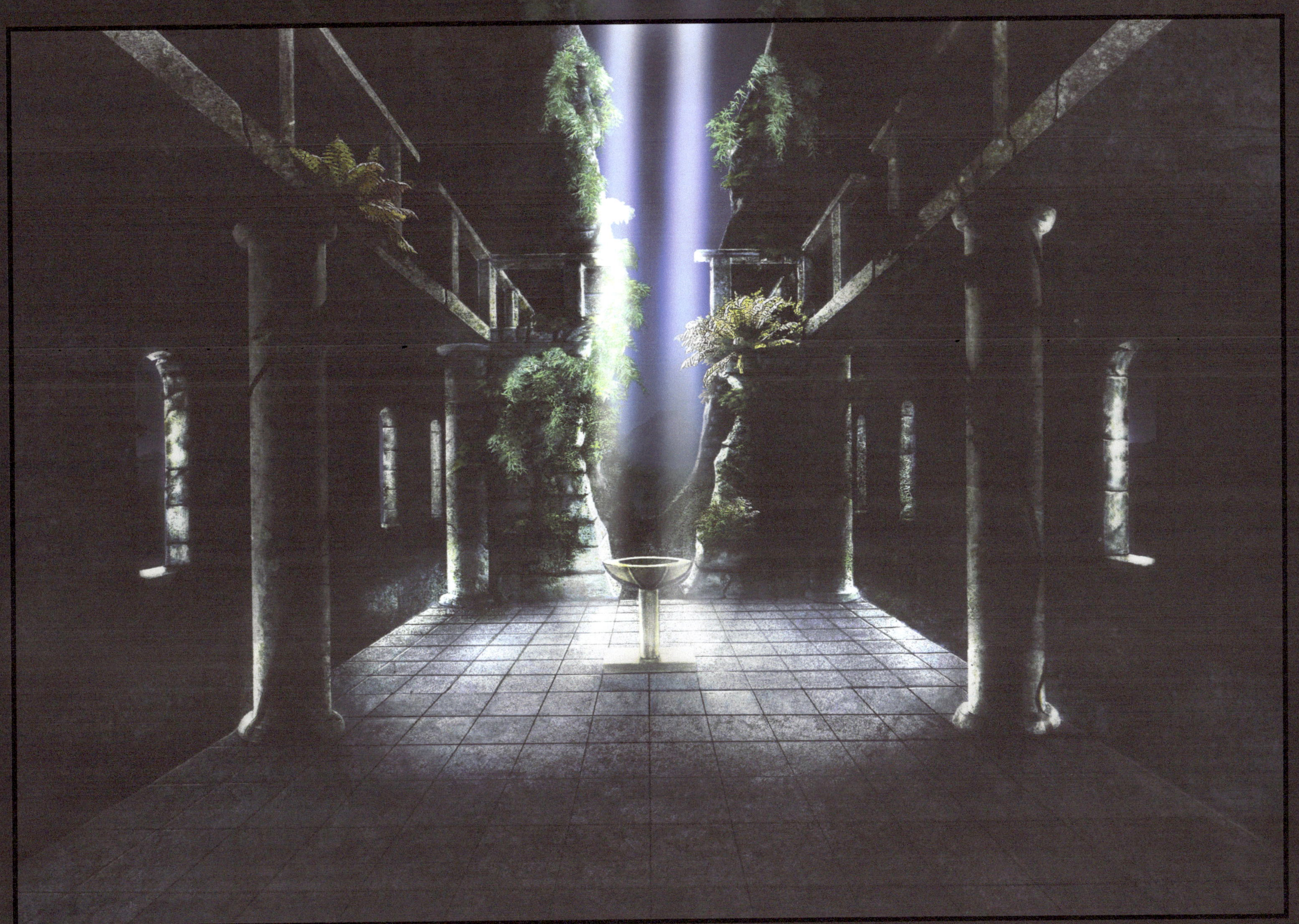